D1038146

The Mark *of a* Giant

The MARK *of a* GIANT

7 PEOPLE WHO CHANGED THE WORLD

TED STEWART

With a Foreword by CHRIS STEWART

Visit us at ShadowMountain.com

Library of Congress Cataloging-in-Publication Data

Stewart, Ted, author.
The mark of a giant : 7 people who changed the world / Ted Stewart ; Foreword by Chris Stewart.
pages cm
Includes bibliographical references and index.
ISBN 978-1-60907-181-3 (hardbound : alk. paper)
1. Religious leaders—Biography. 2. Scientists—Biography. I. Title.
CT104.S744 2013
920—dc23 2013009323

Printed in the United States of America
Edwards Brothers Malloy, Ann Arbor, MI

10 9 8 7 6 5 4 3 2 1

To John Braithwaite
and other giants in my life

Contents

Foreword by Chris Stewart ix

Introduction Giants 1

Chapter 1 Abraham of Ur 7

Chapter 2 Pericles the Greek 23

Chapter 3 Paul—Apostle to the Gentiles 47

Chapter 4 The Incomparable Mr. Newton 79

Chapter 5 Madame Marie Curie 110

Chapter 6 Dr. Martin Luther King Jr. 157

Chapter 7 Mother Teresa 206

Conclusion Are There Giants among Us? 240

Bibliography 251

Index 255

Foreword

It has been my great honor to work with my brother, Ted Stewart, on several national bestselling books over the past few years. One reason I have so enjoyed working with him is the fact that he is a brilliant observer of history. He sees things that many historians don't see, or that they may see but not judge as being very important. Part of the reason he has such an interesting perspective on history is that he is able to see things from a "30,000-foot level." (The big picture is always the most important—and the most interesting—part of the story to tell.) Part of it is his ability to recognize patterns in the unfolding of the human story and then to tie them together in ways that help us understand why these events were important in their day and why they still matter to us now. Finally, I think he is a marvelous storyteller. He is able to set the scene and to provide insight into the minds and intentions of the characters that is compelling and helps us to see the wonder in life.

The Mark of a Giant is a great example of those abilities.

History is the most fascinating of hobbies. It lets us dive into the realm of human emotions and the most vivid dramas while giving us the added satisfaction of knowing they are real. That's why books such as this are so important—and so much fun to read. They give us a better understanding of our world. They help us appreciate the struggles of the past, the price that was paid to move us forward, and how a few men and women have shaped and benefitted our world. They sharpen our minds and entertain us. What more could we ask!

In *The Mark of a Giant* we get to ask ourselves some fascinating questions. How did Abraham of the Old Testament alter our modern world? Did an ancient Greek political leader called Pericles really change the way our government was formed? How did a small and humble woman who earned the title "Mother" change so many hearts in a world where so many seem so heartless? Who was the most brilliant scientist ever born, and why have his discoveries changed the outcome of time? All of these were giants who helped to change and shape the world.

Then we get to ask perhaps the most important question of them all: If there were giants among us then, are there giants among us still?

These are the questions that this book is going to answer. And though it is impossible to take the grand sweep of human history and boil it all down to a few hundred pages, Ted has done a brilliant job of highlighting a few men and women who have truly changed the scope of history, individuals whose impacts have remained with us through all the generations and will remain with us for a thousand years to come.

There's an old adage that my father used to quote—youth is wasted on the young. The same is true of history; too often it is valued only by those who have lived enough of it to appreciate the past. But for those of us who have come to love history and the lessons that it teaches, for those of us who would rather curl up with a good history book than with anything else, *The Mark of a Giant* is treat that is to be savored and enjoyed.

My only regret is that I didn't get to help him write it—how much fun it would have been to have learned all of these great stories for myself!

—Chris Stewart

Introduction

Giants

This is a book about history. More specifically, it is a book about how strong-minded men and women have changed the course of history.

Through the centuries, the image of a dwarf sitting on the shoulder of a giant has been used to express the idea that we owe our own successes largely to the contributions of great people. A short man who finds himself sitting on the shoulder of a giant can actually see farther than the tall man because his sight is at the higher level of the two. As long ago as A.D. 1159, John of Salisbury wrote: "Bernard of Chartres used to say that we are like dwarfs on the shoulders of giants, so that we can see more than they, and things at a greater distance, not by virtue of any sharpness of sight on our part, or any physical distinction, but because we are carried high and raised up by their giant size."

We live in a remarkable era. In so many ways, it is the best of all times. More of the earth's people live with freedom than at any time in world history. The pursuit of social equality is more widespread than at any time in the record of mankind. Medical advancements help us to live longer and to enjoy those extended years with less pain and more comfort. Economic prosperity is more pervasive and within the reach of a larger number of people than ever before. Science is harnessed not only to enrich our lives but to expand our horizons into the far reaches of the universe.

With all of the tyranny and poverty and assault on traditions that exist in today's world, it is still a truly wonderful time in which we are fortunate to live!

Why is that so? Can *we* take credit for this remarkable age? Ought we not to be honest enough to acknowledge that today's world, with all that is amazing and beautiful about it, exists as it does because of those giants who went before us?

This book is about seven of those giants, seven men and women who left their mark upon the world in which we now live. Thanks to them, we have not just the ability to gaze farther but the opportunity to live the abundant life in countless ways.

What is it about those few that makes them different? Are there character traits that they share in common? Or were they merely in the right place at the right time?

Do these notable ones craft their own destiny? Or are they somehow chosen?

Famed American essayist Ralph Waldo Emerson, in memorializing the recently assassinated Abraham Lincoln, said in his tribute to that great man, "There is a serene Providence which rules the fate of nations. . . . It makes its own instruments, creates the man for the time, trains him in poverty, inspires his genius, and arms him for the task."

There is no doubt that Abraham Lincoln was such a man. His imprint upon the history of this nation and the world is beyond dispute. There are many who contend that he was a gift of God to the human race.

Are all of those giants in world history in fact men and women called by "serene Providence"? Were they all, truly, gifts of God?

Or were they the product of their own genius or their own unique gifts? Were they giants because they were brave, or determined, or full of faith?

This book will not attempt to answer those questions. Instead, it encourages readers to draw their own conclusions after they have read something of the lives and exploits of certain men and women who have lived great and earned the title of "giant":

1. Abraham of Ur (generally accepted to have lived in the early part of the second millennium before Christ) is claimed by three of the world's great religions—Judaism, Christianity, and Islam—as one of their own, since Judah, Jesus Christ, and Muhammad are all said to be descended from Abraham. His life itself was a major turning point in world history. He was born into a world where idolatry and the worship of multiple gods were universal. He died with the practice of monotheism firmly implanted, never to be extinguished. He instituted, by his example and through the teachings of his descendants, a system of morality and justice that has survived and served as a standard for four millennia.

2. The Athenian Greek Pericles, who lived from 494 to 429 B.C., left a heritage that altered the history of mankind. In the lengthy history of Athens's experimentation with democracy there were many individuals whose lives could be heralded. Pericles, however, celebrated as the "first citizen of Athens" by the Greek historian Thucydides, was responsible for a major expansion of the rights of the non-elites of Athens. Under his guidance, the ordinary citizens of Athens became more powerful, the rule of law was enshrined, and obligations of citizenship were demanded of both the rich and the poor. In a world where "might made right" and tyranny of the powerful was the historical norm, the bright light of Athenian democracy pierced the darkness for a brief period. Although of relatively short practice, it remained an emblem that has inspired the high-minded of many nations down to the present day. Because of the Athenian experience, the modern-day giants known as the founders of the United States of America were inspired to attempt self-government. But, in addition, those founders learned from the Athenians what not to do. It was what our founders

refused to copy of the Athenian system that has allowed us to survive our own experiment in self-government for as long as we have.

3. The Apostle Paul (A.D. 4 to 64), often referred to as St. Paul, affected the world after the death of Jesus Christ in two major ways. First, his writings, which make up a major portion of the Bible's New Testament, contributed mightily to an understanding of the doctrine of Christianity. Second, his missionary efforts spread Christianity throughout the Roman Empire. These combined efforts planted Christianity firmly in soil from which it would never be rooted out. And the impact of Christianity on the world thereafter is beyond dispute.

4. There are many men and women who have altered world history because of their achievements in science, music, art, and other areas where human genius is demonstrated. None, however, equal the exploits of Sir Isaac Newton, the English scientist who was born in 1642 and died in 1727. Newton is considered by many to be the greatest scientist who ever lived. Before him, the advances in science and mathematics of previous centuries were a conglomeration of isolated, unrelated facts and theories. Newton brought them together, proposed unified theories to explain them, and launched the scientific era that turned science and mathematics into useful tools for mankind. His genius and tenacity allowed him to make major advances in mathematics, optics, mechanics, astronomy, and other fields. It was largely his scientific discoveries that made possible the Industrial Revolution, which altered the world unlike anything before or since.

5. Marie Curie, commonly known as Madame Curie, was born in 1867 in Poland. This was an age when women struggled to gain any opportunity for educational or personal accomplishment, and yet Marie Curie overcame the societal handicaps of her era to become one of the greatest scientists in history. She was the first person to win two Nobel Prizes, and the only person to ever win Nobel Prizes in multiple sciences (physics and chemistry.) The work of Marie and her husband, Pierre, resulted in the discovery of two new elements, with one, radium, opening the doors to the entire line of scientific inquiry known

as nuclear physics. Further, they were responsible for the medical miracle of radiation therapy for cancer.

6. Throughout the history of the United States, many have struggled to assure that the "American Dream" was shared by all of its citizens, regardless of their background or country of origin. Sadly, that dream was denied a major block of American citizens for the first two hundred years of our nation's history—those Americans whose ancestors came from Africa. Slavery ended with the American Civil War. However, following the failure of the United States Supreme Court to prohibit it, segregation of blacks and whites became the official policy of many states. Laws and practices that discriminated against African Americans were common in all regions of the nation. This shameful condition might not have been brought to an end when it was, or as peacefully as it was, had it not been for the efforts of the Reverend Martin Luther King, Jr., who was born in 1929 and died at the hand of an assassin in 1968. As the highly visible and dynamic leader of the American Civil Rights Movement he triggered a reexamination of the accepted way of thinking of many Americans, both black and white. He led the movement that broke down barriers and helped extend justice and equality of opportunity to millions of Americans.

7. The world may not recognize the name Agnes Gonxha Bojaxhiu, but practically everyone knows this heroine by her adopted name, Mother Teresa. Born in 1910 in modern-day Macedonia, at the age of eighteen she committed herself wholly to caring for the poor and indigent of India's slums. Her efforts to help those whom no one else cared for and her founding of an order committed to assisting the world's most unfortunate earned her the Nobel Peace Prize in 1979. Although she passed away in 1997, her charitable organization has survived and her marvelous example of self-sacrifice is permanently enshrined in the minds of all who hear of her. Her example of selfless service must be duplicated many times over if the world is to ease the pain of severe poverty.

This list is obviously too short. Instead of including seven giants, it could list seven hundred or seven thousand. It is undeniably true that many, many women and men have been responsible for altering history for the good of all mankind. Readers are free to debate whether any or all of the seven here included are worthy of such attention.

In the end, the hope is to provide some insight as to how these seven became great. What traits did they share that marked them as giants? To answer that question will require at least a cursory account of how human history was affected by their actions. To accomplish that, each story will include an explanation of what the world was like when the person was born and how it was changed by his or her existence. We will examine how each person truly altered the course of history. Perhaps understanding how the great ones became so may motivate some to become giants!

For this book is not just about the giants, it is also about the dwarfs. It is about those of us who live ordinary lives in this remarkable time in world history, and about the responsibilities we bear because of that which we have been gifted. Perhaps, as a result of reading these accounts, there will be more people inspired to make their own mark upon the world.

Chapter 1

Abraham of Ur

And I will make of thee a great nation,
and I will bless thee, and make thy name great.

Jehovah to Abraham (Genesis 12:2)

Philosophers assert that each of us possesses a worldview—the lens through which we view the world and everything in it. It is a collection of biases and prejudices that dictate how we interpret the world. It is the source of all of our opinions, mores, and ethics.

Some philosophers further assert that there are just two worldviews: the spiritual worldview and the materialistic or rational worldview. The spiritual worldview is one that has "its emphasis on moral truth and right conduct and its motto of Thus said the Lord." It is "rooted primarily in ancient Israel."[1]

The spiritual worldview has been possessed by billions of the earth's inhabitants. It is perhaps worth inquiring as to the origin of that worldview. That inquiry might well lead to a man who lived four millennia ago. His name was Abraham.

Abraham of Ur

The Bible tells us that ten generations after the flood, in a land called Ur of the Chaldees, a man was born named Abram. As with many of the details of his life, there is dispute as to exactly where Ur of the Chaldees actually was. Most Christian experts claim that Ur was the capital of Sumer, an ancient civilization in the southern area of Mesopotamia, in modern-day Iraq. Muslim scholars claim that Ur was in Southern Turkey.[2]

In the seventeenth century, a famous churchman by the name of James Ussher (Archbishop of Armagh in Northern Ireland, the Primate of All Ireland, and Vice-Chancellor of Trinity College in Dublin), a highly regarded scholar, attempted to calculate the dates of the earth's creation as well as all of the Old Testament milestones. According to his calculations, Abram was born in 1996 B.C., roughly two thousand years after the earth was created.[3]

An early legend tells us that Abram lived at the time of Nimrod, the mighty hunter and the first great King of the Earth. It was Nimrod who conjured up the idea of building a tower into heaven. One legend has it that Nimrod tried to have young Abram killed because of Abram's rejection of the stairway to heaven project. But Abram was saved from death in a fiery furnace.[4]

There appears to be little dispute that Abram's was a time of great wickedness among the descendants of Noah. According to Ussher's calculations, only 350 years had passed since the flood had destroyed all but a handful of the earth's inhabitants.[5] But in that brief time the descendants of Noah and his sons had degenerated into a wicked throng of idol worshippers:

> Some of them through their error adored the heavens, and some of them worshipped the sun, and moon and stars, and some of them the earth, and wild beasts, and birds, and creeping things, and trees, and stones, and the creatures of the sea, and the waters, and the winds. . . . The land became filled with idols in the form of men and women.[6]

Eventually, the worship of idols, of the elements, of the cycles of the sun, moon, and stars, and of every other form of life and even the dead, led to other conduct unbecoming descendants of the survivors of the Great Flood—that prodigious punishment inflicted on the people in Noah's time for their enormous wickedness.

Sorcery was introduced. There was great violence throughout the land. Human life was treated as something of little worth. The odious practice of sacrificing children to idols became common. Justice was nonexistent. Nothing was sacred except the pervasive and widespread worship of dumb idols.[7]

As a young man, Abram rejected idolatry. He came to the conclusion that idolatry was irrational in a very rational way. According to the account contained in an ancient text called the *Apocalypse of Abraham,* one day Abram (his name had not yet been changed to Abraham) was guarding the idols of his father, Terah, and his brother, Nahor. Terah and Nahor believed in covering all of their bases by worshipping a variety of idols made from wood, stone, gold, silver, copper, and iron. On this occasion, one of the stone idols fell over. While Abram and Terah were lifting it back to its upright position, the head fell off. Undeterred, Terah simply used his tools to carve a new idol from stone, without a head, and put the broken head upon it.

This got Abram to questioning.

One day thereafter Abram was sent into the streets to market some of the idols produced by his father, Terah, who was engaged in the trade of crafting and selling idols. The idols were strapped to a donkey. A braying camel caused Abram's donkey to panic, and several of his father's idols were smashed. Abram gathered up the pieces and, not knowing what else to do, he threw them into a river. He observed that they simply sank.

The young Abram began to think: *Who is the god here, these idols or the man who makes them—my father? When the idol falls over, it can't lift itself up, my father and I have to do it. A head falls off and my father simply carves a new body and puts on it the head from the broken god. These idols get smashed by an ass and my father will make some more. I throw the smashed idols into the water and they sink. If they cannot make themselves, nor lift themselves up, nor save themselves—how is it that they can help me or save me or my father?*

The boy Abram rejected the gods of his fathers. For this his father was furious with him.[8] Some accounts assert that he even tried to kill the young boy.[9]

But Abram was soon to discover Jehovah, for Jehovah called out and revealed himself to Abram in what was to be the first of a number of remarkable conversations between God and man.

Abram thus became a man unique among his entire generation: He became a believer in one God, the creator of heaven and earth and all things therein—Jehovah of the Old Testament. He not only believed, but Abram was to display over and over again his unparalleled faith in Jehovah and His commands. Because of this faith, Abram was to receive abundant blessings during his own life and the promise of even greater blessings for his posterity.

Abram of Canaan

The biblical account of Abram's life is quite full.[10] From it we learn that Terah (apparently reconciled to his son) took Abram and his wife, Sarai, as well as his grandson Lot, and they left Ur of the Chaldees and traveled to the land Haran in what is now southern Turkey. There Terah died.

Here, another of those conversations between Jehovah and Abram occurred. Abram was told by Jehovah to leave Haran. For his faithfulness he was promised that Jehovah would make of him a great nation and would also make his name great. Of considerable significance, Abram was promised that through him all the families of the earth would be blessed.

Abram was seventy-five years old when he left Haran. Considering that he was to live to be one hundred and seventy-five years old, he was just entering middle age.

Abram took with him his nephew Lot, who had become a most

fortunate addition to Abram and Sarai's household. He was joined by all those whom Abram had already converted to his belief in one true God.

For Abram was a missionary! Once he became converted to the worship of Jehovah, he did not hesitate to try to convert others. The great Jewish priest, general, and historian Flavius Josephus said of Abraham:

> He was a person of great sagacity, both for understanding all things and persuading his hearers, and not mistaken in his opinions; for which reasons he began to have higher notions of virtue than others had and he determined to renew and to change the opinion all men happened then to have concerning God; for he was the first that ventured to publish this notion, That there was but one God, the Creator of the universe.[11]

Abram was led to the land of the Canaanites. Jehovah promised that land to him.

Although it was a "promised land" for Abram and his heirs, it was not without its challenges. A great famine hit the land of the Canaanites and Abram was forced to leave his land of promise to find food for himself and his household in the land of Egypt.

This led to one of the more interesting events in Abram's life. Sarai, his wife (who was also either his niece or his half-sister[12]), was apparently a woman of remarkable beauty. In one of the Dead Sea Scrolls, ancient texts discovered in 1947, Sarai was described thus: "Above all women her beauty stands out; her loveliness is far above them all. And with all this beauty there is in her great wisdom."[13]

In that day, the Egyptian king, the Pharaoh, got what he wanted. Abram realized that if it were known that the lovely Sarai was his wife, the Egyptians would simply kill him so that the Pharaoh could take her as his own. To avoid that fate, and not dishonestly, Abram asked Sarai to tell the Egyptians that she was his sister.

Upon entering Egypt, Sarai was immediately noticed. She was, as predicted, taken to the king, but Jehovah protected her virtue by bringing multiple curses upon the Pharaoh. Eventually, Pharaoh figured out what was happening. Abram was called and healed the king. In gratitude Pharaoh bestowed upon him great riches of gold, silver, fine clothing, and excellent cattle. He was also given Hagar as a handmaiden to Sarai. Abram and Lot returned to their promised land much richer men than they had left it.[14]

But Abram did not leave the Egyptians without bestowing gifts of his own. Ancient records reveal that he was a man with great knowledge about astronomy and that he taught the Egyptians all he knew about astrology and other sciences.[15]

Abram—A Man of Justice and Mercy

Upon returning to Canaan, Abram encountered a crisis of sorts: The land was not big enough for both Abram and Lot now that they were men of great wealth in cattle, flocks, and tents. Fights over the land, and presumably over water, erupted between the herdsmen of Abram and those of Lot. Abram then displayed a character trait that the worship of Jehovah must have nurtured—unselfishness. He gave Lot the choice, "Do you take the lands to the left or to the right?" Lot, not quite as soft of heart, took those lands that were the plain of Jordan, near the cities of Sodom and Gomorrah, primarily because there was so much water to be found on that plain.

Perhaps in recognition of Abram's selflessness, Jehovah again visited Abram and renewed his promise that all of the lands in every direction would be his and that his posterity would be as numerous as the dust of the earth.

The history of the Middle East, then as now, was one of constant warfare. The cities of Sodom and Gomorrah were attacked and sacked. Many captives were taken, along with all of the wealth of those two cities. Lot was among the captives. Abram raised a private army and pursued the plunderers. He succeeded in recovering both the captives and the plunder.

The king greeted Abram upon his return to the city of Sodom. Filled with gratitude, he offered to let Abram keep the spoil of plunder if Abram would give up the captive people. Abram again displayed his tempered soul by refusing to keep any of the valuable loot that he had recovered.

Shortly thereafter, Abram was going to bargain with the Lord to try to save the cities of Sodom and Gomorrah from total destruction because of their wickedness. Again, he demonstrated compassion and mercy unusual for the age.

These individual acts of unselfishness and mercy may not seem like much—except when viewed in light of the era in which Abram lived. Moral creeds were almost nonexistent. The acclaimed Code of Hammurabi, a Babylonian code of conduct that included protection of the weak, was still a hundred years in the future. The ethical constrictions of the Old Testament law of Moses were centuries away. This was an age where "might made right." A convenient advantage of worshipping idols was that they did not demand much from one in the way of restrictions on personal conduct. Individual acts of kindness or mercy were undoubtedly extended, but there was little by way of overarching morality that demanded it.

Abram was a rarity.

And among his rare gifts was that of great faith. He had been promised an innumerable posterity, yet, to this point, he and Sarai had produced no offspring—not one.

After the rescue of Lot, Jehovah again appeared to Abram in a vision. Abram was shown the heavens and was promised that he would have more posterity than the stars in the night sky. Genesis tells us, "And he believed in the Lord; and he counted it to him for righteousness."[16]

Abram Receives a New Name

Sarai, faithful wife that she was, knew that her husband desired children. She did not have faith that they were to be born to her, however.

Sarai had been given the handmaiden Hagar by the Pharaoh of

Egypt. Jewish tradition claims that Hagar was, in fact, a daughter of Pharaoh.[17] Sarai suggested that Abram take Hagar as a wife—which offer Abram accepted. Hagar promptly became pregnant.

Upon learning this, Sarai reacted very badly. She drove Hagar from her home. As Hagar fled into the wilds, she was approached by an angel and told to return to Sarai, to submit to her, and to be reassured that she was pregnant with a son. The angel also told Hagar that she was to name the son Ishmael. She was promised that Ishmael would be the source of a multitude of grandchildren and other posterity for Hagar and Abram. Hagar did as she had been instructed, Ishmael was born, and the angel's prophecies came to pass.

Thirteen years later, as Abram approached one hundred years of age, Jehovah appeared to him and renewed His promises. Abram's name was changed to Abraham and Sarai's name was changed to Sarah. Abraham was told that he would be the father of many nations and kings and much posterity. Abraham entered into a covenant with Jehovah that Abraham's posterity would worship Jehovah and none other. The entire land of Canaan was promised to Abraham's posterity. As a sign of their covenant, Abraham was told to circumcise all males in his line when they were eight days old.

Finally, Abraham was told that Sarah would yet bear him a son and that she would be a mother of nations, kings, and people.

To this point, Abraham had been a faithful man—but one reading the biblical account might conclude that he did not receive this news with much faith. In fact, it relates that he fell on his face and laughed. How was he, almost one hundred years old, to father another child, by a woman who was ninety? The account may also be interpreted to mean that, upon receiving the news that he and Sarah were yet to have posterity, he rejoiced.

Isaac Is Promised

Shortly thereafter, the man with a new name was again visited by the Lord. Again the promise was made that he and Sarah would become the parents of a son. This time Sarah was eavesdropping on the conversation. She too laughed to herself upon hearing that news.

But Jehovah kept his promise, and Sarah bore a son and named him, according to the Lord's command, Isaac.

Genesis reports that Isaac became the chosen son, the son through whom the great promises made to Abraham were to be fulfilled—the kings, the nations, and the multitudes of people.

At the demand of Sarah, Abraham reluctantly forced Hagar and Ishmael out of the community. Abraham was assured by Jehovah not to worry about Ishmael. As promised, after Hagar arranged for Ishmael to marry an Egyptian, he became the father of twelve princes, with a great posterity of his own.

With Hagar and Ishmael in exile, Isaac was the sole heir to Abraham's pledged noble and plentiful posterity. That is why the next chapter in the Abraham story is so significant.

The Great Trial

Jehovah again visited Abraham and gave him an ultimate test: He was to take his son of the promise, Isaac, to the land of Moriah and offer him up as a burnt offering. With no recorded hesitation, Abraham complied.

Moriah was a three-day journey away. Abraham took with them fire and wood for the fire. As they approached the place where the sacrifice was to occur, the young Isaac became curious. How old Isaac was is not known, but he was old enough to observe that his father was bringing the fire and the wood but no lamb to be sacrificed. When he asked his father why, Abraham assured Isaac that the Lord would provide a lamb for the sacrifice.

When Abraham and his son reached the spot designated by Jehovah, an altar was built. Abraham arranged the wood, then bound Isaac and laid him on the altar. He took his knife and stretched out his hand to kill his dearly loved son. At the last moment, an angel called out from heaven and stopped the test.

The angel praised Abraham and his faithfulness. A ram was provided to complete the sacrifice. Abraham and Isaac returned to their home.

Abraham demonstrated his ultimate faith in Jehovah by his willingness to comply with Jehovah's command to sacrifice the son of the promise. In the New Testament, the great Apostle Paul asserts that Abraham was willing to sacrifice Isaac because he had the simple faith that even if he killed his son, Jehovah would raise Isaac from the dead.[18]

Once more, all the promises of kings, nations, and posterity were reaffirmed. Abraham was again promised that through his posterity all the nations of the earth were to be blessed.

Before his death Abraham arranged for Isaac to marry one of his kindred, a cousin named Rebekah. To them was born a son named Jacob, whose name was changed by Jehovah to Israel. To Israel and his wives were born twelve princes whose posterity became known as the twelve tribes of Israel. One of those tribes, headed by Israel's son Judah, became known as the Jews. Jesus Christ was a descendant of Abraham through Isaac, Israel, and Judah.

What If There Had Been No Abraham?

What is it about this man who lived four thousand years ago that qualifies him to be deemed a giant among men?

The best way to answer this question is to imagine what this world would have been like if there had been no Abraham.

What if he had never been born?

What if he had been sacrificed by his father as a youth?

What if the Pharaoh of Egypt had murdered him in order to be free to marry Sarai?

It would be a world without a belief in God, a Father in Heaven. The pillar of all of Abraham's legacy was monotheism—the belief that there is just one God, Jehovah of the Old Testament, and that Jehovah is the creator of heaven and earth, the God of all mankind, and that we are all his children. Abraham was not the first monotheist, but he was the one who made it stick. "He is the first person to understand that there is only one God. This is his greatest contribution to civilization and the shared endowment of the Abrahamic faiths."[19]

President John Adams said:

> The Hebrews have done more to civilize men than any other nation. . . . [God] ordered the Jews to preserve and propagate to all mankind the doctrine of a supreme, intelligent, wise, almighty sovereign of the universe . . . [which is] to be the great essential principle of morality, and consequently all civilization.[20]

Monotheism had existed before Abraham, but its practice had been lost. It had even been abandoned by those whose memory of God's punishment by way of the Great Flood was very vivid.

Why? Why was Abraham's God so hard to follow?

History shows that a belief in a God who cannot be seen is not the norm. Belief in a God who requires faith to worship is the rare exception. The worship of tangible idols, multiple gods, and one's ancestors is just much easier.

In addition, worshipping idols that do not require one to exercise discipline, follow a moral code, or do the "unnatural" unselfish thing is vastly easier than following a God who expects his followers to conduct themselves in ways that require sacrifice and self-control in their personal conduct.

The world in which Abraham lived—and in which all of those who followed his teachings of monotheism have lived down to the modern day—is a world that naturally rejects the Abrahamic concept of God.

It is also a world that resists the spiritual worldview that Abraham's life and example gave birth to. Yet Abraham somehow resurrected that belief and instilled the spiritual worldview in his posterity. Abraham and his adherents have kept alive the exceptional.

Let us take this analysis further.

Imagine a world in which Judaism, Christianity, and Islam did not exist.

Those who consider Abraham part of their religious heritage are, to put it mildly, numerous. One author asserts that "half the people alive today claim to be descended from him."[21]

All Jews descended from Abraham. Those who are literally descended from one of the other twelve tribes of Israel are direct descendants as well. Anyone who converts to Judaism is also deemed to be a descendant of Abraham.

Imagine a world without the contributions of the direct descendants of Abraham throughout the history of the world, especially those descended from his grandson Judah.[22]

The Muslims consider Abraham to be a quasi-founder of their faith. They believe that eighteen of the twenty-five acknowledged prophets of Islam come through the family of Abraham. He is a significant figure in the Islamic holy book, the Koran. He figures prominently in historically significant events in Islamic history, such as the rebuilding of the Ka'ba—a black cube, forty feet along each side, that lies at the center of Islamic worship in Mecca and is part of the required hajj: the sacred pilgrimage to Mecca expected of all faithful Muslims. Abraham also played a significant role in Muhammad's night journey wherein he saw Abraham and learned that he even resembled him physically. To the Muslims, Abraham represents faith.[23]

He does to Christians as well. Christians also believe that those who have been baptized unto Christ become part of Abraham's seed and heirs to the promises made to him.[24]

But of most importance to Christians, it was through the lineage of Abraham that Jesus Christ was to be born.

Imagine a world that had never heard of Jesus Christ or his teachings!

It is true that Abraham did not leave a lengthy compilation of teachings. He did not generate a list, such as the Prophet Moses did centuries later, of those things his posterity were to do or not to do.[25]

But the biblical account of Abraham's life, found in the book of Genesis, did contain specific examples of moral behavior that were very enlightened for his time. The examples of selflessness and mercy displayed by Abraham are not insignificant, especially considering the violent and ruthless times in which he lived.

Genesis tells us that Abraham and his posterity kept "the way of the Lord, to do justice and judgment."[26] Again, among people for whom justice was an alien concept, a man and household who did do justice were of no small consequence.

Abraham's example of faith in Jehovah is, without doubt, one of the most significant elements of his legacy. His faith was expressed in his willingness to accept Jehovah as the one and only God and to obey the command to leave his home in Haran. ("This is an extraordinary request at any level, but it's made even more profound by the fact that he's aging, that his wife is barren, and that he doesn't even know where he's going."[27]) Unquestionably, his passing of the ultimate test, Abraham's willingness to sacrifice his son of the promise, is unparalleled in religious history. These examples of faithful obedience have served to bolster the faithful obedience of all of those who consider Abraham part of their religious heritage—Jews, Christians, and Muslims.

Despite the fact that Abraham did not personally leave a written belief system, his acceptance of monotheism did lead to certain distinctive behaviors by its adherents. One scholar of the subject asserts:

> Once the Jews accepted the idea of monotheism (the doctrine that there is only one God), they began to behave in a special way without consciously knowing they were doing so. This change in behavior was at first imperceptible, but became ever more noticeable, setting them farther and farther apart from others.[28]

Among those behaviors that distinguished Abraham's followers was the rejection of human sacrifice. The killing of humans as a part of religious ritual has been common in multiple societies throughout the history of mankind: It existed among those people who encircled Abraham and his descendants. It existed in China, India, Europe, and both North and South America. It is rumored to exist in some areas of the world even today. The followers of Abraham rejected human sacrifice, and from that belief emerged the concept that human life is sacred.

Abraham and his descendants refuted the pagan fertility rites and sexual perversions that dominated the pagan worshippers among whom they lived.[29] They taught that sexual morality was required of the followers of Jehovah. This teaching has been a distinguishing feature of Abraham's legacy throughout the ages.

From his adherents have come other great and notable teachings that have enlightened the world, a few examples being: the concept of loving one's neighbor as oneself,[30] freedom of religious choice,[31] and a code for the conduct of judges and the administration of justice.[32]

These enlightened beliefs in the human condition have been the foundation for most of the advances in humanity since the time of Abraham. Again, they are the foundation of the worldview that has as its emphasis "moral truth and right conduct and its motto of Thus said the Lord."[33]

Wherever Abraham's influence has been most powerfully found, philosophy and religion have been very different from where there is no such influence. Justice, respect for human life, and the pursuit of equality are traits uniquely the offshoot of Abraham's intellectual offspring.

Let it be said that Abraham's discovery, conversion, faithfulness, example of obedience, and his zeal in spreading his belief to all who would listen did change the world.

Before Abraham, monotheism did not exist. After him, the spiritual worldview and its attendant blessings to the human condition have survived, among populations tiny and large, surrounded by pagans, without exception—for four thousand years.

Abraham was a giant!

Notes

1. Nicholi, *Question,* 7.
2. Feiler, *Abraham,* 20–21. For a review of the scholarly debate as to whether

Abraham did or did not exist, see ibid., 18–21. So much of the information about the life of Abraham, besides that which is found in the Bible, comes from ancient Jewish, Christian, and Muslim sources. Feiler argues that each of those sources was motivated by a desire to enhance the role of Abraham and to tie him to their unique religious doctrine. One scholarly source suggests: "Two themes run through his story of Abraham: God's promise of land and descendants, and the patriarch's struggle for sure faith that the divine promise will be fulfilled. The resulting story must be read as neither straight biography nor pure allegory" (Crim, *Interpreter's Dictionary,* 16).

3. Ussher, *Annals,* 22.
4. Tvedtnes, *Traditions,* 21–24, 44–45, 164–77. This book is a major collection of the various written references to Abraham from ancient sources outside of the biblical account.
5. Ussher, *Annals,* 19, 22.
6. Tvedtnes, *Traditions,* 190.
7. Ibid., 11, 14, 39, 190–91.
8. Ibid., 52–57; see also 14–16.
9. See those multiple sources cited at ibid., 540–41.
10. The Bible's account of Abraham is found in Genesis, chapters 11–25, although there are miscellaneous references to him sprinkled throughout the entire Bible, both Old and New Testaments.
11. Josephus, *Works*, 37.
12. Genesis 20:12.
13. Tvedtnes, *Traditions*, 28.
14. Ibid., 26–29; Genesis, chapter 12.
15. See Tvedtnes, *Traditions*, 7–9; see also the multiple sources cited at the same source, 544–45.
16. Genesis 15:6.
17. Tvedtnes, *Traditions*, 46, 67, 99.
18. Hebrews 11:17–19.
19. Feiler, *Abraham*, 11.
20. Federer, *America's God*, 12.
21. Ibid., 10. "He is the father—in many cases, the purported biological father—of 12 million Jews, 2 billion Christians, and 1 billion Muslims around the world" (ibid., 9).
22. Just one graphic example: 22 percent of all of the Nobel Prizes awarded for science have been awarded to Jews or those with three-fourths Jewish lineage, 185 in total (Jinfo.org).
23. For a discussion of the relationship between Abraham and all three of the Abrahamic religions (Judaism, Christianity, and Islam), see Feiler, *Abraham*, and Levenson, *Between Torah and Gospel.*

24. See Galatians, chapter 3, in the New Testament.
25. As one author said, "We have said that in Genesis Abraham has no teaching; he is a father and not a founder like the Buddha or Jesus or Muhammad" (Levenson, *Between Torah and Gospel*, 16).
26. Genesis 18:19.
27. Feiler, *Abraham*, 40.
28. Dimont, *Jews*, 33.
29. Ibid., 33–34.
30. Leviticus 18:19.
31. Joshua 24:15.
32. Exodus, chapter 23.
33. Nicholi, *Question*, 7.

Chapter 2

Pericles the Greek

Great men have two lives: one which occurs while they work on this earth; a second which begins at the day of their death and continues as long as their ideas and conceptions remain powerful.

ADOLPH BERLE

Throughout the history of mankind, if one considers the opportunity for men and women to govern themselves as enlightened, the world has been essentially dark.

Typical was the era five hundred years before the birth of Jesus Christ in the region of the Mediterranean Sea. This area was then dominated by the Persian and the Egyptian Empires. Both of these empires were governed by totalitarian monarchs who ruled their kingdoms arbitrarily and ruthlessly. These kings had standing armies not only to protect their borders from outside invaders but also to protect the ruling class from those being ruled. Centralized bureaucracies existed to enforce the rulers' mandates and to collect taxes to supply the rulers' desires. Independence among the governed cities was nonexistent. Freedom among the ruled people was unknown.

What was to become known as the nation of Greece had its own example of totalitarianism in the city-state of Sparta. Although this Greek city-state was vigorous in defending its independence as a city, it had long ago adopted a system that rejected personal freedom for its citizens as the means of protecting that independence. The recognized citizens of Sparta made up a distinct minority among the population of the community. In order to maintain order and to preserve their privileges, citizens of Sparta adopted an incredibly disciplined, militaristic existence. Family ties and affection were minimized (until much later in an adult male's life). Individual freedom was completely subordinated to the needs of the community. There was no belief in the importance of personal privacy; no economic freedom; no developing the talents of its citizens in the arts, sciences, philosophy, or any other form of enrichment of the soul. The Spartan system was typical of governments everywhere else in the world at that time: A small minority of noblemen ruled over the citizens of Sparta and enslaved all those deemed unworthy of citizenship.[1]

If there is anything that is obvious to any observer of world history, it is this: Tyranny and rule by the elite are the norm, the natural order, the way things are. It has always been so. Such darkness has been the rule not only in the Mediterranean world but in every other nation on every continent since the beginning of humankind.[2]

In the midst of this darkness—this prevailing form of tyrannical governance—a candle was lit just before the beginning of the fifth century B.C. in the Greek city-state of Athens. The candle was Athenian self-government—Athenian democracy. The candle was to grow into a full-fledged flame, which was destined to shine brightly for almost two hundred years. More important, the relatively brief era of Athenian self-government was to serve as an example of "what could be" to men and women of enlightenment for the next twenty-five hundred years.

How Did It Come to Be?

The development of the Greek city-state is a fascinating bit of history. In the centuries before Athens lit its candle, the Greeks refused a centralized government. Instead, they formed themselves into independent city-states, each organized around a single city.[3] Within what we now consider to be the nation of Greece, there were hundreds of such city-states. They were fiercely competitive with each other. Because they would compete in everything from athletic events (the Olympic Games began in ancient Greece), to trade, to political influence, and in war, simple survival demanded that it was excellence that mattered—not inherited name or title.

Because they were so competitive, the Greeks would never think of surrendering their personal allegiance to another city-state or allowing their city-state to become subsumed in a greater empire. This fierce independence and loyalty to a local government fostered a sense of personal independence—the emergence of an innate desire for individual freedom and the power to control one's personal destiny.

These city-states were relatively poor (Greece was not very favorable for agriculture and possessed only a limited amount of mineral wealth), and there was not a lot of difference in the living standards between the economic classes in the period when the city-states evolved. This prevented the emergence of a wealthy and powerful elite in most of the Greek city-states.

Perhaps most essential for the appearance of the Athenian democracy was the method of warfare adopted by the Greeks. On the land, dependence on the cavalry, a small number of men fighting from horseback, had been abandoned centuries earlier. It was replaced by men fighting in massed formation—large numbers of men.

The Athenians did not have a professional army available to protect the city-state. Rather, they relied on citizen soldiers who would serve when called and would otherwise go about their normal lives and engage in their customary livelihoods. The average citizen of a Greek city-state was expected to arm himself and to be prepared to fight alongside his fellow citizens.

Such men demanded a voice in the political decisions that mattered, most important of which was the decision to send them to war. Thus, a broad-based political class was born.

The Athenians' reliance on another element of their military, the navy, also resulted in demand for the inclusion of a broader base of citizens in government.

In this era Athens emerged as a great naval power. This came about from both its military needs (it was Athens's navy that saved it from being conquered by the Persians in 480 B.C.) and also its reliance on trade. Because they had so little agriculture or mineral wealth, the Greeks needed trade within the greater Mediterranean world to survive and to thrive. For trade, a navy was essential.

Further, during the fifth century B.C. Athens developed an empire, or at least a large number of cities over which it exercised political and military influence and from which it could demand tribute. This empire extended throughout much of the eastern Mediterranean region. Athens's empire depended on its navy.

In turn, its navy depended entirely on those who would row the boats, for the ships of that era could never rely on sails for propulsion. The Athenian citizen who was going to row a boat—a miserable profession, to say the least—demanded a voice in all of those political decisions that involved war, trade, and empire.[4]

This combination of factors was unique in world history. It resulted in the emergence of a broad-based, activist citizenry in Athens.

But it did not happen overnight:

> Precisely why she became a democracy is of course as important a study as that of her democratic constitution. It was a long process, from monarch to democracy, and the first step taken could not have been with any conscious knowledge of the ultimate goal. In a general way, however, we can say that the Athenians vaguely knew what they wanted and were able through the centuries finally to embody their wants in a code with the proper machinery for smooth operation.[5]

Who Was Responsible?

There is some dispute about who should be given credit for Athenian democracy. In the long journey that led to this unique method of governance, many helped the process along.

Some of the recognition must be given to Solon, who became a dominant political figure in Athens in 594 B.C. Solon was a man of many achievements in politics and business, and he was also a poet of some acclaim. Most important, he was recognized to be a very wise man. Upon achieving political power, he set about to solve a number of challenges, primarily economic in nature, then faced by the Athenian people. The outcome of his reforms was the weakening of rule by the royalty of Athens. No longer could one expect to retain a position of power simply because of birth, nor was all political power vested in a handful of powerful and noble families. Instead, a timocracy emerged—a government in which wealth played a major role in deciding one's position at the political table. As Athens evolved into a more wealthy city, this meant that all but the very poorest of the city's citizens would qualify for office.

Although the old aristocracy and the most wealthy still controlled the high offices, organizations known as the Assembly (which consisted of all of the citizens of Athens) and the Council of the Four Hundred gave the average citizen a check on the power of the elite. This check was made even more secure by Solon's creation of the *heliaea.* These were courts in which all men over the age of thirty were expected to participate as jurors. These courts considered appeals from decisions made by the archons, the nine chief magistrates of Athens. Perhaps of greatest importance to the evolution toward democracy, these courts could judge the conduct of the archons themselves.

The sum of Solon's efforts was described by one scholar: "The net result was that the rich and noble were to fill the offices, the commons were to have only enough power to check them and preserve their own liberty."[6]

The author of this quote most seriously understates the matter.

Considering the dominance of the elite in every other empire on earth, the fact that the commoner—the average farmer, merchant, artisan, soldier, sailor, and such—had even a *check* on the power of the nobleman was an enormous step forward!

The candle had been lit.

The man often given credit for being the founder of the Athenian democracy was a nobleman who proved himself willing to ignore the demands of his own class and to expand the power of the common man. His name was Cleisthenes.

In the decade before 500 B.C., Cleisthenes undertook serious reforms of the Athenian constitution. He set about to destroy certain clans and associations of long standing that were the foundation of the enduring power of nobles and certain families. He created an organization that consisted of ten tribes based upon geography within Athens and the adjoining area of Attica. A new Council of Five Hundred was created to replace the old Council of Four Hundred. Membership in the Council of Five Hundred was decided annually when fifty members from each of the ten tribes were chosen by lot. The random selection guaranteed that no one could be guaranteed membership in the Council.

The Council of Five Hundred was responsible for certain administrative tasks, specifically financial matters and foreign affairs. It also decided what matters of business were to be taken before the Assembly.

Cleisthenes wisely understood that certain citizens would always seek for absolute power. To discourage such individuals from attempting to reestablish the power of noblemen, powerful families, or individual tyrants, he instituted the mechanism of the "ostracism." Once a year, at a meeting of the Assembly, an individual deemed to be a menace to Athenian democracy could be "ostracized," sent into exile for ten years. There had to be at least six thousand members of the Assembly in attendance for such a vote to occur, and it was the person with the highest number of votes who was cast out of the city for a decade.

The final reform brought about by Cleisthenes was the establishment of a board of ten generals, the *strategoi.* These men were elected and had as their chief responsibility the typical duty of all generals—conducting the military affairs of the city-state.

The citizen courts were also continued.

Cleisthenes must be given credit for what he accomplished. For the first time in human history, and the last time until the late eighteenth century after Christ, the average citizens of a great community were given the opportunity, and the responsibility, to govern themselves.

The candle was now glowing.

But, despite the brilliance of these reforms, there were still problems in the Athenian democracy. Chief among them was the fact that the average citizen had to make a living. That required almost constant attention to his farm, his shop, his trading affairs, or the like. Leaving the farm or shop to attend to public business was often a great sacrifice. Many of the citizens of Athens simply could not take the time to do so. The result was that only the more wealthy citizens actually participated in the Council, the courts, even the Assembly. The second weakness was that the Council of the Areopagite, a council made up exclusively of aristocrats, continued to wield great power in the Athenian government.[7]

The Rise of Pericles

Among the great things that Cleisthenes left to Athens was his grand-nephew, Pericles.

Born in 494, Pericles was the son of Cleisthenes's niece Agariste. He was born into one of Athens's most prominent families, if not its most prominent. His father, Xanthippus, was a war hero. His was a privileged life. His associations were with the elite of Athenian society.

Pericles received the traditional education of an Athenian youth: studying Homer's epic poetry, training in athletics, mastering musical instruments. Pericles also displayed an early intellectual curiosity and aptitude that compelled his parents to provide him with more education. The primary influence on Pericles's intellectual development came from a non-Athenian named Anaxagoras who became his hired tutor. Anaxagoras was a native of a Greek city famous for producing men of philosophy and science. He rejected the superstition and belief in the supernatural that were common among the population as a whole. Pericles was taught to rely on reason. He was also taught to question and challenge the status quo.

Pericles made his first appearance on the public scene when he was given the honor of producing a play that won an annual contest. In the Athenian world, a world where poetry and theater were so important, this feat was significant. The fact that Pericles was only eighteen years old at the time showed him to be somewhat of a prodigy.

He then diverted his attention from the arts to the field of battle. For the next decade he served in the Athenian military. He became known for his daring and bravery as well as his leadership abilities.

By this time Athens had succeeded in establishing a significant empire, although not an empire in the traditional sense. Following the Persian invasions of the early decades of the fifth century, many of the Greek city-states that encircled the Aegean Sea banded together to form an alliance known as the Delian League. This alliance was created as a defensive bulwark against future Persian aggression. Athens became its leader. From the many participants, Athens demanded tribute to help pay for an expanded navy and army to deter Persian attack. The League also took on the role of ridding the seas of pirate bands that disrupted trade. When Athens succeeded in both of the League's objectives, it naturally rose to a position of influence and power within the League. The net effect was that the League evolved into an Athenian empire.

This empire provided adventurous and brave men such as Pericles a superb opportunity to find glory on the land and on the sea. Pericles made much of that opportunity.

By the time he was thirty years old, the earliest age at which he could do so, Pericles ran for the office of general and was successful. Thus began his leadership role in Athenian politics—a role he was to play until his death.

Pericles came to political power at a time when the fragile Athenian democracy was under attack.

For years, the most popular politician in all of Athens was Cimon. A war hero, wealthy, very generous, he commanded the respect of both the prosperous and the poorer citizens of the city-state. However, he was closely wedded to the aristocracy. He supported the ancient Council of the Areopagite, whose members were the elite of Athenian nobility. Cleisthenes had been afraid to weaken the power of that council in his reforms several decades before. After the Persian War, it reestablished itself as the overseer of all administrative and military matters in the empire. It was the ultimate power in Athens.

Despite the growing dependence of the city-state on its poorer members, particularly those in the navy, these commoners were not being awarded with more political power because the Council of the Areopagite would not surrender it. Cimon saw to that.

After Pericles had served for several years as a general, he became the chief supporter of a reformer named Ephialtes. Ephialtes and his supporters seized the power of the Council of the Areopagite and transferred it to the Council of Five Hundred. Cimon was ostracized and sent into exile. Shortly thereafter, the nobles took revenge, and Ephialtes was assassinated.

Pericles succeeded him. It was the year 461 B.C. He was thirty-three years old. He was suddenly the leading citizen of a powerful city-state with an extensive empire. He was to remain so for the next thirty years.

What would he do with his power?

The Great Democrat

Pericles inherited leadership in a limited democracy. As a general, Pericles had some political sway, but in the end any reform that he sought to bring about had to pass through the gauntlet of public opinion. As a general, he was just one of ten. As a general, he had to stand for election every year, and he could be recalled from his generalship at any time. He had no personal fortune, political party, or access to public funds.

In sum, although he was a leader, his was not an inherently strong political position. Yet he was able to bring about reforms that were to make Athens the most democratic nation in the history of the world.[8]

Why did he do it? Why did Pericles, a member of one of Athens's most aristocratic families, turn his back on his family and elite associates and work to weaken their power? Why did he not use his considerable political skills to gain more power for himself and his class?

Because he actually believed in the power of democracy.

Arguably the most important characteristic possessed by Pericles was his sincerity. He truly believed in expanding the power of average Athenians over the decisions so important to their happiness. It was in his blood, literally, being the grand-nephew of the great democratic reformer Cleisthenes.

He had been taught by his tutor, Anaxagoras, to believe in man's ability to reason, and the capacity to reason dictated that man possessed the ability to govern himself.

Finally, he saw the greatness that Athens could aspire to, but he believed that only through unleashing the freedom, the genius, and the vigor of all its people could that greatness be reached: "Only democracy held the prospect of releasing the full energy of all the people, thereby creating a polis of unprecedented potential. Perhaps that prospect, more than anything else, made Pericles the convinced democrat that he always was."[9]

Pericles "was one of those rare individuals who do not merely accept the conditions of the world they find but try to shape it to an image in their own minds."[10] He believed that Athens could become "the greatest political community the world had ever known."[11] He foresaw Athens and its people possessing great glory. Unlike the rulers, kings, and emperors to be found in every land throughout history, he did not believe such glory could come about only through conquest, pillaging, ruthless terror, and tyranny—he believed it could best be achieved by assuring equality for all of the citizens of his city-state; he believed it could be achieved by making the citizens of Athens accountable for their public lives; he believed it could best be achieved by persuading the citizens of Athens to do their duty—to actively govern themselves.

How did he manage to accomplish it? What qualities did he possess that allowed him to succeed in expanding the power of Athens's nonelite?

Because he believed in democracy so earnestly, his power of persuasion was greatly enhanced. Absent such powers, he had no way of achieving what he sought to do. "Pericles tried to shape a new kind of society and a new kind of citizen, not by the use of force or terror but by the power of his ideas, the strength of his personality, the use of reason, and his genius as a uniquely persuasive rhetorician."[12]

Pericles was a most gifted speaker. His power of persuasion is perhaps best captured by the words of one of his political opponents. When asked who was the better wrestler, he or Pericles, Thucydides replied, "When I have thrown him and given him a fair fall, by persisting that he had no fall, he gets the better of me, and makes the bystanders, in spite of their own eyes, believe him."[13] He was "the greatest orator of his day by common consent."[14] Such powers of persuasion could have been misused in the Athens of the mid-fifth century. Pericles might have easily used this extraordinary ability to reverse the course of democratization, but he chose to do the opposite.

One of the most common criticisms of political leaders of any kind, but in particular those found in democracies and republics, is that they are prone to tell the people what they want to hear. Pericles could easily have justified in his own mind the need to do so. He was, after all, subject to rejection every time the Assembly met; he had to stand for reelection every year. But he did not:

> Yet he refused to flatter the people and appeal to their prejudices. Instead, when the occasion demanded, he informed them of the realities and advised them how to cope; he called upon them to rise above their fears and short-range self interest, and inspired them to do so. When necessary, he was willing to chastise them and risk their anger.[15]

The Greek historian Thucydides, a contemporary of Pericles, summarized Pericles's own philosophy of what a leader was expected to do: "to know what must be done and to be able to explain it; to love one's country and to be incorruptible."[16] To his great credit, Pericles lived what he preached.

Because of this vision, and through his focus, powers, and resolve, Pericles set about to create a more perfect democracy.

Athenian Democracy Is Perfected

In the years following his ascension to leading citizen, relying on the system for changing the constitution and the laws of Athens that he inherited, Pericles brought about major reforms. Of most importance, all levels of the government, including the Council of the Areopagite, were finally opened up to every Athenian citizen regardless of wealth or status. At last the great power that had rested exclusively in the aristocratic and wealthy minority was shattered. One might be from an old family, one might be more wealthy than others, but such a one had no more say in the affairs of Athens than the small farmer or shopkeeper, sailor or soldier.

The Assembly became the exclusive body for making laws. A simple majority vote within that Assembly was all that was required. All citizens of Athens were entitled to vote in the Assembly. During the Pericles era there were an estimated forty thousand citizens of Athens.[17] Some actions required a minimum of six thousand citizens to make a quorum. Presumably, this was the average number of those in attendance.

The Assembly would meet at least forty times each year. The sessions would begin with a prayer. Everyone was entitled to speak. "Thus a man, with no family connections whatever, could urge a particular policy and win a position for himself among his fellow citizens."[18] Matters of great import—war, foreign affairs, removal of officials from office, ostracizing, trade arrangements—were decided. In addition to these weighty matters, anything else could be raised in the Assembly, including private feuds or neighborhood disputes.

Sometimes, when the matters to be decided did not seem particularly interesting, it was difficult to get the citizens to take the day off from their labors to attend. In those cases police officers would be sent into the streets to literally "rope" citizens into the meetingplace using ropes drenched in wet red paint.

Those who today observe governing bodies—be they Congress, parliaments, state legislatures, city councils, or PTA meetings—and find them to be unruly and disorganized should consider just what these Athenian mass town meetings would have been like: impassioned speeches, shouted insults, vocal groans of disagreement not just from a single member but from hundreds, perhaps thousands. Following the debate, every decision, small or great, would be decided by the vote of the citizens in attendance, and the majority would carry the day.

The primary means of controlling this mass of citizens was the Council of Five Hundred. The members of this group were chosen by lot from the ten tribes created earlier by Cleisthenes. Their primary job was to prepare legislation for the Assembly to consider—the agenda for the meeting, if you will. However, the Assembly was by no means limited by what this Council suggested.

The closest thing to executives within the Athenian system were the ten generals. However, they were severely limited in their authority. They were elected for one-year terms and even then were subject to being recalled at any time by the Assembly. Their responsibility was to conduct wars. Here, however, they were subject to the Assembly as well, for the Assembly assigned them to specific campaigns and allotted them their men or ships. At the end of each year they were held accountable by an audit and job review by the Assembly.

Other than commanding their assigned military forces, they had no inherent political authority. The extent that they were able to affect political outcomes was due solely to their powers of persuasion in the Assembly.

Almost all of the other administrative offices in Athens were filled randomly by lot.

The popular law courts, the *heliaea,* were continued. Each year up to six thousand citizens would be empaneled to hear cases during the coming year. Because the Athenians were a litigious people, trials were conducted almost every day. The usual jury had 501 members. There were no judges. A simple majority decided the issue. In order to avoid corruption, the jurors would not know what cases they were to hear until the day that they would show up for trial.

The time demands of the Assembly and the courts put great pressure on the less wealthy Athenians—those who had to tend to fields, flocks, customers, and employees. Before Pericles's reforms, many commoners simply could not find the time to participate in their appointed duty. This left the richer citizens with greater say in the political process than their numbers would have suggested.

Pericles solved this critical flaw in Athenian democracy by encouraging a law to allow for jurors and members attending the Assembly to be paid. This simple solution dramatically altered the Athenian democracy. For the first time, every citizen was not only allowed but capable of attending the Assembly and passing judgment in the courts. Eventually the payment for public service was extended to all other public servants as well as members of the military.

One last reform of significance was the increase in the number of public offices that were selected by lot—randomly—with no politicking allowed. The assumption was that all citizens were equal in both ability and duty; thus service in the higher offices was to be open to all and to be required of all. Only a handful of offices remained subject to popular vote. For those offices, the terms of office were shortened.

In the Athenian system under Pericles, rights of citizenship were confined to those men who were the sons of both a mother and a father of Athens. Those who may have come from other communities, Greek or barbarian, were not entitled to citizenship. Women, slaves, and men under the age of twenty were not citizens. In sum, those entitled to exercise the rights of citizenship in Athens were nearly identical to those allowed to exercise rights of citizenship in the United States of America until the American Civil War freed the slaves and the passage of the nineteenth amendment to the Constitution of the United States in 1920 extended the right to vote to women.

A Perfect Form of Governing?

Was this a perfect system of governance? History would say no. In the decades following Pericles's death, many critics arose among the Athenian elite, including the famous Athenian philosopher Plato. These critics rejected the idea that masses of common people should be deciding complicated matters of state. They also found fault with the use of random selection—selection by lot—for key administrative positions. These critics also assumed that the rights of property were always at risk and that minority rights were in jeopardy under the Periclean democracy.

Sometime during Pericles's era a criticism of the Athenian experiment in democracy was written by an unknown author referred to as the "Old Oligarch." His critique details his concerns, but also acknowledges the system's strengths and praises Athens for bringing democracy about:

> Now, as for the constitution of the Athenians, and the type or manner of constitution which they have chosen I praise it not, in so far as the very choice involves the welfare of the baser folk as opposed to that of the better class. I repeat, I withhold praise so far; but, given the fact that this is the type agreed upon, I propose to show that they set about its preservation in the right way; and that those other transactions in connection with it, which are looked upon as blunders by the rest of the Hellenic world, are the reverse.[19]

The great Greek historian Plutarch was another writer who was not a fan of Pericles's efforts to bring democracy to Athens. Because Plato and Plutarch got to write the reviews that survived, history has not been so kind in its appraisal of Periclean democracy.

Athens at the Height of Its Glory

Although Plutarch did not like Athenian democracy, he wrote much in praise of what Pericles accomplished—for Pericles had much to praise beyond his reform of Athenian democracy. Those praiseworthy deeds included his innovative efforts in colonizing. Recognizing that Athens could sustain only a limited number of citizens, Pericles organized large groups of citizens, sometimes in the tens of thousands, and established them in new colonies throughout the Mediterranean world. This not only removed the threat from the impossible demands of a surplus population but also expanded the wealth and influence of Athens manyfold. The resulting empire was a notable one.

Pericles tapped the talents and energy of the Athenian people in remarkable ways. "Pericles also sponsored a great outburst of artistic and intellectual activity. . . . His patronage of the arts and his personal support and encouragement of thinkers and their activities made Athens a magnet that drew to it the leading creative talents from the entire Greek world."[20]

It was Pericles who came up with the idea of building the temples and other buildings that adorned the Acropolis and surrounding area. He envisioned the sculptures and effigies that the world marvels at 2,500 years later. He raised the money and hired the sculptors, architects, and builders to accomplish those tasks.

Encouraged by Pericles, and as a direct consequence of the incredible human energy unleashed by democracy, the Greeks of the fifth century became intellectual giants:

> The Greeks, and pre-eminently the Athenians, whose city became "the teacher of the Hellas," placed intellectual inquiry high among the things that really counted in life. As a result, they asked practically every great question that has ever engaged mankind: the advantages of wealth; the

> nature of the gods and the immortality of the soul; the true character of democracy; the meaning of justice and tyranny, cruelty, beauty, and love. Athens in the fifth century B.C. very obviously did not answer these questions with a finality, nor always with marked success, but some of her best minds made a noble attempt, and it is by its best minds that any civilization may fairly ask to be judged.[21]

Pericles had a vision of what humans could be. He brought Athens to the "summit of civilization never before reached by the human race."[22]

The Noble Athenian

Pericles perceived a concept of the "noble Athenian." This concept, along with an expression of his love for Athens and what it represented, were articulated in one of the few speeches delivered by Pericles that has survived. The occasion was a funeral oration for those who had died in the first year of what was to become known as the Peloponnesian War. This war between Athens and Sparta began in 431 B.C. and was to last for ten years. In many ways, it proved to be the undoing of the greatness of all Greece.

Pericles's funeral oration seemed designed less to honor the dead and more to motivate the living, the audience, to a greater love and admiration for Athens. Pericles hoped to inspire the citizens of Athens to even greater achievements. The words of Pericles:

> But before I praise the dead, I should like to point out by what principles of action we rose to power, and under what institutions and through what manner of life our empire became great. . . .
>
> Our form of government does not enter into rivalry with the institutions of others. We do not copy our neighbors, but are an example to them. It is true that we are called a democracy, for the administration is in the hands of the many and

> not of the few. But while the law secures equal justice to all alike in their private disputes, the claim of excellence is also recognized. . . . Neither is poverty a bar, but a man may benefit his country whatever be the obscurity of his condition. . . . In our private intercourse we are not suspicious of one another, nor angry with our neighbor if he does what he likes; . . . a spirit of reverence pervades our public acts; we are prevented from doing wrong by respect for the authorities and for the laws, having an especial regard to those which are ordained for the protection of the injured. . . .
>
> Wealth we employ, not for talk and ostentation, but when there is a real use for it. To avow poverty with us is no disgrace; the true disgrace is in doing nothing to avoid it. . . . We alone regard a man who takes no interest in public affairs, not as a harmless, but as a useless character. . . . The great impediment to action is, in our opinion, not discussion, but the want of that knowledge which is gained by discussion preparatory to action. . . . We alone do good to our neighbors not upon a calculation of interest, but in the confidence of freedom and in a frank and fearless spirit. . . .
>
> I have dwelt upon the greatness of Athens because I want to show you that we are contending for a higher prize than those who enjoy none of these privileges.[23]

This description of the noble Athenian may have been in the eye of the beholder, Pericles. However, there was undoubtedly more than just a sliver of truth to his description of the people of Athens. The best evidence of that truth is found in the fact that this rare and truly unique form of governance lasted as long as it did. It could not have done so if the average Athenian did not possess to some degree the patriotism and high ideals expressed in the words of Pericles. The Athenians under Pericles believed in the equality of men and the rule of law. They believed that individuals, by performing their duty, could set their own destiny. They further believed that the proper form of government could unleash the potential of all men to true greatness. Their beliefs were proven by the success of their society and political community.

Again, the question: Was Athenian democracy a perfect form of government? The answer is decidedly *no.* Support of this conclusion can be found in how Pericles's democracy treated him. When the Peloponnesian War began to go bad, and Athens was struck by a plague that killed much of its population, the people turned against Pericles. Despite all that he had done for them, the Athenian Assembly ousted him from office, accused him of fraud, fined him, and almost had him executed. He died of the plague shortly thereafter in the year 429 B.C.

Democracy was to survive the death of Pericles. Despite several coups and brief periods of usurpation, Athens managed to hold on to its basic democratic system for another century. It was the rise of Alexander the Great and his successors that finally ended Athenian independence in foreign affairs and domestic governance, roughly 320 years before the birth of Christ.

Why Athens Matters

There are three points about the Athenian experience that must be made.

First, it was an extraordinary experiment in self-government that, despite its faults, succeeded for a considerable period of time:

> Starting with the fuller democracy instituted by Ephialtes and Pericles from 461, we discover an almost unbroken, orderly regime that lasted 140 years. Twice it was interrupted by oligarchic episodes. . . . On each occasion the full democracy was restored without turmoil—without class warfare, revenge, or confiscation of property. Through many years of hard warfare, military defeat, foreign occupation, and oligarchic agitation, the Athenian democracy persisted and showed a restraint and moderation rarely equaled by any regime.[24]

The second point is of greater significance. It cannot be overemphasized how incredibly rare Athenian democracy was. It came about when the inhabitants of the rest of the entire world, no matter what nation or continent we are considering, were ruled by tyrants and kings and emperors with controlled, centralized authority. A notable scholar makes this point:

> Although in our time democracy is taken for granted, it is in fact one of the rarest, most delicate and fragile flowers in the jungle of human experience. It existed for two centuries in Athens and less than that in a small number of Greek states. When it reappeared in the Western world more than two millennia later, it was broader but shallower. . . .
>
> Only in ancient Athens and in the United States so far has democracy lasted for as much as two hundred years. Monarchy and different forms of despotism, on the other hand, have gone on for millennia. A dynasty or tyranny or clique may be deposed, but it is invariably replaced by another or by a chaotic anarchy that ends in the establishment of some kind of command society. Optimists may believe that democracy is the inevitable and final form of human society, but the historical record shows that up to now it has been the rare exception. . . .
>
> If we are to understand the Greeks' experience we must recognize that it was a freakish exception to that of the overwhelming number of human beings and societies that came before and after.[25]

The third point is this: The United States of America might not have come about, nor would it have survived as long as it has, if not for the Athenian experience.

The fact that one group of people in world history had proved that self-government worked was of incredible importance to the founding of America. It was long recognized that Athenian democracy had unleashed the power of the people in such a way that Athens became the hallmark of human progress. But for millennia, these ideals always remained just a flicker in the hearts and minds of the enlightened ones.

In the United States of America, that flicker of an ideal finally came to full flame—but that flame might not have been lit if not for the knowledge that it had existed before.

The Athenian view of equality was the inspiration for the American system that has moved inexorably toward treating all Americans equally under the law. The Athenian view of the rule of law is a pillar in the American representative democracy today. Rewarding excellence, making one earn respect instead of being born to it, has been a hallmark of the American experiment. These were all things learned from Athens.

It was, in sum, Athens that proved that even with an imperfect system, men could govern themselves.

Had there been no single example in the entire history of mankind of successful self-government, would the American Founders ever have attempted the grand experiment that they did?

In addition, it must be acknowledged that the United States of America has survived its own experiment in self-government because Athens taught the Founders *what not to do.*

The Founders were students of world history. They had examined the experience of Athens, as well as those of Rome and other notable forms of government, to see what worked and what did not work.

Noting the weaknesses of the Athenian system, they were critical of it. Specifically, the Founders were wary of the "pure democracy" practiced by the Athenians—that is, the system of simple majority rule. Pericles and his form of government were considered and specifically rejected by the Founders.

Why? The Founders clearly understood that pure democracy was unstable. They observed in the Athenian experience that pure democracy is by definition the rule by the majority, and sometimes that majority is just a mob. Majority rule lends itself to the temptation for the majority to trample the rights of the minority. The Founders also recognized that a pure democracy could result in the rights of the majority being trampled by an agitated minority.

They perceived that in a pure democracy the inalienable rights which governments are created to protect could be at risk. They foresaw the possibility of the mob depriving a minority of their property. They foresaw the possibility of the majority deciding to dictate a national religion. They saw the possibility of a mass of citizens supporting a charismatic leader who would overthrow self-government altogether and institute a monarchy or dictatorship.

To avoid this, the Founders specifically rejected pure democracy. The Constitution of the United States contains no elements of pure democracy.

Instead, a republic was created in which the citizens are allowed to exercise their democratic rights through the election of representatives. To those representatives, the members of Congress and the president, the right to exercise the power of government is entrusted. But that power is bestowed upon the elected ones only by the people, through legitimate and frequent elections. Further, those persons exercising those powers can do so only so long as the people choose to grant them that right. They can be deprived of that right by the ballot box.

One of the most telling explanations of why the Founders rejected the Athenian system and implemented a republic is to be found in *The Federalist* #63, in which the system of government organized under the new Constitution of the United States was set forth and then contrasted with Athens's pure democracy: "What bitter anguish would not the people of Athens have often escaped if their government had contained so provident a safeguard against the tyranny of their own passions?"[26]

We have thrived as a nation under the form of government the Founders gave us. We have survived wars and economic turmoil and attacks upon our freedoms because we are a republic. The genius of the Founders is a fact proven by the 225-plus years of America's triumphant existence.

That genius was, at least in part, a result of the Founders learning from Athens what the new government ought not to be.

What of the Future?

And as for the future? It is a proven fact that for any system of self-government to survive, it requires both a citizenry that is wise and possessed of a modicum of selflessness and leaders who can instill within citizens the understanding that those virtues are demanded.

This is as true for a republic as it is for a pure democracy.

Self-government requires citizens and leaders who will resist the temptation to demand equality of result by abuse of the law. In a republic, both citizens and leaders must understand that it is individual freedom and equality of opportunity that will lead to both economic prosperity and the fullness of advances in all aspects of civilization. This requires a citizenry that performs its public duties, is informed, and elects leaders who are wise and possess a true public spirit.

The Founders understood that.

Pericles understood that. As a leader, he struggled to help the Athenians understand that. That is why he is a giant.

What about us?[27]

Notes

1. Kagan, *Pericles,* 30, 41–43, 139–40, 145. In one interesting account, Kagan tells of an occasion when Sparta called on Athens to help quell a rebellion of the slave class in Sparta. The Athenians sent soldiers to help, but they were quickly dismissed by the Spartans because the Spartans were both appalled at, and threatened by, the behavior of the independent thinking Athenian soldiers. See ibid., 41–43.
2. Until the late eighteenth century and the emergence of the United States of America. For more information on this topic, see Stewart and Stewart, *The Miracle of Freedom.*
3. The central city was the focus of the city-state; however, the actual borders of the city-state usually included areas, sometimes fairly large areas, of surrounding countryside. For example, the city-state of Athens included all of the Attic Peninsula, an area of about a thousand square miles. See Botsford and Robinson, *History,* 85 and Robinson, *Athens,* 6.
4. For a discussion of the factors that resulted in the emergence of democracy in Athens, see Kagan, *Pericles,* 4–5, 16, 29, 34.
5. Botsford and Robinson, *History,* 84.

6. Ibid., 92. For a summary of Solon's reforms, see 89–93.
7. For information about the reforms instituted by Cleisthenes, see ibid., 95–98, and Kagan, *Pericles,* 15–16.
8. See Kagan, *Pericles,* 47. When we use the term *democracy,* or *democratic,* we are referring to the ability of the people to make the political and policy decisions for themselves, directly, by simple majority rule.
9. Ibid., 64. For Pericles's motivation, generally, see ibid., 63–64. *Polis* was the Greek term for city-state. The Greek historian Plutarch, who lived five hundred years after Pericles, took a dimmer view of the motivation of Pericles. Plutarch suggests that he had seen what had happened to Cimon and had become a democrat to avoid the same fate. There is little support for this position in the historical record. It should be noted that Plutarch did not have much respect for the Athenian democracy, perhaps believing the critique of Plato. See Plutarch, *Lives,* 206.
10. Kagan, *Pericles,* 136.
11. Ibid.
12. Kagan, *Pericles,* 7.
13. Plutarch, *Lives,* 207.
14. Kagan, *Pericles,* 7.
15. Ibid., 8.
16. Ibid., 9.
17. Ibid., 49. It is estimated that the total population of Athens in this period was 150,000 citizens (including the men and their wives and children), 35,000 alien noncitizens, and 80,000 slaves (see Robinson, *Athens,* 93).
18. Robinson, *Athens,* 29.
19. Ibid., 21.
20. Kagan, *Pericles,* 6–7.
21. Robinson, *Athens,* 51.
22. Botsford and Robinson, *History,* 181.
23. Ibid., 40–44.
24. Kagan, *Pericles,* 61.
25. Ibid., 2–3.
26. Hamilton, *The Federalist,* 342. For more information about the decision of the Founders to reject the pure democracy of the Athenians, see *The Federalist* generally.
27. For additional information about Pericles and the Athenian democracy, see Botsford and Robinson, *History,* 84–215; Kagan, *Pericles;* Plutarch, *Lives,* 201–34; Robinson, *Athens;* Strain, *Contribution,* 136–49.

Chapter 3

Paul—Apostle to the Gentiles

The Church of Christ needed also "the Apostle of Progress."

Frederic W. Farrar

Toward the end of the first century after the birth of Jesus Christ, a Jewish-Roman historian by the name of Josephus wrote:

> Now, there was about this time Jesus, a wise man, if it be lawful to call him a man, for he was a doer of wonderful works; a teacher of such men as receive the truth with pleasure. He drew over to him both many of the Jews, and many of the Gentiles. He was [the] Christ; and when Pilate, at the suggestion of the principal men amongst us, had condemned him to the cross, those that loved him at the first did not forsake him; for he appeared to them alive again the third day, as the divine prophets had foretold these and ten thousand other wonderful things concerning him; and the tribe of Christians, so named from him, are not extinct at this day.[1]

How is it that Christianity, considered a cult, with its origin in one of the backcountries of the Roman Empire, survived the decades after the crucifixion of Jesus Christ at the insistence of the "principal men amongst us?"

The man Jesus had left no written words. There were no extant records of his spoken words. How did his followers of later decades and centuries know what he taught or what he represented?

Why were "the tribe of Christians" not only not extinct but thriving throughout the reaches of the Roman Empire and in its capital of Rome as well?

Why did this religion, whose Messiah was a Jewish carpenter, draw to it Gentiles—the Greeks, the Romans, the Egyptians, and so many others who often looked upon the Jews with contempt?

One key to answering these questions is to be found in knowing Paul, the man from Tarsus.

It should be noted that, as with the study of any individual, particularly one who lived two millennia ago, it is difficult to find source materials about Paul's life. It is even more difficult to know what to believe in that which one finds. Even though the life of the Apostle Paul is the best documented of the early followers of Jesus Christ, controversy abounds over what is to be believed about the biblical account of his life and what he is assumed to have written.

For example, historically he was afforded credit for writing the fourteen Epistles, or letters, that make up the bulk of the New Testament. However, many scholars now assert that he was not the author of one of those Epistles, the book of Hebrews. Other scholars dispute his authorship of others of the Epistles. Some contend that his personal history as contained in the book of Acts, which was written by Luke, is not fully authoritative.[2]

Notwithstanding these contentions, there is a sufficiently large, accepted knowledge base on the life and teachings of Paul to allow us to draw certain conclusions. These conclusions fully support the argument that Paul was the pivotal player in the expansion of Christianity from a religion focused in the confines of Asian Palestine to *the* religion of Europe and eventually much of the world. Because of the role of Christianity in the development of Western philosophy and the unfolding of world history, Paul is highly qualified to be called a giant among men.

The Younger Paul

It is not known when Paul was born, but it seems safe to assume that he was born in the same decade as Christ.[3] We do know that he is first mentioned in the New Testament as a participant in the stoning death of the martyr Stephen, which took place, by tradition, about the year 37 A.D. Paul is there characterized as a "young man."[4] Shortly thereafter, he is sent off on a significant assignment by the Jewish authorities. Likely he would have been at least thirty years old for such an important task to be given him.

The world into which he was born was a pagan world. The city of Tarsus, where he was born, was notorious for its worship of the Zoroastrian god Mithras. The worship of Mithras required that "the initiates either drank the blood of the sacred bull or drank a chalice of wine as a symbolic representation of blood. The steer would be held over a platform and ritually slain. Under the platform stood the initiate, who would be literally bathed in the blood which dripped down from the platform. He would rub the blood in his eyes, ears and nostrils."[5] Mithras was the god of battles and the patron deity of soldiers.

"Any child born or brought up in Tarsus could not fail to have been impressed by the great religious ceremonies which took place there in honour of Herakles."[6] Herakles to the Greeks, and Hercules to the Romans, was considered a savior for all mankind.

The number of pagan gods was immense. With few exceptions, the Romans were tolerant in allowing the subjects throughout their empire to worship who or what they wanted. There were official public or state cults that had to be worshipped empire-wide, as well as official cults that were recognized locally. There were also private cults practiced by certain groups or individuals. The gods included Jupiter,

Juno, Minerva, Mars, and Isis. There were so many different gods and goddesses that it would be impossible to name them all. Religion within the Roman Empire consisted of the worship of a cornucopia of European and Asian religious figures.[7]

Much of the pagan worship was sensual and sexual in nature. To those few of the era who believed in sexual purity, such degrading public displays exacted great pain.

The Jews, who were dispersed throughout the Roman Empire, were just such sexual purists. They were also the monotheists, the inheritors of Abraham of Ur's worship of Jehovah, the God and creator of heaven and earth and all things therein.

Paul was an Israelite, a Hebrew, from the tribe of Benjamin.[8] However, those who were Benjamites had been so thoroughly assimilated by the tribe of Judah that they too were considered Jews.

His birthplace, Tarsus, was a commercial center of some importance. Paul came from modest circumstances. He was a tentmaker, which was a craft common in Tarsus. It appears that throughout the many years of his ministry he continued to engage in this trade, for he believed that he had no right to rely on the charity of others, especially those whom he was responsible for converting.[9]

Paul was a citizen of Rome.[10] How he came to achieve that status, which provided a substantial advantage to those who possessed it, is not known. Citizenship might have been purchased by one of his forefathers, or perhaps it was earned by his family for providing tents to a Roman army.[11] Among its most significant benefits was the right to be free from torture or execution. The citizen also possessed the right of *appellatio,* the right to appeal to Caesar from a criminal prosecution by a lower tribunal.[12] This right of Roman citizenship was to play a significant role in Paul's later life.

He was also a Pharisee and the son of a Pharisee.[13] The sect known as Pharisees had a presence in the kingdom of Judea as early as the second century before Christ. They were to remain influential long after Jerusalem was destroyed by the Romans in 70 A.D. The Pharisees would become the rabbis of the Jewish diaspora, the forced exile of Jews throughout the known world under Roman rule.

During the time of Christ, and through the years of Paul's ministry, the Pharisees were one of the four sects or schools that dominated Jewish society.[14] The members of these sects were intensely loyal to their teachings. The Pharisees' dogma included belief in the afterlife, in an ultimate judgment and resurrection, and in angels and spirits. They followed strict regulations involving observance of the Sabbath and other religious rites as well as food laws.[15]

Paul was totally immersed in everything Jewish and Pharisaic. "St. Paul, then, was to the very heart a Jew—a Jew in culture, a Jew in sympathy, a Jew in nationality, a Jew in faith."[16] Throughout his writings he made constant reference to the customs, laws, and celebrations of the Jewish people.

It is likely that when he was a young teenager, about the age of thirteen, Paul (then Saul) was sent from Tarsus to Jerusalem to be trained by Rabban Gamaliel.[17] Perhaps there he lived with a sister, for we later learn that he had a nephew, a son of his sister, living in Jerusalem.[18]

Rabban Gamaliel descended from a distinguished line of Jewish rabbis. He was known as a "liberal" Pharisee—humane and thoughtful, although loyal to the teachings of his fathers. The image of Pharisees portrayed in the New Testament, in particular the Gospels, is not a positive one. However, as with any large group, there were exceptions. Unlike the hypocritical, strict, and close-minded Pharisees so often condemned by Jesus, there were some who were sincere in their beliefs yet steeped in the higher law, that of love and peace and righteousness. Gamaliel was one of those exceptions. Whether Saul adopted his mentor's liberality is unknown, but there is little evidence of it until after his miraculous conversion.

Under Gamaliel's tutelage, Saul would have learned the law and become immersed in Pharisaic teachings. He would have mastered the Old Testament scriptures—the Pentateuch, the Prophets, the Psalter.

Throughout his writings in the Epistles he quotes these scriptures repeatedly and with wonderful effectiveness.

From the age of thirteen until he appears in the scriptures at the martyrdom of Stephen, Saul would have lived the consuming life of a Pharisee. He would have been obsessed with:

> the colour of fringes, and the tying of tassels, and the lawfulness of meats and drinks. We know the tithings, at once troublesome and ludicrous, of mint, anise, and cummin, and the serio-comic questions as to whether in tithing the seed it was obligatory also to tithe the stalk. We know the double fasts of the week, and the triple prayers of the day, and the triple visits to the Temple. We know the elaborate strainings of the water and the wine, that not even the carcase of an animalcula might defeat the energy of Levitical anxiety. We know the constant rinsings and scourings of brazen cups and pots and tables, carried to so absurd an extreme that, on the occasion of washing the golden candelabrum of the Temple, the Sadducees remarked that their Pharisaic rivals would wash the Sun itself if they could get an opportunity. We know the entire and laborious ablutions and bathings of the whole person. . . . We know how this notion of perfect Levitical purity thrust itself with irritating recurrences into every aspect and relation of ordinary life, and led to the scornful avoidance of the very contact and shadow of fellow-beings, who might after all be purer and nobler than those who would not touch them with the tassel of a garment's hem. We know the obtrusive prayers, the ostentatious almsgivings, the broadened phylacteries, the petty ritualisms, the professorial arrogance, the reckless proselytism, the greedy avarice, the haughty assertions of pre-eminence, the ill-concealed hypocrisy, which were often hidden under this venerable assumption of superior holiness. And we know all this quite as much, or more, from the admiring records of the Talmud—which devotes one whole

> treatise to handwashings, and another to the proper method of killing a fowl, and another to the stalks of legumes.[19]

Paul did not ever shrink from his status as a Pharisee; he proclaimed later in life, "Men and brethren, I am a Pharisee, the son of a Pharisee . . ."[20] If the young Saul was as completely faithful and consumed as the older Paul after his conversion to Christianity, it is clear that he would have been a totally devout Pharisee. He would have pursued perfect allegiance to and exactness in his Pharisaic practices.

A question that has intrigued many throughout history is whether Paul ever met or listened to Jesus Christ before His crucifixion. A modern scholar speculates that Paul might well have been employed at the temple of Jerusalem in providing security—in essence, a "policeman" of the temple. As such, this scholar speculates, he likely would have seen or heard Jesus and perhaps even been involved in his arrest and prosecution by the Jewish authorities.[21] A scholar of earlier years rejects this notion, arguing that if Paul had heard or met the Messiah, such an event would have been recorded or referenced in one of Paul's writings. It is further implied by this scholar that had Paul in fact heard the Messiah, he would have been converted by Him.[22]

Another interesting question is whether Paul was ever married. The great Bible scholar Frederic Farrar builds a case that he was. He refers to Paul's statement in 1 Corinthians 7:8 in which he refers to the widows and encourages them to "abide even as I." Farrar also provides as evidence the Jewish teaching that marriage was a moral duty, a positive command for all Jewish men. Farrar contends that, in light of Paul's devotion to Jewish law, it would have been highly unlikely if Paul had never married. He suggests that Paul was likely a widower and had no surviving children.[23]

The Troubling Christians

Following the crucifixion of Jesus Christ, it was assumed by the Jewish leaders that his followers would disappear. Much to their chagrin, such did not happen:

> For the death of Jesus had been followed by a succession of events, the effects of which will be felt to the end of time—events which, by a spiritual power at once astounding and indisputable, transformed a timid handful of ignorant and terror-stricken Apostles into teachers of unequalled grandeur, who became in God's hands the instruments to regenerate the world.[24]

Following the resurrection, Christ mingled with and taught his followers for a brief time. He then ascended into heaven. He left the disciples and Apostles in apprehension of a promise—for he told them immediately prior to his final departure that they would receive power through the Holy Ghost and that they should then take Christ's gospel to the "uttermost part of the earth."[25]

Waiting, they spent time in the temple,[26] for they were still, above all, Jews—just Jews that believed in Jesus Christ as the Messiah and the Savior of the world. But they were beginning to separate themselves from the Jews in subtle ways. When they gathered together, for example, they did so as both men and women, unlike the Jewish practice.[27] By this they were beginning to put into practice what was to become a defining characteristic of Christianity, the belief that "There is neither Jew nor Greek, there is neither bond nor free, there is neither male nor female: for ye are all one in Christ Jesus."[28]

But they were still far from that, as we will see.

The followers were few. The 120 who were then located in Jerusalem gathered together in a council and selected a replacement for the traitor Judas as one of the Twelve Apostles: a man named Matthias.[29]

And then the anticipated day came—the day of Pentecost. The followers of Christ were again all together. Perhaps they were partaking of the sacrament, the consuming of bread and wine in remembrance of Christ and his sacrifice. Suddenly the Holy Ghost fell upon them all—the promised baptism of fire:

> Suddenly on the rapt and expectant assembly came the sign that they had desired—the inspiration of Christ's promised Presence in their hearts—the baptism with the Holy Ghost and with fire—the transforming impulse of a Spirit and a Power from on high—the eternal proof to them, and through them, in unbroken succession, to all who accept their word, that He who had been taken from them into heaven was still with them, and would be with them always to the end of the world.[30]

This great event was accompanied by physical signs—sound and light—and manifestations of the newly acquired gift by the faithful who had received it. A crowd gathered. The leader of the group, the great Apostle Peter, preached a sermon. Powerful testimony of the resurrection of Christ was offered, and three thousand were converted that very day.

From that eventful date forward, the little group became a church: learning the doctrine from the Apostles, breaking bread together, praying. Among one of the most notable characteristics of the new faith was that they "had all things common"[31] and none went without. Wonders and signs accompanied the new converts, including very public healings, and the fledgling faith continued to grow in numbers.

At first the followers of Christ were received with favorable regard by the population generally. The miracles performed by the Apostles and the genuine goodness reflected in the community as a whole were viewed positively. These new Christians were still Jews. They adhered with great care to the law of Moses. They preached primarily in the synagogues. They were deemed to be a bit heretical, having accepted Jesus of Nazareth as the Messiah, but beyond that they did not stand out much.

But as the Christian message spread, converts were made among both the Jews and the Gentiles. The importance of this fact to the future of Christianity, and the role that the Apostle Paul would play in that future, is worthy of a brief departure from our narrative.

The dispersion of the Jews (including members from all of the twelve tribes of Israel, but primarily from Judah and Benjamin) began with the Babylonian conquest in the sixth century before Christ. Many were taken captive and carried off into Babylon. Shortly thereafter, Babylon was conquered by the Persians. When the Persian king, Cyrus, gave permission for the Jews to return to Palestine, some did, but many did not—they remained and dispersed throughout the mighty Persian Empire. With this beginning, the Jews ultimately found themselves scattered throughout the "habitable earth," as Josephus asserts.[32]

In most of these dispersed locations, the Jews made permanent homes. They were usually afforded full rights to practice their religion and to participate in the commercial life of their adopted communities. And they did so. But they kept themselves separated from their neighbors in their religious practices, remaining true to the law of Moses and all of its commands as well as adhering to the other unique teachings of the Jewish faith.

This dispersion of Jews among the heathen was a mixed blessing. The uniqueness of the Jewish faith—in particular its monotheism, its emphasis on the sanctity of life, and its belief in sexual purity—resulted in much persecution from those among whom the Jews now lived. That persecution was to continue throughout history. However, those same teachings were also attractive to some. Many Gentiles rejected the worship of pagan gods and became converts to the Jewish faith.

In the decades after the death of Jesus Christ, both Jews and converts to Judaism could be found worshipping Jehovah in the Jewish synagogues that were established in cities far and wide. When Christianity began to be preached throughout the Roman Empire, it was often preached in those Jewish synagogues. Gentile converts to Judaism, having already adopted monotheism and the teachings of morality that were an essential part of the Jewish creed, were primed for the enlightened appeal of Christianity. Having abandoned their pagan or heathen past, they were prepared for the message of a resurrected Christ and his teachings of purity, brotherly love, and eternal life.

Two other events of major historical consequence had already impacted the world of the New Testament and cultivated the prospects for the spread of Christianity.

Alexander the Great's conquest of much of the then-known world—from the Mediterranean Sea to the Himalayan Mountains—350 years before the birth of Christ had led to the adoption of Greek as the common language throughout the entire region. The Jews of the dispersion adopted it. Greek was spoken in the synagogues of the Jews wherever they were found. A common language made it easier for Christian missionaries to preach in whatever nation they might proselyte in.

The second event, the rise of the Roman Empire, resulted in a unified political structure throughout the Near East, including Palestine, and the rest of the Mediterranean region. Roman roads made travel convenient. Roman fleets made travel by sea safe. Roman armies allowed commerce and trade to thrive.[33]

These major twists in world history bring us to the story of the unfolding of Christianity to become the religion of Europe, and of Paul's unique role in that unfolding.

Persecution of the Christians

Public tolerance of the early Christians was short-lived. The signs that accompanied the followers of Christ, including healings and other miraculous manifestations, began to bring out the worst in the Jewish leadership. Beset by feelings of jealousy, or perhaps even from some noble impulse that Peter and his followers were apostates and heretics who had to be dealt with, the Jewish leaders began to persecute the little band of Christians.[34]

The first to feel the full wrath of their fury was Stephen. Stephen was a follower of Christ whose zeal and enthusiasm had brought him to the attention of Peter and the other Apostles. When their duties became too much for them to handle, the Apostles had appointed "seven men of honest report, full of the Holy Ghost and wisdom"[35] to assist them in the work of the growing religious community. Stephen was one of those seven.

We do not know his age for certain, but the image of Stephen is one of youthful exuberance. He was "full of faith and power" and performed "great wonders and miracles among the people."[36]

One day, while contending with certain members of a Jewish synagogue, Stephen frustrated his rivals with his skill in defending his faith. They became angry and accused him of blasphemy—speaking evil of Moses and God. He was summoned before a tribunal and, through the testimony of false witnesses, found guilty. He was dragged out of the city and stoned. In order to allow the fullness of their fury to be exercised, those hurling the stones removed their robes and laid them down at the feet of a young man named Saul, who by that act "was consenting" to the death of Stephen.[37]

We are thus introduced to the giant whose name would soon be changed to Paul.

The Road to Damascus

Saul was a great tormenter of the Christian church. He set about to find those who professed the Christian faith to see that they were punished. He did not hesitate to persecute both men and women, dragging them from their very homes with great zeal. Saul would testify against them as blasphemers and hope for their execution—most likely by stoning. In his own words, he "made havock of"[38] the church.

This fact was to haunt him for the remainder of his life.

Hearing that the Christians were making their presence known in Damascus, 150 miles north of Jerusalem, Saul sought permission from the high priest to travel there to stamp out the heresy. He asked specifically for the right to find the Christians, bind them, and return them to Jerusalem for prosecution.

As Saul neared Damascus, his mission of persecution was suddenly interrupted. He and his fellow travelers were unexpectedly surrounded by a great light. It was about midday, with the sun at its brightest, yet this light was brighter than the sun.

Saul fell to the earth.

A voice addressed him, "Saul, Saul, why persecutest thou me?"

The shock of that question must have shaken him to the core. Jesus Christ stood before him[39]—yet Saul did not know him.

"Who art thou, Lord?"

"I am Jesus of Nazareth, whom thou persecutest."[40]

The thoughts that must have coursed through Saul's mind! The image of those whom he had seen persecuted for following that very Jesus who now confronted him must have seared his memory!

"Lord, what wilt thou have me to do?"

"Rise, and stand upon thy feet: for I have appeared unto thee for this purpose, to make thee a minister and a witness both of these things which thou hast seen, and of those things in the which I will appear unto thee; delivering thee from the people, and from the Gentiles, *unto whom now I send thee,* to open their eyes, and to turn them from darkness to light, and from the power of Satan unto God, that they may receive forgiveness of sins, and inheritance among them which are sanctified by faith that is in me."

Saul's entire life was altered forever in that brief moment.

"Saul rose another man: he had fallen in death, he rose in life; he had fallen in the midst of things temporal, he rose in awful consciousness of the things eternal; he had fallen a proud, intolerant, persecuting Jew; he rose a humble, broken-hearted, penitent Christian."[41]

Saul was told to continue to Damascus, where it would be made known to him what he was to do. Having been made blind, he had to be helped by those men who were his fellow travelers. He was to be without sight for three days.

Meanwhile, in Damascus, a disciple by the name of Ananias had received his own vision. He was told to find Saul. Ananias was taken aback at this request, for he was well aware of Saul and his efforts to destroy the disciples of Christ. But Ananias was assured, "He is a chosen vessel unto me, to bear my name before the Gentiles, and kings, and the children of Israel."[42]

Ananias obeyed. He found Saul, healed him of his blindness, and set about to instruct him. Saul, now called Paul, had experienced a conversion that was all consuming. It was never to be questioned or doubted. He was baptized. Soon he was preaching Christ in the synagogues.[43]

The shock to those hearing Paul bear witness of Jesus of Nazareth as the Son of God—this testimony from a man who only days before had been seeking to destroy those who bore the same witness—must have been immense.

But Paul was not yet ready for the full responsibility of an Apostle, a special witness of Christ. Although it is not clear from the scriptures, it appears that he spent but a short time in Damascus and then disappeared for three years.

He was to sojourn for at least part of that time in Arabia before returning to Damascus. What he did is not known with certainty, but during that period it is clear that he absorbed the teachings of Jesus. Perhaps he was visited by the Savior himself, for he had been promised in his vision outside Damascus that he would be visited again.[44]

There is no reason to believe that Paul had heard Jesus Christ teach during Christ's mortal life. Yet Paul learned enough, through revelation and study, to be able to write and teach regarding all aspects of Christ's life and teachings: "And to what does he testify respecting Jesus? To almost every single primarily important fact respecting His Incarnation, Life, Sufferings, Betrayal, Last Supper, Trial, Crucifixion, Resurrection, Ascension, and Heavenly Exaltation."[45] This collection of knowledge was understood by Paul so thoroughly that he could teach and write about it as if he himself had been an intimate companion of Jesus during His earthly ministry.

When Paul returned to Damascus, he proved to be a powerful teacher. He displayed a potent talent for convincing the Jews that Jesus was in fact the promised Messiah and Savior. Soon his own life was in danger, for the Jewish leaders saw that he had to be destroyed. Ironically, they chose to resort to violence against Paul in the same way that he had dispensed violence before his conversion. The city gates were watched to assure that he did not escape. He did escape, but in a unique fashion—in a basket, lowered by his fellow disciples from a window that looked out over the wall of the city.

Paul then journeyed to Jerusalem for the first time since his conversion. How he was to be received must have been prominent in his thoughts. He had left Jerusalem after wreaking havoc among the fledgling Christian church there. Those he was about to seek out, in order to associate with and learn from them, might well have been incidental victims of his hateful persecution. Some of their loved ones could have been stoned at Paul's insistence. All of them would have known and loved Stephen.

Peter was among his first contacts. This great man, who would have suffered so much as he witnessed Paul's efforts to destroy his flock, apparently accepted him totally. Paul was invited into Peter's home and "abode with him fifteen days."[46] Of the other Apostles, only James was there to greet the converted Paul. As far as the other members of the Christian faith, likely with some hesitation, they accepted Paul, and he was allowed to come and go with them in Jerusalem.

Paul preached Christ. His compelling testimony soon raised the ire of the enemies of the Christian faith in Jerusalem. There seems little doubt that those who had worked so diligently alongside the old Saul to persecute the Christian faithful would have reacted with abject horror to hear the new Paul testify of Christ's divinity. There is no hatred so intense as that of former friends who feel betrayed.

With the threat rising, Paul was visited by Christ and told to flee Jerusalem.[47] He was forced again to flee, this time to his home in Tarsus, where he was to spend the next six or seven years teaching in the surrounding area.

At some time during this period, an event occurred involving the leader of Christ's disciples, Peter, that was to open the door for Paul to accomplish the mission to the Gentiles to which he had been so convincingly and unquestionably called.

Peter's Vision and Conversion

The twelve Apostles of Christ, those who had been with him throughout much of his ministry, were great men. But, in some ways, they were slow learners—slow to comprehend the true nature of their Master's mission. For example, although he had talked frequently of his death, they appear to have been taken by complete surprise when he was crucified. Despite the fact that he had told them that he would be resurrected, they were completely taken aback by—and slow to accept—his reappearance in the flesh after that resurrection.

In one other very significant way they had not fully comprehended the message of Jesus of Nazareth: his teachings pertaining to the law of Moses. They did not understand when he instructed them that the law of Moses had simply been a tool to direct its adherents to him, the Messiah. These simple men, totally steeped in the law of Moses, could not comprehend their Master's instruction that the law of Moses was not only fulfilled in him but was to be replaced by his new teachings. "They were not yet ripe for the conviction that to attach primary importance to Mosaic regulations after they had been admitted into the kingdom of Heaven, was to fix their eyes upon a waning star while the dawn was gradually broadening into boundless day."[48]

Jesus had sent clear signals that the law of Moses, as it was then taught and practiced by the scribes and Pharisees, was extreme. He had criticized the strictures of Sabbath observance frequently. He had refused to attend ceremonial festivals at Jerusalem. He had frustrated the stoning of an adulteress. He had spoken of the importance of mercy and minimized that of sacrifice. Had he not, in answer to the question as to what was the great commandment in the law, answered with, "Love the Lord thy God"?[49] In so many ways he had sent the message that the law of Moses as interpreted by the Jews of his age was not necessary. He had, in fact, said, "The law and the prophets were until John."[50]

It seems that the martyr Stephen had understood this message before the Apostles did. One of the accusations made against him was that he dared to repeat what he had heard Jesus say, that he was going to "change the customs which Moses delivered us."[51] This blasphemy doomed him to death.

But among the very first Christians, even among their leadership, the notion of abandoning the law of Moses to any degree was beyond their comprehension. Thus, although Christians, they remained Jews in daily practices, rituals, and observances. This included the practice of circumcision of all males.

But what of the Gentile converts to Christianity?

The book of Acts contains accounts of a few early successful missionary efforts among the Gentiles. For example, Acts, chapter eight, tells of Philip, one of the seven, and his conversion of Samaritans and an Ethiopian eunuch. These he baptized without hesitation despite the fact that they were Gentiles.

Undoubtedly some Gentiles were receiving baptism at the hand of those Christians who had been scattered throughout the Near East region because of the depredations of the old Saul and his ilk. Others would have been converted by those three thousand who had been converted and baptized on the day of Pentecost. They were natives of distant regions of the Mediterranean world.

The relevant question was whether circumcision was required of those Gentile converts to Christianity. Were they expected to adopt and live the rituals of the law of Moses as well as the teachings of Jesus Christ?

In sum, were they expected to become Jews as well as Christians?

Paul would have been particularly troubled by these questions, for he had been called specifically by Jesus of Nazareth to be an Apostle to the Gentiles. How was he to succeed at that calling if it was not clear what would be expected of the new Gentile converts? Was Paul also frustrated by the fact that he had received a separate revelation in which a "mystery" was revealed to him that the "Gentiles should be fellowheirs, and of the same body, and partakers of his promise in Christ by the gospel"?[52]

These questions must have occupied much of the thinking of the

Church's chief Apostle, Peter. He likely sought earnestly and frequently for answers to the questions in his heart.

While abiding in the home of a man named Simon in the seaside city of Joppa, Peter received a vision. He was shown an assortment of animals that the law of Moses forbade him to eat. He was told by a voice to eat them. He said, "No, I never have!" He was told that what God had cleansed, he had no right to call unclean. Three times the message was repeated. Peter pondered on what the vision meant.

Just then, three men arrived at the home of Simon and asked for Peter.

The men were there at the request of a Roman centurion named Cornelius, a man admired by the Jews for his generous spirit, who resided in Caesarea. Cornelius had shortly before received a vision of his own. He was told by an angel to send men to Joppa to find Peter, and that Peter would tell him what he was to do. Faithfully, Cornelius did as commanded and sent three men to ask for Peter.

The spirit told Peter of their mission. He agreed to join them to travel to Cornelius's home.

Upon arriving at the home of the centurion, Peter found a gathering of family and friends of Cornelius. This was an awkward moment for Peter, for the law of Moses forbade a Jew to go into the home of a Gentile.

But things were now beginning to make sense to him. He realized that his vision pertained to the Gentiles. God intended that the Gentiles not be left out. He declared, "Of a truth I perceive that God is no respecter of persons: But in every nation he that feareth him, and worketh righteousness, is accepted with him."[53]

His conclusion was quickly confirmed, for, as Cornelius and his gathered intimates heard Peter's testimony, they wholeheartedly accepted his message and received a spiritual outpouring from the Holy Ghost. They were baptized, and Peter stayed in Caesarea to teach them.

When Peter returned to Jerusalem, a council was called for. He reported on his vision and his experience with the Roman centurion.

The Church accepted his leadership—the Gentiles were to be received into full fellowship.

But this did not end the controversy. Yes, it might be true that Gentiles could be received in baptism and receive the Holy Ghost and expect a remission of sins through the sacrifice of Jesus Christ, but were they also required to abide by the law of Moses?

Most specifically, were the men required to be circumcised?

The matter was soon to demand resolution. Paul and his longtime missionary companion, Barnabas, had been preaching and baptizing in the city of Antioch in what is now southern Turkey. They were finding great success among the population of Gentiles. But then a group of men from Judea arrived and began to stir up contention, arguing that in order to *really* be saved, the newly baptized Christian men had to submit to circumcision.

Paul and Barnabas said that was not so!

It was clear that a decision had to be made by those at the top.

Paul and Barnabas traveled to Jerusalem, and another council was held. On the one hand were Christians who were also Pharisees. They argued that not only was circumcision necessary, but the entire law of Moses had to be followed.

On the other side were Paul and Barnabas, who revealed to the assembled Apostles and elders of the Church all of the miracles and wonders that had occurred among the Gentiles.

Peter spoke in favor of Paul and Barnabas.

James, the brother of Jesus, proposed a compromise—that the Gentiles be burdened only with a bare minimum of the law of Moses: the commandments that forbade the eating of meat offered to idols, the consuming of blood and things that were strangled, and fornication.

The compromise was accepted. The message was sent to Antioch.

The issue was settled—although some Jews would not let it die and it was to resurface frequently throughout the remainder of Paul's life. It would turn out that Paul's greatest enemies would be those who simply could not accept his teaching that even believing Jews need not follow the law of Moses.[54]

For Paul, however, the controversy was no more—there was no doubt. Paul was freed to minister to the Gentiles—to the uncircumcised and the not-required-to-be circumcised. The word of God was to grow and to multiply and would find a welcoming audience throughout the entire Roman Empire, including in the capital of Rome itself.

It cannot be overstated how important this series of events, visions, and pronouncements was. As the great scholar of Paul's life, Frederic William Farrar, asserts:

> To this outward peace and inward development was due an event which must continue to have the most memorable importance to the end of time—the admission of Gentiles as Gentiles into the Church of Christ. . . .
>
> The struggle of St. Paul against the hostility of Judaism from without and the leaven of Judaism from within was severe and lifelong, and even at his death faith alone could have enabled him to see that it had not been in vain. But the glorious effort of his life must have been fruitless had not the principle at stake been publicly conceded—conceded in direct obedience to sanctions which none ventured to dispute—by the most eminent and most authoritative of the Twelve. And yet, though St. Peter was thus set apart by Divine foresight to take the initiative, it was to one whom even the Twelve formally recognised as the Apostle of the Uncircumcision, that the world owes under God the development of Christian faith into a Christian theology, and the emancipation of Christianity from those Judaic limitations which would have been fatal to its universal acceptance.[55]

The Missionary Journeys

Before the second Jerusalem council was called, Paul and his companions had been laboring in Antioch for about three years. The success they experienced in that city of perhaps 500,000 was striking; so much so that this city of Gentiles, mostly Greeks and Romans, would eventually become the capital of Christianity.[56]

It was while in Antioch, before the second council, that Paul had undertaken the first of three missions. He and his companion, Barnabas, had traveled to cities in what is now southern Turkey and the island of Cyprus. They taught wherever they could find an audience, and that was often in the synagogues of the Jews. They were successful in converting both Jews and Gentiles, and in each city where converts were made, elders were ordained to lead the local congregation. However, Paul and his companions were often greeted with contempt by the nonaccepting Jews and were driven from some cities. In Lystra, the Jews stirred the people up to such rage that they stoned Paul and left him for dead.

At the end of this mission, Paul returned to Antioch, and it was then that the men from Judea arrived and stirred up the Christian Gentiles, which action led to the second Jerusalem council. Following that council, Paul and Barnabas had returned yet again to Antioch.

"And some days after Paul said unto Barnabas, Let us go again and visit our brethren in every city where we have preached the word of the Lord, and see how they do."[57] With this somewhat casual suggestion, Paul undertook his second mission, a mission that was to last for three years and would include a monumental event, the spreading of the work of the Lord into Europe.

At the outset, Paul and Barnabas got into a tussle over who should accompany them. The partnership of Paul and Barnabas was severed—Barnabas went his way and Paul went his. In the city of Lystra in southern Turkey, Paul met and was joined by a young man named Timothy. Timothy's mother was a Jewess and his father was a Greek. Thus commenced the second great missionary companionship in Paul's life.

Paul, his Apostle-companion, Silas, and the new missionary, Timothy, labored through the cities of what is now Turkey, slowly making their way to the West. Somewhere along the way they were joined by the physician Luke, who became a frequent companion and the chronicler of Paul's life. They eventually came to the city of Troas in far western Asia.

One night, Paul had a vision in which a "man of Macedonia" appeared to him and said, "Come over into Macedonia, and help us."[58]

Paul saw in the vision the will of the Lord being expressed, and he obeyed the message.

"With such brevity and simplicity is the incident related which of all others was the most important in introducing the Gospel of Christ to the most advanced and active races of the world, and among them to those races in whose hands its future destinies must inevitably rest."[59]

Paul and his companions sailed across the Aegean Sea and embarked upon European soil. Thus Christianity was introduced into Europe.

This European mission included stops at the ancient cities of Philippi in Macedonia and Thessalonica, Berea, Athens, and Corinth in Greece. On his return trip, Paul stopped at Ephesus on the southwestern coast of modern-day Turkey. He finished his mission by returning to Jerusalem.

In this three-year undertaking, a certain pattern evolved. First, if the city had a Jewish synagogue, Paul and his companions would usually seek it out to begin their preaching. Second, they often found receptive audiences of both Jews and Gentiles, but most receptive were the Gentiles. Third, in keeping with the Christian belief in equality, women were among the most prominent targets of his preaching and the most choice of his converts.[60] Fourth, the most active and antagonistic opponents were the nonaccepting Jews. Finally, negative reaction was sometimes reflected in violence (Paul was beaten and imprisoned in Philippi) or pure contempt (mocking by the philosophers of Athens.)

After reporting his missionary activities to the leadership of the Church in Jerusalem, Paul returned to Antioch.

Sometime thereafter, Paul undertook his third missionary journey. On this mission, which was to last three and a half years, Paul returned to strengthen and comfort many of those small congregations that he had established on his second mission. During this mission, Paul performed many miracles, including healing the sick and casting out evil spirits. Perhaps most notable of these miracles was the raising from the dead of a young man named Eutychus. Eutychus was attending one of Paul's sermons. Paul preached late into the night. The young man, sitting in a window, fell into a deep sleep and tumbled out the window three floors to the ground below. He was taken up as dead, but Paul restored his life.

During his third mission, Paul spent much time in Ephesus. When he was taking his leave of his flock there, he brought tears to the congregation with the prediction that he would never return. Paul had begun to sense what his future held. While making his return to report to Jerusalem, Paul stopped at Caesarea and spent time with Philip. There Paul was approached by a man possessed of the gift of prophecy who foretold that if Paul returned to Jerusalem, the Jews would bind him and deliver him up to the Gentiles.

Paul's companions and friends begged him not to go up to Jerusalem.

Paul's response, "What mean ye to weep and to break mine heart? for I am ready not to be bound only, but also to die at Jerusalem for the name of the Lord Jesus."[61]

By this statement, Paul prophesied his own fate.

Jerusalem and Rome

Upon Paul's arriving in Jerusalem, as was his habit, he reported to the leadership of the Church. James was the foremost of those who heard his report of great success among the Gentiles of both Asia Minor and Europe. James, in turn, reported on the thousands of Jews that had been converted. But then, the bad news: James revealed to Paul that it had been reported that Paul was teaching to the Jews scattered among the Gentile cities that they did not need to follow the law of Moses.

In a gesture to those believing Jews, Paul went up to the temple.

This proved to be a mistake, for the Jews saw him there and enraged a crowd by proclaiming that Paul was the man who was teaching against the law and the temple. The crowd demanded blood. Paul was seized and was taken out of the temple to be killed. Paul avoided the same fate as Stephen only by the intervention of Roman soldiers. The Romans intended to deal quickly with this troublemaker, but when informed that he was a Roman citizen, they were forced to treat him with the respect such citizenship demanded.

The next few years of his life were eventful. Paul was forced to defend himself before the Jewish high priest and Jewish Sanhedrin; he escaped death at the hand of forty oath-bound assassins; he defended himself before the Roman Governors Felix and Festus; he spent two years of captivity in Caesarea; he made his famous defense before King Agrippa; and, to avoid a return to Jerusalem and certain death, he invoked his right as a citizen of Rome to be judged by Caesar.

Accordingly, Paul was sent to Rome under Roman safeguard.

Paul's journey to Rome was interrupted by a shipwreck and months of delays. Eventually, Paul arrived in the capital of the mighty Roman Empire.

When he arrived in the city of Rome, probably in the spring of A.D. 61, he entered a city with a population of two million people. He was given the privilege of living in his own house with just one Roman guard—but that guard was chained to Paul.

Paul found a small Christian community in Rome. He was permitted to entertain visitors and to preach to crowds. He first sought out the Jewish community, which may have been as large as 60,000 in number.[62] As was usually the case, he found only limited success among the Jews. He then turned his attention to testifying to the Gentiles of the capital city.

During his confinement Paul enjoyed the visits of old friends and likely new friends in the form of Christian converts and Jewish acquaintances. He also spent the time composing many of his most celebrated epistles.

After two years of captivity, he was released. Although now into his later years, he did not rest. Paul embarked on an ambitious mission to cities in Asia, Macedonia, Crete, and, tradition has it, Spain. He did not, however, venture into Jerusalem. He knew that to do so would have been reckless—if not suicidal.

Two years after his release, he was again taken prisoner and returned to Rome. This time, his imprisonment was likely very different: severe, lonely, and painful.

It was while so incarcerated that he wrote his last letter to his most faithful missionary companion and friend, Timothy. In it Paul asserts, with undeniable faith in its truthfulness: "For I am now ready to be offered, and the time of my departure is at hand. I have fought a good fight, I have finished my course, I have kept the faith: Henceforth there is laid up for me a crown of righteousness."[63]

Tradition claims that Paul suffered martyrdom, being executed in A.D. 65.

Thus ended the untiring decades of missionary work and preaching Christ to multiple cities on two continents.[64]

> Laboring as no other Apostle had labored, he had preached the Gospel in the chief cities of the world, from Jerusalem to Rome, and perhaps even as far as Spain. During the short space of twenty years he had proclaimed Christ crucified to the simple Pagans of Lycaonia, the fickle fanatics of Galatia, the dreamy mystics of Phrygia, the vigorous colonists of Macedonia, the superficial dilettanti of Athens, the sensual and self-satisfied traders of Corinth, the semi-barbarous natives of Dalmatia, the ill-reputed islanders of Crete, the slaves and soldiers and seething multitudes of Rome.[65]

Paul and Christianity

The New Testament of the King James Bible contains twenty-seven books. Historically, Paul was deemed to be the author of fourteen of them. Although some modern scholars claim that he was not the author of the epistle to the Hebrews, it is clear that it, too, contains the doctrine of Christianity as espoused by Paul.[66] Collectively, these epistles contain many of the fundamental, central, and unique doctrines of Christianity, including the doctrine that Christ was in fact divine, not just a prophet; that Christ died for our sins and that through that sacrifice, we can have our personal sins forgiven; that we must accept Christ as our Savior to be saved, we cannot do it by simply conforming to a series of laws.[67]

> Paul, more than any other man, was responsible for the transformation of Christianity from a Jewish sect into a world religion. His central ideas of the divinity of Christ and of justification by faith have remained basic to Christian thought throughout all other intervening centuries. All subsequent Christian theologians, including Augustine, Aquinas, Luther, and Calvin, have been profoundly influenced by his writings. Indeed, the influence of Paul's ideas . . . has been vastly greater than that of any other Christian thinker.[68]

Farrar says this of Paul's writings:

> For it is his Epistles—casual as was the origin of some of them—that we find the earliest utterances of that Christian literature to which the world is indebted for its richest treasures of poetry and eloquence, of moral wisdom and spiritual consolation. It is to his intellect, fired by the love and illuminated by the Spirit of his Lord, that we owe the first systematic statement, in their mutual connexion and interdependence, of the great truths of the Mystery of Godliness which had been hidden from the ages, but was revealed in the Gospel of the Christ. [69]

Among the important doctrines that Paul taught was that all those who became Christians, those "which are of the faith," become the literal children of Abraham. It was by such means, Paul explained, that the promise made to Abraham by Jehovah, that through Abraham would "all nations be blessed,"[70] would be fulfilled.

Paul's greatest accomplishment was that he freed Christianity from the constrictions of Judaism. Had he not persevered, had he not pressed the other Church leaders to do so, had he not been willing to confront them when those leaders bowed to the demands of the Pharisees among the Jewish converts and backslid on the principle, Christianity could not have found the worldwide audience that it did. Again, quoting Farrar:

> It is to his undaunted determination, his clear vision, his moral loftiness, that we are indebted for the emancipation of religion from the intolerable yoke of legal observances—the cutting asunder of the living body of Christianity from the heavy corpse of an abrogated Levitism. It was he alone who was God's appointed instrument to render possible the universal spread of Christianity, and to lay deep in the hearts of European churches the solid bases of Christendom. As the Apostle of the Gentiles he was pre-eminently and necessarily the Apostle of freedom, of culture, of the understanding.[71]

Paul did this at no small cost. From the moment he became a convert to Christianity he was a marked man—by both Jews and Gentiles. Five times he was beaten with a whip—thirty-nine stripes each beating. Three times he was beaten with rods. He was stoned and left for dead. He was many times imprisoned. Three times he was shipwrecked. His epistles are filled with references to his sufferings, his mental and physical trials, his depression, his illnesses.[72]

It must be kept in mind that all of Paul's accomplishments were achieved by a man who was, when all is said and done, *just* a man! He was a sinner, by his own confession.[73] He argued with a longtime friend in the gospel (Barnabas) and they severed their relationship. One of the early accounts of his physical presence described him as "little of stature, thin-haired upon the head, crooked in the legs, of good state of body, with eyebrows joining, and nose somewhat hooked."[74] Apparently, he was not an imposing physical specimen. He was by no means a perfect soul.

Yet this tentmaker from Tarsus rose to meet his every challenge. He spoke of the weak things of the world that confounded the mighty.[75] Whether intended or not, he aptly described himself.

Christianity and the History of the World

Today, approximately 2.3 billion people in the world are Christians, roughly one-third of all those who inhabit the earth. Christianity is the most favored of all of the world's great religions, with Islam second with 1.5 billion adherents.[76]

Would this be the case but for Paul?

Today, a greater percentage of the world's population lives with a degree of liberty and the opportunity for self-government than at any other time in the world's history. This is a direct result of the spread of the Western view of personal freedom, equality, rule of law, and the right of individuals to self-government, which, in turn, is directly tied to the Christian faith adopted by the Western world.[77]

Would this be the case but for Paul?

A contemporary scholar of the life of Paul, A. N. Wilson, observes:

> The fact that the Gentile world adopted Christianity is owing almost solely to one man: Paul of Tarsus. Without Paul, it is highly unlikely that Christianity would ever have broken away from Judaism. Only a moment's reflexion tells us what a different world it would have been. The whole Jewish inheritance, which is woven inseparably into the Christian religion, would never have been available to the Gentile imagination. The stories which, until our generation, were told to almost every child in the Western world, would have been the exclusive preserve of the Jews: Adam and Eve, Noah's Ark, Daniel in the Lions' Den. The concept of moral law as a divinely-given set of precepts, spoken

by the Almighty to Moses on Sinai, underpinned, at least until the eighteenth century, the ethical, political and social fabric of Western statecraft. God himself is, for Western Man, the God of Israel. If metaphysicians for the first two millennia after Christ have drawn on non-Jewish traditions—above all on those of Plato and Aristotle—for talking about God, it is nonetheless to the Hebraic tradition, of a God who created the world of matter and who is involved with his creation, that Western philosophers have always returned. And this is the inheritance which Paul opened up to the Gentile world.[78]

Wilson adds:

Even if we do not subscribe to the old view that the Faith is Europe, and Europe is the Faith, the very idea of European civilization is impossible to extricate from the story of Christendom. Would the writings of Plato have survived to us if they had not first been filtered through the Fathers of the Greek Church? If the monks of Benedict had not preserved manuscripts in their libraries, how much of classical literature would have survived in the West? Even if we posit that there would have been other powerhouses of "civilization" during the "dark ages," it is still unimaginable because what history in fact provided was a Christian civilization. Europe without Benedict . . . Dante . . . cathedrals . . . mediaeval universities . . . fifteenth century humanists . . . the Reformation . . . the Crusades . . . Aquinas, no Marsilius, no Duns Scotus. No Hume, Marx or Voltaire reacting against them. No Bach, no Michelangelo, no Shakespeare. . . . Of course, if the Faith had not been European, and Europe had not adopted the Faith, there would have been some other story. But it would not have been our story.[79]

Paul of Tarsus may have been short of stature with crooked legs. But he was a giant among all men!

Notes

1. Josephus, *Works,* 474.
2. See, generally, Wilson, *Paul.*
3. Farrar, *Life*, 8–9.
4. Acts 7:58.
5. Wilson, *Paul*, 25.
6. Ibid., 26.
7. For a discussion of the religions of the Roman Empire in this era see Boak, *History*, 392–97.
8. Romans 11:1.
9. 1 Thessalonians 2:6, 9.
10. Acts 22:25.
11. Wilson, *Paul*, 29.
12. Ibid., 224.
13. Acts 23:6.
14. The Sadducees, the Essenes, and the Zealots were the other three.
15. Brown, *Lost*, 122–25.
16. Farrar, *Life*, 20.
17. Acts 22:3.
18. Acts 23:16.
19. Farrar, *Life*, 35–36.
20. Acts 23:6.
21. Wilson, *Paul*, 51–55.
22. Farrar, *Life*, 41–44.
23. Ibid., 44–46.
24. Ibid., 47.
25. Acts 1:8.
26. Luke 24:53.
27. Acts 1:12–14.
28. Galatians 3:28.
29. Acts 1:15–26.
30. Farrar, *Life*, 51–52.
31. Acts 2:44.
32. See Josephus, *Works*, Book Fourteen, Chapter 7, Section 2.
33. Farrar asserts: "This dispersion of the Chosen People was one of those three vast and world-wide events in which a Christian cannot but see the hand of God so

ordering the course of history as to prepare the world for the Revelation of His Son." The other two events were the mentioned rise of Alexander and the spread of the Roman Empire. See Farrar, *Life*, 66.

34. The first reference to the title of Christians appears in reference to the followers of Christ in Antioch; see Acts 11:26.
35. Acts 6:3.
36. Acts 6:8.
37. Acts 8:1.
38. Acts 8:3.
39. Acts 26:16.
40. Farrar makes the astute observation that Christ used the title "Jesus of Nazareth" very purposefully. If he had used other titles, such as "the son of God," Paul may not have recognized him, or at least he would likely not have identified him as the one whom he was persecuting. Paul had to be confronted with the stark truth that it was that Jesus of Nazareth, the man whose followers he was wreaking havoc among, who was there before him, and none other.
41. Farrar, *Life*, 112.
42. Acts 9:15.
43. For the three separate accounts of the vision of Paul on the road to Damascus, see Acts 9:1–20; Acts 22:6–16; and Acts 26:9–19. It is believed that this conversion took place in the year A.D. 37.
44. Acts 26:16. See Galatians 1:17 for reference to his three years in Arabia and Damascus.
45. Farrar, *Life*, 114–15.
46. Galatians 1:18.
47. Acts 22:17–18.
48. Farrar, *Life*, 81.
49. Matthew 22:36–37.
50. Luke 16:16.
51. Acts 6:14.
52. Ephesians 3:3–6.
53. Acts 10:34–35.
54. For the account of the visions of Peter and Cornelius and the Jerusalem council, see Acts 10, 11, and 15. Ironically, one of those who subsequently backslid on the issue of Gentiles and the law of Moses was Peter (see Galatians, chapter two).
55. Farrar, *Life*, 145.
56. Ibid., 162.
57. Acts 15:36.
58. Acts 16:9.
59. Farrar, *Life*, 271.

60. See, for example, Lydia (Acts 16:14), "chief women" in Thessalonica (Acts 17:4), and honorable Greek women in Berea (Acts 17:12).
61. Acts 21:13.
62. The numbers for the population of the city of Rome and the Jewish population therein are found in Farrar, *Life*, 580.
63. 2 Timothy 4:6–8.
64. For the account of Paul's last years, see Farrar, *Life*, 577–688. For the entire history of Paul, see the New Testament book of Acts and the Pauline Epistles; Farrar, *Life*; Wilson, *Paul.*
65. Farrar, *Life*, 665–66.
66. Other authors dispute his authorship of others of the Pauline Epistles, but the grounds for doing so are not universally accepted by any means.
67. Hart, *100,* 33–34.
68. Ibid., 34–35.
69. Farrar, *Life*, 2.
70. Galatians 3:6–9.
71. Ibid.
72. For details, see Farrar, *Life*, 175–76 and 218, as well as the book of Acts and the epistles of Paul.
73. 2 Corinthians 12:7, for example.
74. Wilson, *Paul,* 77.
75. 1 Corinthians 1:27.
76. Central Intelligence Agency, *World Factbook*, located at www.cia.gov/library/publications/the-world-factbook/geor/xx.html.
77. See Stewart and Stewart, *Tipping Points*, and the sources cited therein.
78. Wilson, *Paul,* 14.
79. Ibid., 137.

Chapter 4

The Incomparable Mr. Newton

God said "Let Newton be!" and all was light.

ALEXANDER POPE

The year 1642 was a singular one in the midst of a momentous age. In China, war was under way between the Manchu and the Ming dynasty. As part of the warfare, man-caused floods killed hundreds of thousands. Very soon, the Ming Dynasty would be overthrown and the Qing Dynasty would be established—a dynasty that was to last until 1912.

In the New World, the European powers were establishing for themselves colonies in what were to become the United States of America and Canada as well as in Central and South America. York, Maine, became the first city to be incorporated in the United States. The city of Montreal, Canada, was founded by the French. The Spanish were continuing to establish new communities throughout the entire Western Hemisphere. The possibility that the discovery of the New World might alter the course of history was beginning to be recognized by a few.

In Europe, religious conflict was rampant. Catholics and Protestants were at war with each other. New religions were being born.

The printing press had ushered in the original "information age." For the first time in history, the written word, in the form of books and mass-produced pamphlets, was flooding the popular market.

In England, King Charles I was in conflict with most of his subjects. His affection for Catholicism was suspect. The conflict with Parliament over his power and prerogatives finally came to a head in 1642 when war erupted between Charles I and Parliament. Soon he was to be defeated and beheaded—ushering in the age of Cromwell and the Puritans. Although the monarchy was reestablished in 1660, it was never again to possess the power it had once held.

In January of 1642 Galileo died in Italy. This great physicist and scientist left behind a legacy that has dimmed but little in four hundred years. He was a major force in the scientific upheaval that was taking place in the first half of the seventeenth century, the so-called "Scientific Revolution." Other great minds—Englishmen Francis Bacon and William Harvey; Frenchman Rene Descartes; German Johannes Kepler, and myriad others—were active and proposing and theorizing in every area of the "natural philosophy."[1]

On Christmas Day of the year in question, in an obscure village in the midlands of England, a baby boy was born to a young widow. She named him Isaac Newton.

Isaac Newton was to become one of the most influential men in the history of the world. One expert assessed him to be the second most influential man who has ever been born and "the greatest and most influential scientist who ever lived."[2]

A song that was to become popular the year after the birth of Isaac Newton was entitled "The World Turned Upside Down." As dramatic as were the changes experienced by the people of England prior to 1643, those that were to follow as the result of the mark left by the giant Isaac Newton dwarfed them all.

The Evolution of Natural Philosophy

In order to appreciate the impact of Isaac Newton on the world, it is necessary to have some understanding of the world of science at his birth.

As Europe emerged from the Dark Ages, the philosophical teachings of the Greeks, specifically those of Aristotle, were revived. In particular, Aristotelian teachings were the established explanation for two questions that are significant for our story, two questions that have intrigued men forever: first, what are things (matter) actually made of, and second, what makes things move?

These questions have been asked from the beginning of time. As early humans watched the night sky and admired the magnificence of the heavenly bodies, they wondered, "What are those remarkable things, and what are they made of?"

As they detected the regular motion of the sun, the moon, and the stars, they would ask, "What makes them move, and how do they do it with such constancy?"

As they perceived the differences between fire, water, earth, and wind, as well as the variety to be found in all solid materials, they pondered, "What makes these things so different in every way?"

Understandably, not all men and women have taken the time to ponder such basic questions, but many thinking humans have. It was the Greeks, however, who were the first to actually suggest answers to these fundamental questions of nature. Aristotle, the teacher of Alexander the Great, proposed an answer to the question of what things are made of. He contended that everything in the universe consisted of just four elements: fire, water, earth, and air. Aristotle argued that the variety in the makeup of all material things is determined by the proportion of fire, water, earth, and air to be found in them. His answer to the question of why things move was based on his basic proposition about the four elements:

> To Aristotle, the earthly realm was composed of a blend of the four elements which, if left to settle, would

> form layers: water falling through air (or air moving up through water, as do bubbles), solid earth falling through water and air, and fire existing in the top layer because it moves up through air. Using this model, Aristotle would have explained the fall of an apple as being due to the earthy and watery parts of the solid apple trying to find their natural place in the universe, falling through air to reach the ground. . . . Aristotle also pioneered the concept of the Unmoved Mover—the name he gave to the omnipotent being who maintained the movement of the heavens, keeping the Sun and the planets travelling around the Earth.[3]

Logic was Aristotle's strong suit. He arrived at his conclusions by relying on logic, specifically, the use of deductive logic. In the mind of Aristotle, things that were provable could be established by the reliance on two premises followed by a conclusion. For example: all humans have two eyes, you are a human, therefore, you have two eyes. This Aristotelian method works as long as both premises are correct. In Aristotle's world, experimentation was not necessary or desirable.

Ironically, another Greek natural philosopher who lived just before Aristotle, Democritus, had proffered an alternate view of matter. He proposed that all matter is made of tiny, invisible things called "atoms." Aristotle rejected the theory of Democritus and prevailed on the public relations front; thus Democritus's theory sat in darkness for about two millennia.

The Romans did little but pass along the Greek natural philosophy. The Arabs preserved what they inherited from the Romans and added to it, primarily in the area of mathematics. Finally, in the thirteenth century, Europeans rediscovered Aristotle.

Interestingly, his theories became enmeshed with Christian orthodoxy. His view of an Unmoved Mover fit very nicely with the Christian belief in a God who was the creator of heaven and earth and all things therein. It supported the Christian belief that God was responsible for maintaining order in the heavens and the earth. As the next centuries passed, the two were deemed to be inseparable:

> This meant that any attack upon Aristotle's science was also seen as an attack upon Christianity. Together, the two doctrines formed a powerful alliance and created a world-view that was taught by rote almost unchallenged in every university in Europe for almost half a millennium, from the thirteenth to the seventeenth century.[4]

One of the other approved beliefs of the era was that the earth was the center of the universe and the sun and all other heavenly bodies revolved around it. This view was consistent with the Christian teaching that man was central to God's creations, that the earth was created just as an abode for His highest creation—man.

The Christian intellectuals of that period were not without their honest pursuits, to be sure. They believed it was imperative that man attempt to understand God's creations and encouraged the active exploration of how nature worked.

Accordingly, in Europe the brightest minds continued to ask questions and from time to time even challenged the accepted orthodoxy.

Some contend that the Scientific Revolution began in 1543 when Copernicus proffered his theory that the earth and other planets circled the sun. Such theological heresy was not well received by either the powerful Catholic Church or the infant Lutheran Church.

It was the Italian scientist Galileo who not only dared to challenge the orthodoxy of Aristotle but added substantive new notions to the philosophy of matter and motion.

Galileo must be recognized for having employed the "scientific method"—that is, reliance on experiments, repeatable by himself or others—to prove his advanced theories in astronomy and to answer questions about how things move. His use of the newly invented telescope allowed him to prove that Copernicus was correct in arguing that the sun, not the earth, was the center of the universe. He was the first to suggest the concept of inertia, that is, that all objects are prone to move unless stopped, and he proved it by experiments. This was a rejection of Aristotle's concept of the Unmoved Mover, the omnipresent force that was always pushing or pulling at things.

Among the most influential of the natural philosophers of the Scientific Revolution was the Frenchman René Descartes. With credit for major advances in mathematics and general philosophy to his name, he also proffered a theory of motion and matter that was to be widely accepted: the theory of ether as a substance that fills the universe and through which all of God's creations move:

> In Descartes's image of the universe, matter is immersed in an unseen, immeasurable medium called the ether. God endowed the universe with movement at the beginning of time and allows it to run spontaneously but in accordance with his will . . . all motion is produced by matter impressing on other matter within the medium of the ether. Descartes expressed this in his famous theory of vortices, in which he pictured movement, such as the fall of a stone to the earth, as being like the movement of a feather or a straw caught in an eddy or a whirlpool.[5]

The theories advanced by Descartes were being received very favorably at the time that Isaac Newton began his foray into the world of natural philosophy.

Another notable contributor to the Scientific Revolution was Sir Francis Bacon. Although his contributions to society were far-flung, including in politics and law, it was his rejection of the routine teaching of Aristotle in the universities of England and his insistence on the adoption of a scientific method within those universities that particularly affected the world in which Isaac Newton was to become immersed.[6]

In sum, the Scientific Revolution was resulting in a broad-based challenge to the theories of Aristotle and the rest of the established theories of natural philosophy. Even though Aristotelianism remained the accepted curriculum among the intellectual elite, it was being contested by notable thinkers who dared to advance new theories for how things worked.[7]

Still, all that was being produced by those who contributed to the scientific movement sweeping across Europe were reports on isolated experiments, the posing of single propositions, or the demonstration of a significant, but narrow, scientific breakthrough. There was no proffering of a unified explanation for nature's system.

It was for the man born on Christmas Day 1642 to bring some sense of order to it all.

A Challenging Beginning

That baby boy born near the end of 1642 was so tiny that he was not expected to survive. He was born prematurely, and reportedly was small enough to fit into a small pot. His father, Isaac, had died three months before his birth. His widowed mother, Hannah, named him after his father.

Young Isaac was born in the small village of Woolsthorpe, north and west of London, in Lincolnshire. It was not a rich town. Most villagers were simple farmers and relied on the raising of sheep for their livelihood. The Newtons were not wealthy, but they had raised themselves above the peasant class several generations before; because Isaac's father owned sixty acres of land, they were considered to be of the yeoman class. But the Newtons were not educated—Isaac senior, in fact, could not read or even sign his own name.

To his credit, Isaac senior did marry above himself. Hannah came from a family that was part of the gentry, the Ayscoughs. Their sons had been educated at Oxford and Cambridge. However, the family Ayscough had fallen on hard times, and because of declining wealth they were slowly descending the class scale to yeoman status. Thus, the marriage between Hannah and Isaac was not deemed inappropriate in the class structure.

At her husband's death, Hannah had inherited the farm and small manor as well as cattle and sheep. So Hannah and Isaac junior were left with enough to be comfortable.

When Isaac was three years old, an event occurred that was to shape both his intellectual growth and his social skills: Hannah remarried. The rector of a nearby village, Barnabas Smith, negotiated a marriage contract with the widow Newton. It contained a provision that seems somewhat harsh: She was to move into his home but to leave her three-year-old son behind to be raised by her parents. That provision does not appear to have implied a lack of love for her son on the part of Hannah, but rather was a condition imposed by the new husband. As a widow, she was not in the best position to resist.

Regardless of the reason, this change left Isaac without a mother. This was very hard on him because Hannah was, after all, the only parent he had. Although she did live with Barnabas but a short distance away, her visits were irregular and usually very short. Isaac hated his stepfather and thought none too kindly of his mother. In later years, Isaac confessed that he had harbored youthful thoughts of burning to the ground the house in which Hannah and Barnabas lived.

Isaac turned out to be less than sociable. His relationships with women throughout his life were almost nonexistent, except with a stepniece much later in life. He never married. He had few friends. His social skills and ability to bond with either women or men were stunted by the separation from his mother that was to last for eight years until Barnabas died.

Isaac was raised by Hannah's parents during this period. Newton apparently did not connect with these elderly folks, for they were never mentioned by him in his later life.

In sum, Isaac Newton was a very lonely boy.

But there is reason to speculate that this situation did aid Isaac in one very significant way. He came under the influence of the Ayscoughs, who did favor the education of their men. Had Hannah not remarried and abandoned Isaac for eight years, Isaac's expectations about education might have been very different.

If Isaac Newton had been a farmer, as he almost certainly would have if his father had lived, he probably would have channeled his extraordinary mental power into becoming a superb farmer. He might even have been responsible for dramatic improvements in agricultural practices. But it seems highly unlikely that the world would have been altered as it was with the path that he was to follow.

Schoolboy

When Hannah returned upon the death of Barnabas, she brought with her three children that had been born to their union. The new situation at Woolsthorpe, a mother who was viewed with suspicion plus three new step-siblings, unnerved the eleven-year-old Isaac.

A year later, however, he was able to escape. He was sent to attend grammar school in Grantham, some seven miles away. He boarded with a local family, the Clarks, whose father was an apothecary—what we would today call a pharmacist. This exposure to primitive chemistry piqued Isaac's interest.

The headmaster of the King's Grammar School, Henry Stokes, was a graduate of Cambridge. He was to exert substantial influence on the future of Isaac Newton.

Isaac studied the standard curriculum for the age: Latin (the language of both scientists and scholars in Europe), Greek, and Hebrew. The Bible was also a major topic of study. Math was barely touched upon.

The young Master Newton was not a particularly good student. He appeared to be bored by the memorization and rote learning style of King's School. He was ignored by his teachers and bullied by his fellow students. He made no fast friends.

He was to find his escape in the books that he found in abundance in Grantham—some that he had inherited from Barnabas, others to be found at the library in the local church, and those that he bought. One in particular, *The Mysteries of Nature and Art,* inspired him greatly. Stimulated by its instructions for building things, Isaac began to construct remarkable working models of windmills, mousetraps, water clocks, kites that would carry a lantern, and sundials. He displayed an extraordinary ability in the mechanical skills, a talent that was to serve him well in his future.

This sideline did not help Isaac with his standing at King's School. Memorizing and repeating passages in Latin simply did not capture Isaac's fancy. It was not until he found himself the victim of a bullying classmate that he decided to take his schoolwork seriously. The classmate, who happened to be ahead of Isaac in class standing, kicked Isaac on the way to school. Although smaller, Isaac challenged the aggressor to a fight after school, a fight in which Isaac was to prevail because he possessed the fire in the belly. Not content to have beaten his classmate physically, Isaac taunted him by asserting that he was also going to overtake him in class standing.

Suddenly motivated, Isaac began to take his studies seriously. Headmaster Stokes took note, and he eventually determined that young Newton should follow in his footsteps and attend Cambridge.

There was a slight detour that first had to be finessed. Hannah, despite her family custom, was not sold on the idea of Isaac attending the university. When Isaac was seventeen, he was ordered home by his mother and given responsibility for running the Woolsthorpe farm. By his own admission, Isaac did not take this command well.

Beginning when he was nineteen, Isaac kept a notebook in which he listed his "sins" dating back to his early youth. For this period in his life he reported that he was guilty of hitting his siblings, fighting with the servants, and being "peevish" with his mother.[8] He ignored the farm because he preferred reading a book to watching the sheep. As a result he found himself in trouble with the law from time to time for allowing his animals to trespass on the land of neighbors.

On Saturdays he and a servant would journey into Grantham to sell the farm's produce. Often Isaac would bribe the servant to do the marketing while he snuck off to Clark's Apothecary to read and converse about chemistry.

Isaac's mind was always somewhere else. On one occasion he and his servant were returning from Grantham with Isaac leading a horse. The horse slipped the bridle and ran home ahead of Isaac. Isaac dragged the empty bridle home and did not realize that the horse was not in tow until he walked over a hill and saw his horse standing in front of Woolsthorpe.

Headmaster Stokes continued to badger Hannah to surrender Isaac to Cambridge University. Hannah did not give up easily. She was, after all, a widow with three young children to care for and a farm to run. In her mind, as the oldest son, Isaac should have accepted his responsibility gracefully and performed his duty. What was to be gained at the university in any event? Isaac could have a good life on the farm, as his father and grandfather and generations of Newtons before him had done. Of what great value was a university education?

But in the end, Hannah did surrender. Encouraged not only by Stokes but also by family members, she finally relented. How the world would have unfolded had Hannah prevailed is an interesting question.

At the age of nineteen, Isaac Newton entered Cambridge, a place he would be wedded to for the next thirty-five years.[9]

The Cambridge Undergraduate

In early June of 1661 Isaac Newton presented himself at Trinity College at Cambridge University. He was assessed by school authorities to determine whether he was qualified to attend lectures. He passed and was admitted to the College. Shortly thereafter he was admitted to the university itself.

When Isaac entered Cambridge, the university was in its fifth century of existence. It was a tradition-bound institution with close ties to the English crown and the Church of England. A hundred-year-old English law dictated the exact curriculum and the requirements for receiving a bachelor of arts degree.

As with society as a whole, Cambridge had a class system. At the top were the nobles; a rung down were the regular students, usually the sons of wealthy businessmen or farmers; and at the bottom were the subsizars. Isaac was a subsizar. Although Hannah had let Isaac go, she did not intend that his life as an academic would be easy. She provided him such a meager allowance that he struggled to survive. Perhaps she was trying to starve him home.

A subsizar was a servant to the students on higher rungs of the social ladder. Isaac was forced to run errands for, and clean the rooms and empty the bedpans of, the more wealthy students. He was held in contempt by those wealthier students. This did not sit well with young Newton. A motivation to rise above his class was ignited within his bosom.

As with his years at King's School in Grantham, Isaac led a very solitary life in his first months at Trinity College. He made no close friends. The fact that he was a subsizar made his relationships with other students a challenge. Further, he had been raised as a Puritan, and the Cambridge links to the Church of England placed him in the distinct minority. He consciously hid his Puritan faith.

It was not until Isaac had been enrolled at Trinity College for about a year and a half that he made a friend in a new roommate named John Wickins. For the next twenty years, these two would share rooms at Cambridge. Wickins became an indispensable assistant in the far-flung scientific adventures that Newton was yet to embark upon.

The Cambridge curriculum was simple and consisted of the classics, chiefly the Greeks and predominantly Aristotle. For the first year and a half, Newton attended the lectures and followed the rules. He was undistinguished. Presumably he would follow a track where he would receive his bachelor's degree in four years and then go on to become a teacher or a church rector.

But in early 1663, when Isaac was twenty years old, something took hold of him that completely altered his future.

Despite the College's devotion to Aristotle, Newton had been surreptitiously reading Galileo and Descartes. He began to realize that what his lecturers were saying did not ring true. He was not yet ready to abandon Aristotle, but he was not going to accept what he was being taught without examination.

In a notebook where he had been taking notes on Aristotle, he made a new entry: "Some Problems in Philosophy." What followed was a list of "Quaestiones" (Latin for "questions") that Isaac Newton wanted the answers to. He did not believe that he would find the answers from the conventional lecturers of Trinity College. He determined to seek them for himself.

The depth and breadth of questions that leapt into the mind of this twenty-year-old, seventeenth-century farm boy are astonishing. Under forty-five different headings he wrote down the things he felt he needed to research and the experiments that had to be undertaken. Eventually he began to provide answers to his questions:

> He set down forty-five headings under which to organize the fruits of his reading, beginning with general topics on the nature of matter, place, time, and motion, proceeding to the cosmic order, then to a large number of tactile qualities (such as rarity, fluidity, softness), followed by questions on violent motion, occult qualities, light, colors, vision, sensation in general, and finally concluding with a set of miscellaneous topics not all of which appear to have been in the initial list. Under some of the headings he never entered anything; under others he found so much that he had to continue the entries elsewhere. The title "Quaestiones" adequately describes the whole in that the tone was one of constant questioning. . . . Newton had left the world of Aristotle forever.[10]

Newton began to research and read with a passion. As he explored the writings of Descartes, Galileo, and other fresh philosophers, he refused to accept their theories at face value. In fact, he questioned their conclusions as forcefully as he questioned the dry, uninspiring, Aristotelian lecturers of Trinity College.

Newton's "Quaestiones" featured several of the areas that were to make him famous in future years, including discussions of motion, gravity, light, and colors. But, in some ways, it was his approach to philosophical inquiry as contained in the "Quaestiones" that set Newton apart:

> Nevertheless, if the essence of experimental procedure is active questioning whereby consequences that ought to follow from a theory are put to the test, Newton the experimental scientist was born with the "Quaestiones." In 1664, such a method of inquiry had been little used. Newton's example was to be a powerful factor in helping experimental procedure convert natural philosophy into natural science.[11]

Isaac Newton was not the first to use the scientific method—Francis Bacon is generally credited for that—but Newton was the one who made it an imperative for those serious scientists who would follow him.

Presumably with Wickins's consent, Newton turned their rooms into laboratories. The rooms were small, but they became the home for Newton's documents, instruments, and eventually furnaces and containers of chemicals. John Wickins was Isaac's dutiful scribe and assistant. Newton was not to obtain a real laboratory until 1673.

In 1664 another light clicked on in Newton's mind. He realized that he could not further the exploration of his "Quaestiones" without mastering mathematics. In that year, he began to make notes in a separate notebook. This young man, with only a smattering of mathematical training, taught himself mathematics to the highest degree simply by reading and digesting available textbooks. There is no evidence that he was taught mathematics by anyone.

Meanwhile, there was the matter of his Cambridge education that he had more or less let slip. Fortunately for him, Cambridge was rather lax in what it demanded of its undergraduates. In the spring of 1665 he managed to graduate with his BA, but only with a second-class status. Still, it was the means to an end. The previous year, he had been granted a scholarship. Combined, these two events guaranteed him at least four more years at Trinity College.

He now had his able assistant, a secure place to study, no desire or need to prove himself to anyone, and a mind full of remarkable thoughts.[12]

A Mind and Focus without Peer

It is a fair question to ask: How does one become the greatest scientist in the history of the world? It is a particularly good question when we consider Isaac Newton's troubled youth, simple farm background, and limited education. It is also a legitimate question in light of the fact that most of what he invented or discovered he did in a relatively brief period of time while he was still a young man.

It is obvious that Newton's success resulted primarily from the fact that he was born possessing intellectual powers that were magnificent. But there have been numerous superior intelligences in world history who failed to achieve what Isaac Newton achieved.

Newton became what he became because of two factors that distinguished him. First, his motivation for seeking answers to the questions that unsettled his psyche and for his pursuit of scientific excellence was a lofty one—it was to please God. Second, he possessed amazing powers of concentration and an ability to focus on whatever his then-chosen intellectual undertaking was. To this was coupled a tenacity that was astonishing.

Motivation

Without question, Newton's complete devotion to his religious beliefs was a key to his success. He followed his intellectual pursuits because he thought that God expected him to do so. "As a 'natural philosopher,' Isaac Newton tried to understand more about the universe. His aim, as was the case with many other scientists in that age, was a religious one. He wanted to shed light on the wonders of God."[13]

Isaac Newton was a devoted Christian, raised as a Puritan:

> His was not the Puritanism of the political extremist (of which there were still many following the turbulent days of civil war and regicide); nor was he the Puritan of the Victorian caricature—the solemn kill-joy who saw debauchery and evil in all the doings of his fellow man. Newton was

> of the type that elevated the principles of hard work and dedication to learning as the highest hopes of humanity. He believed that the acquisition of knowledge and the unraveling of Nature's truths were to the greater glory of God.[14]

Isaac's religious awakening apparently occurred when he was nineteen. In the summer of 1662, he started to keep his notebook wherein he listed the sins of his youth as well as those of his current life as a Cambridge undergraduate. Those "sins" of his younger years included those thoughts, previously mentioned, that he ought to burn the house where Hannah and Barnabas lived and that he was mean to his siblings and rude to his mother. Those that he listed as current weaknesses included such weighty matters as "Having uncleane thoughts words and actions and dreamese;" failing to keep the Sabbath day holy as he should by "Making pies on Sunday night," "Squirting water on Thy day," and "Swimming in a kimnel [a tub] on Thy day." That he was truly devoted to his religion is proven by his great concern that he was falling short in loving the Lord with all his heart and soul by "Setting my heart on money learning pleasure more than Thee"; "Not turning nearer to Thee for my affections"; "Not loving Thee for Thy self."[15]

It is somewhat remarkable that Isaac acquired this ultrasensitivity to being in tune with the Lord at an early age. It is also remarkable because it occurred within the confines of a college environment that was not much different from a typical college environment of today—that is, one filled with a myriad of temptations and vices, including ready access to prostitutes and ample opportunity for drinking and gambling.[16]

Isaac never lost his devotion. In fact, his commitment to God and Christ only grew as he aged. "If anything, his fundamentalism became more pronounced in later life. He never swayed from his assertion that God was responsible for maintaining planetary motion through the device of gravity. . . . Although in many intellectual areas Newton was generations ahead of his time, his notion of God was simplistic and as orthodox as the next person's."[17]

Toward the end of his life, after a lifetime of unparalleled scientific discovery and achievement, after he had attained universal fame and some fortune, his belief was as simple and enduring as it had been in his youth. In a later writing, he said: "The most beautiful system of the sun, planets, and comets, could only proceed from the counsel and dominion of an intelligent and powerful Being. . . . This Being governs all things, not as the soul of the world, but as Lord over all; and on account of his dominion he is wont to be called *Lord God*."[18]

As has been noted, Newton was raised a Puritan and was expected to adhere to the Anglican faith as a member of the Cambridge community, but he was, in fact, an Arian. "The Arian doctrine had its origins in the teachings of a fourth-century Alexandrian priest named Arius, and held (in defiance of orthodox Trinitarianism) that Jesus and God are not of one substance but that Christ, although divine, was created by God as *the first creature*."[19]

Arianism rejected the orthodox doctrine of Trinitarianism, approved by all mainstream Christian faiths of the time, that God the Father, Jesus Christ, and the Holy Ghost are distinct yet exist as one being.

Newton's commitment to Arianism was a constant threat to his career. It put at risk his standing as a member of the Cambridge hierarchy. At Cambridge he was expected to confirm his adherence to the Thirty-Nine Articles of the Anglican Church—which included Trinitarianism. This public commitment was expected of him at various stages of his academic life.

As to his reputation and standing within the broader scientific community and society as a whole, his belief in Arianism would have been viewed as most unorthodox and with great disfavor. In the era of heightened religious tolerance that England enjoyed at that time, there were still two religions that were considered fair game when it came to discrimination against their members: Catholicism and Arianism.[20]

Yet he clung to it, although privately, throughout his adult life. He not only clung to it, but he devoted an incredible amount of his precious time and attention to justifying it:

> He studied the documentary evidence, analysed it, and then produced his own deductions in a notebook divided into headings. By asking himself the direct question What does the Bible actually say on the matter of the Holy Trinity? he pinpointed what he saw as two major flaws in the Trinitarian credo. Together these led him to believe that Trinitarianism was a deliberate, calculated lie, perpetuated through the ages by a series of self-interested pontiffs.[21]

Once the question of the nature of the Godhead grasped him, he did not let it go. His study of the early history of the Christian faith and the teachings of its Fathers forced him to reach but one conclusion:

> The conviction began to possess him that a massive fraud, which began in the fourth and fifth centuries, had perverted the legacy of the early church. Central to the fraud were the Scriptures, which Newton began to believe had been corrupted to support trinitarianism. . . .
>
> Newton convinced himself that a universal corruption of Christianity had followed the central corruption of doctrine. Concentration of ecclesiastical power in the hands of the hierarchy had replaced the polity of the early church. . . . It is not hard to understand why Newton became impatient with interruptions from minor diversions such as optics and mathematics. He had committed himself to a reinterpretation of the tradition central to the whole of European civilization. . . . He recognized Christ as a divine mediator between God and humankind, who was subordinate to the Father Who created him.[22]

Why was Newton so obsessed with disproving, if only to himself and eventually a handful of close associates, that orthodox Trinitarianism was false?

The answer may lie in his compulsive desire to learn the truth about God's creation—a desire that motivated Newton unequivocally. If that unquenched search for truth about God's creations was of the highest priority, then was not learning the truth about the nature of God himself an even higher priority? His true identity must be learned![23]

It was not just an attack on Trinitarianism that consumed his passion for religious knowledge. In his later years, he was befriended by the great British political philosopher and intellectual John Locke. Together they shared their unorthodox religious views. On one occasion Locke told his cousin that he knew few who could equal Newton's knowledge of the Bible.[24] That knowledge was acquired as he indulged in a series of in-depth analyses of a myriad of religious topics. He spent years working on a method for interpreting the meaning of biblical prophecies, and he devised a timeline for when the biblical end of the world was prophesied to occur.[25] (For the reader's benefit, Newton predicted the end of the world to take place sometime during the twenty-first century. He also predicted that the "Call to Return to Jerusalem" would take place in 1899, and that the "End of the great tribulation of the Jews" would happen in 1948. It is interesting to note that the Jewish state of Israel was established in 1948.) He also undertook an intense study of the design and dimensions of Solomon's Temple, believing that it held clues as to the future of mankind.

Newton, like many other intellectuals of his age, believed that the most ancient of civilizations also possessed access to the most pure knowledge. He further believed that Israel was the most ancient of civilizations, and that all subsequent civilizations were simply followers of ancient Israel.[26] He believed that ancient Israel possessed the true, pure religion, and that it had been polluted. He believed that there were to be found in that "true religion" the most basic scientific truths.

To Newton, understanding the Old Testament and ancient Israel was not just a sideline, it was the source of pure intelligence.[27] Newton's religion motivated him and elevated his vision in a most meaningful manner.

Powers of Concentration and Tenacity

The second gift possessed by Isaac Newton, beyond his inherited brainpower, was his power of concentration and focus.

> Once at work on a problem, he would forget his meals. His cat grew very fat on the food he left standing on his tray. . . . He would forget to sleep, and Wickins would find him the next morning, satisfied with having discovered some proposition and wholly unconcerned with the night's sleep he had lost.[28]

The reason that he did not seem to need food or sleep was because he was totally focused on whatever project he was then working on. "In the age of his celebrity, Newton was asked how he had discovered the law of universal gravitation. 'By thinking on it continually' was the reply. . . . What he thought on, he thought on continually, which is to say exclusively, or nearly exclusively."[29]

On another occasion, when asked how he came upon his great discoveries, he answered, "I keep the subject constantly before me, till the first dawnings open slowly, by little and little, into the full and clear light."[30]

Not only was Newton able to focus exclusively, but he would do so until he had solved the problem or answered the question. For example, in the case of mathematics, once he began the task of mastering it, he stuck to that task without diversion for one and a half years until he had accomplished what he set out to do.

His single-mindedness sometimes overcame his common sense. In 1664 he was engaged in pursuit of the question "What is light?" His fixation on his subject led him to perform two experiments that almost caused him to go blind. In the first, he stared at the sun for too long and had to lock himself in a dark room for three days to recover his vision. In the second, he took a small dagger and forced it between his eye and the bone and manipulated it so that he would be able to see circles and colors, something that he found important to his research.

The possibility of causing oneself to become blind just might be considered above and beyond the call of scientific duty.

Having explored the nature of Isaac Newton's lofty motivation as well as his astonishing powers of concentration, focus, and tenacity, we can further demonstrate these themes by examining how Newton applied these gifts in bringing about two of his greatest discoveries, discoveries that are among the most notable contributions to man's understanding of nature.

Calculus

In our world, the branch of mathematics known as calculus has widespread use in the areas of science, economics, and engineering. According to the *Encyclopedia Britannica,* "Calculus is now the basic entry point for anyone wishing to study physics, chemistry, biology, finance, or actuarial science."[31]

Prior to 1666, it did not exist.

Eighteen months earlier, Isaac Newton had reached the point where there was no more that he could learn from anyone else about mathematics, but he did not yet have the mathematical tools that he needed to further answer many of his "Quaestiones." What was this highly driven twenty-one-year-old to do?

Of course, looking backward, the obvious answer was to develop an entirely new field of mathematics. Sometime in the spring or early summer of 1664, Newton set about to do so.

He had studied Descartes's text on geometry, Viete on algebra, Wallis on infinitesimals. One writer described his talent in mathematics as "intuitive."[32] Within a few months his notes showed him moving from what was known by others to his own original examinations. Within a year he had moved into an entirely new field of mathematics.

Likely in the winter of 1664–65, Wickins would have begun to observe the foodless/sleepless regimen with which he would become all too familiar. It was during this period that Newton's ability to focus for long periods of time proved to be invaluable. He thought constantly on what he was trying to uncover.

His efforts were interrupted, however. In the summer of 1665 Cambridge was evacuated because it was visited by the Black Plague. An exodus from the city was necessary because its cramped living conditions assured the plague's spread. Isaac escaped to Woolsthorpe, where he was to stay for much of the next two years.

It is worth mentioning what occurred during these two years of forced habitation in the place that he had loathed and had barely escaped from four years earlier. First, it was here that Newton took great strides in the formulation of calculus. Second, it was also during this time that he embarked on the road to the discovery of what he is, perhaps, most famous for: the principle of universal gravity.

Applying his great gifts, and enjoying the benefit of fewer demands of academia, Newton made tremendous progress. In 1666 he produced three papers, the last of which contains what Newton called his "fluxional method," or what is known today as infinitesimal calculus.

In subsequent years, Newton improved on what he had accomplished in mathematics in that frantic, eighteen-month period of 1664–66. He did not publish the tract of 1666, a fact that came back to haunt Newton when, in his later life, his claim to being the inventor of calculus was challenged. He did, however, begin to put it to good use in his pursuit of other scientific truths. It was one of Newton's most significant gifts to the future of mankind.[33]

The Greatest Work of Science Ever Written

In the summer of 1684, English astronomer Edmond Halley paid a visit to Cambridge and its Lucasian Professor of Mathematics, Isaac Newton. He had a question to ask the good professor. Normally, Newton would have avoided a discussion of his research and theories. By this time he had suffered an inordinate amount of pain from having some of his prior research on optics publicly criticized. He had withdrawn from public scrutiny and was content to just work his life away quite alone.

However, the unexpected visitor was allowed entry. Common courtesy demanded such.

Halley posed a question as to the nature of the planets' course around the sun supposing that the force of attraction toward the sun was reciprocal to the square of the planet's distance from it—a question that had gone unanswered by Halley and other notable natural philosophers at the time. Newton told him without hesitation that the course would be an ellipsis. Surprised at the quick response, Halley asked how he knew it, and Newton replied that he had already made such a calculation.

Halley pleaded for the calculation. Newton looked among his papers, could not locate his notes, but promised Halley that it would be forthcoming.

A few months later it arrived, with the promised calculations and much more. Halley saw in it something of incredible value—something so revolutionary that it could not be abandoned.

He visited Newton again. He begged for more. Newton agreed.

The relationship of trust between these two great men of philosophy resulted in Newton's publishing in 1686 and 1687 three volumes of work under the combined title *Principia Mathematica* (Mathematical Principles of Natural Philosophy). It has been called the "greatest single work of science ever written,"[34] "by common consent the greatest of scientific achievements,"[35] "the most influential book in the history of science,"[36] and the book that "transformed the course of Western science."[37]

Writing the *Principia* did not come easily to Newton. First, he had to overcome the inordinate fear of criticism that had crippled him throughout his career and had, in the past, driven him to total seclusion for long periods of time. Second, to this point in his career (he was now forty-one years old), he had engaged in and made incredible discoveries in a wealth of fields, and he had advanced natural philosophy by great strides in each: light, color, gravitation, motion, matter, alchemy, and religion. But he had finalized very few of his projects and made public almost none of them.

That now all changed.

Over the months following Halley's first visit, from August of 1684 until the spring of 1686, Newton was consumed by his work. His single-mindedness and tenacity were incredible. He did nothing else. He ate sparingly. He was so absorbed that his erratic behavior gave rise to the stories previously detailed.

But this was not just eighteen months of work that was to be presented in the 550 pages that make up the three volumes of the *Principia.* It was the culmination of twenty years of toil.

There is little doubt that Newton's greatest scientific insights had occurred within the period of 1663 to perhaps 1668, when he was but twenty to twenty-five years old. It was during this time that he invented calculus and began to contemplate on gravity.

The story about what prompted Newton's exploration of gravity, a story initially of his own origin, is quite famous. Newton accounts that it all began at Woolsthorpe during the plague exodus, when he was sitting under an apple tree and observed an apple fall to the ground. It got him to speculating about gravity. He wondered whether the gravity that pulled the apple to the earth was the same force that kept the moon in its orbit. He later was able to make mathematical calculations that supported his hypothesis.

From that, much work on gravity was triggered, but it was never completed.

Other hypotheses had been generated by Newton's fertile mind. Some had even undergone the proving step that Newton obsessively required. It was in this requirement that Newton distinguished himself. Other natural philosophers could conjure up hypotheses, and many of those hypotheses were correct. However, those scientists did not possess the ability to prove them, either by mathematics or by repeatable experiments. Newton insisted on both. He did, of course, have the advantage of having invented calculus. This tool he had kept largely to himself, so the others did not possess the tool to prove their hypotheses in any event.

In the course of his work, he had disproven Descartes's theory of ether, by itself a major milestone, but no one else knew it.

This was true of so much more.

Yes, Newton had in twenty years proven much, but he had finalized in paper form and published almost nothing. The visit of Halley triggered an intense effort by Newton to finally complete and summarize the inspired insights of the 1660s and the two decades of work that had followed.

It is very difficult to summarize the full extent of the depth and breadth of the *Principia,* especially as a layman. Its greatest contribution was establishing the universal principle of gravity, proving the fact that every object in the universe attracts every other object. The force of gravity is determined by the mass (size and density) of the two bodies and the distance between the two bodies.

It also detailed the three laws of motion. The first law, the law of inertia, states that every body will continue moving unless acted upon by another force. For example, a spaceship traveling through the emptiness of space will continue to do so forever unless acted upon by gravity or the atmosphere of a celestial body.

The second law deals with acceleration, the principle that the acceleration of an object depends on two things, the body's mass and the force that might be acted upon it.

The third of Newton's laws of motion states that for every action there is an equal action acting in opposition to it. This is illustrated by what happens when a person swims and the water acts upon the swimmer and the swimmer acts upon the water.

The *Principia* contained so much more:

> With the *Principia,* Newton not only unified the disparate theories of Galileo and Kepler into a single, coherent, mathematically and experimentally supported whole: he also opened the door to the Industrial Revolution. Along with solutions to age-old puzzles such as how the tides

> are produced and how comets travel through the heavens, Newton addressed more exotic ideas—for example he explained the Earth's 'wobbling.' . . . The *Principia* laid the cornerstone for the understanding of dynamics and mechanics which would, within a space of a century, generate a real and lasting change to human civilisation. Without being understood, the forces of Nature cannot be harnessed; but this, in essence, is what the Industrial Revolution achieved—it dragged humanity from the darkness, from the whim of Nature, to the beginnings of technology and the yoking of universal forces.
>
> And this was the harvest of dedication, unsurpassed insight, peerless technical powers and a willingness to explore exotica such as alchemy.[38]

Another author has described the impact of the *Principia* as laying

> the foundation for the whole of physics . . . making it clear that laws of physics are indeed *universal* laws that affect everything . . . it achieved what scientists had been groping towards (without necessarily realizing it) ever since Copernicus—the realization that the world works on essentially mechanical principles that can be understood by human beings. . . .
>
> The publication of the *Principia* marked the moment when science came of age as a mature intellectual discipline, putting aside most of the follies of its youth and settling down into grown-up investigation of the world.[39]

One last point must be made about the impact of the *Principia.* "Not only did it become the foundation of physics for the next 200 years, it formed the basis of the scientific method that slowly made its entry into the study of natural phenomena."[40] Because of the discipline displayed by Newton in proving those hypotheses presented in the *Principia,* never again was the suggestion of a hypothesis, without provable experimentation and/or mathematical justification, going to be accepted. So much of all subsequent scientific advancement has been accelerated because of the adoption of the "scientific method" that Newton established.[41]

In providing the details of Isaac Newton's two greatest achievements, we must not neglect to point out that he was responsible for so many more scientific advancements. For example, he was the first to identify the true nature of light and color, he designed and built the first truly functional reflecting telescope, and he dabbled in electricity, building an electrical generator in 1709. Volumes have been written about his incredible range of scientific achievements.

Much More!

A decade after he published the *Principia,* Newton's life took a dramatic turn. He essentially left the world of a scientist and entered the life of a civil servant. It is true that thereafter he published important works and continued to update the *Principia,* but his life as a full-time academic came to an end. He moved from Cambridge to London in 1696.

Newton eventually became responsible for the operation of the English Mint. He did so when the printing of coinage for the British realm was in need of the focus and tenacity of a Newton. As he had done with his scientific endeavors, he wrought great, positive change. For his successful efforts he became wealthy and financially secure.

He became a member of Parliament for a brief period.

With the move he abandoned his life of solitary scientific pursuits and became somewhat of a social icon. His wealth and the addition of a member to his household, a beautiful and charming niece, brought visitors and a greatly expanded social circle. He counted among his friends the politically connected and the intellectual elite, as well as British royalty. Among his associates was the political philosopher John Locke, with whom Newton shared much, including religious unorthodoxy. It was Locke who characterized Newton as being "the incomparable Mr. Newton."

Newton had been a member of the Royal Society of London since he was thirty years old. The Royal Society was an association of natural philosophers who combined in 1660 to encourage the advancement of science and learning. The Society had been the source of the dissemination of the *Principia* and the foundation of much of Newton's fame. In 1703, he returned the favor. He became its president at a time when it was in decline, and he presided over its rejuvenation.

In 1704 Newton published his second great masterpiece, *Optiks.* It contained the results of his studies and experiments in the nature of light and color that he had performed more than thirty years before. It too was considered to be one of the most influential additions to natural philosophy in history.

In 1705, Newton was knighted by Queen Anne and became "Sir Isaac Newton." Not bad for a country boy from Lincolnshire.

To the end, Newton continued with his study of history and religion. He was known for his generosity to his family and friends. He had mellowed much and grown much as a man as his death approached. He died in March 1727. His body was buried in London's Westminster Abbey.

Conclusion

There is much more to the story of Isaac Newton than is related here. There are epic tales of his secretiveness, his obsession with those who criticized him, and his feuds with some of the most notable natural philosophers of his age. Much about his personality, especially when he was a younger man, is not pleasant to learn about.

But a few final observations are in order.

Isaac Newton was without doubt a giant among men. Evidence of his status as the greatest scientist ever, and the value of his work, has been presented throughout this chapter.

Consider a world in which the "Industrial Revolution" had never occurred. One might argue that it would have eventually happened—but how long would it have taken for a genius, or a collection of geniuses, to emerge to duplicate Newton's scientific feats?

Imagine the world without everything that flowed from the Industrial Revolution. It can't be done because everything that we eat, drink, wear, drive, watch, listen to, or touch is the direct result of what Newton introduced to the world.

Finally, there was a disarming hint of humility in Newton's personality. This is reflected in several ways, but two are worth mentioning.

In 1676 Newton engaged in an exchange of letters with the great philosopher Robert Hooke. Hooke had been, and was to be, a man with whom Newton would often feud. In this series of letters the two were making peace (although it proved to be just a temporary truce), and much flattery was exchanged. In Newton's letter he made a statement that reflects the truth about Hooke's role in helping Newton discover the nature of light: "What Descartes did was a good step. You have added much several ways, & especially in taking the colours of thin plates into philosophical consideration. If I have seen further it is by standing on ye shoulders of Giants."[42]

This is a minor concession to the truth about Newton's success, but not one to be ignored.

The second evidence of humility is this. As he was approaching death, he summarized his own life in a rather charming way: "I don't know what I may seem to the world, but, as to myself, I seem to have been only like a boy playing on the sea shore, and diverting myself in now and then finding a smoother pebble or a prettier shell than ordinary, whilst the great ocean of truth lay all undiscovered before me."[43]

His life was summed up by the English poet Alexander Pope in another way:

> Nature and Nature's laws lay hid in night;
> God said "Let Newton be!" and all was light.[44]

Notes

1. The term *natural philosophy* was used to identify the study of our surroundings and universe before the adoption of the term *science* in the first half of the nineteenth century. Those who studied and wrote in the fields of natural philosophy were often referred to as philosophers.
2. Hart, *The 100,* 11.
3. White, *Sorcerer,* 30–31.
4. Ibid., 35.
5. Ibid., 39.
6. The "scientific method" that Bacon proposed has been explained as: "Masses of facts were to be obtained by observing nature at first hand, and from such accumulations of facts deductions were to be made. In short, reasoning was to be from the specific to the general" (Williams, *History,* 93–94). That approach is a contrast to Aristotle's deductive approach to scientific discovery.
7. For information about the status of the Scientific Revolution at the time Newton was born, a subject far too broad to be discussed except in the most cursory way in this book, see Bunch, *History,* 142–46, 195–231; Steele, *Newton;* White, *Sorcerer,* 29–42; Williams, *History.*
8. White, *Sorcerer,* 17, 25.
9. For an account of Newton's early years, see Steele, *Newton,* 8–19; White, *Sorcerer,* 7–42; Westfall, *Life,* 1–18.
10. Westfall, *Life,* 26.
11. Ibid., 28.
12. For information about Newton's undergraduate years, see Steele, *Newton* 22–25; White, *Sorcerer,* 43–65; Westfall, *Life,*19–38.
13. Steele, *Newton,* 28.
14. White, *Sorcerer,* 50.
15. Westfall, *Life,* 23.
16. See ibid., 43–45.
17. White, *Sorcerer,* 149.
18. Westfall, *Life,* 290.
19. White, *Sorcerer,* 149.
20. Westfall, *Life,* 197–98.
21. White, *Sorcerer,* 151–52.
22. Westfall, *Life,* 122, 124.
23. Newton was not the only luminary of his age who was rumored to be Arian: John Locke and Edmond Halley share that distinction (see ibid., 199–200, 205).
24. Ibid., 199.
25. White, *Sorcerer,* 157, 160.
26. Ibid., 154–55.

27. For more detail on the role of religion in Newton's motivation, see Westfall, *Life,* and White, *Sorcerer.* For specific information about his Arian beliefs and study of religious topics, see Westfall, *Life*, 119–40, 199–200, 205 and White, *Sorcerer,* 106, 149–62.
28. Westfall, *Life,* 35.
29. Westfall, *Life,* 40.
30. White, *Sorcerer*, 85.
31. www.britannica.com.
32. Westfall, *Life*, 41.
33. For an in-depth account of this accomplishment, see White, *Sorcerer*, 88–89, 327–42; and Westfall, *Life,* 37–46.
34. White, *Sorcerer*, 190.
35. Williams, *History*, 114.
36. Gribbin, *Scientists*, 164.
37. Westfall, *Life*, 163.
38. White, *Sorcerer*, 221.
39. Gribbin, *Scientists*, 186–87.
40. Bunch, *History*, 195.
41. For more information about the *Principia*, see Gribbin, *Scientists*, 164, 174, 186–88; Steele, *Newton*, 48–50; Westfall, *Life,* 159–94; White, *Sorcerer,* 190–221; and Williams, *History*, 114–21.
42. White, *Sorcerer,* 187.
43. Westfall, *Life*, 309.
44. Williams, *History*, 121. The primary sources for this chapter are Westfall, *Life,* and White, *Sorcerer.* Other primary sources are Hart, *100;* Steele, *Newton;* and Williams, *History.*

Chapter 5

Madame Marie Curie

I am among those who think that science has great beauty. A scientist in his laboratory . . . is also a child placed before natural phenomena which impress him like a fairy tale.

MARIE CURIE, 1933

This is a story about one of the most remarkable women who ever lived.

Marie Curie's contributions to science were enormous. Her work "opened a new field in physics and developed the primary technique for exploring the interior of the atom, that tiny unit of matter that came to dominate twentieth-century science."[1] She is the only woman to ever earn two Nobel Prizes, one in physics and one in chemistry. She became the most famous scientist of her age, yet, as her friend Albert Einstein asserted, "She is, of all celebrated beings, the only one whom fame has not corrupted."[2]

It is also a story about overcoming, for in her life Marie Curie had to overcome much. She was a patriotic Pole at a time when her beloved land was under the brutal domination of Russia. She was determined to become educated at a time when women were not expected to do so. She demanded that she be accepted by the scientific community for her contributions at a time when women scientists were shunned. She accomplished what she did despite suffering from depression throughout much of her life. She overcame it all.

It is also a love story, the story of a French man and a Polish woman who fell in love and whose devotion to each other allowed them to work side by side in the laboratory in full partnership for years.

It becomes the story of a single mother called upon by the early death of her husband to raise two children alone. And, like so many single mothers, she was never able to spend as much time with her children as she wished—yet she raised two remarkable daughters who loved their mother and were totally devoted to her. They were to become among the most accomplished women of their age.

In sum, it is a story about the mark left on the world by a true giant.

The Little Rebel

Marie Sklodowska[3] was born in Warsaw, Poland, on November 7, 1867.

At that time, Poland was not an independent nation and was not to become so until after World War I. It had been partitioned at the end of the Napoleonic Wars among Prussia, Austria, and Russia. Warsaw was in that part of historical Poland under Russian control.

And controlled it was.

The Poles resisted the Russian domination and were in open revolt from time to time. Shortly before Marie's birth, the Poles had rebelled, and the rebellion had been violently repressed. In order to assure that their vassal people would not cause them further problems, the Russians demoted Poland to a province of Russia, the speaking of Polish was outlawed, the teaching of Polish history was forbidden, and Russians replaced all Polish officials. To further guarantee that no more Polish uprisings would occur, secret agents were planted throughout the population.

It was in this atmosphere that Marie was born. She was the youngest of five children. Her parents were educated, but of very moderate means. However, they had big dreams for their children.

When Marie was five, her mother contracted tuberculosis. In order to assure that her disease would not spread to her children, her mother refused to ever again embrace them. The young Marie was allowed to hug her mother's skirt, but nothing more. Throughout her young life, Marie was to witness the coughing attacks, the blood on the handkerchief, her mother's body growing thinner and weaker.

Her father was a patriot. Unfortunately, the principal of the school (or *gymnasium*) where her father taught physics and math was not. They clashed, and Marie's father was fired. It meant not only the end of his employment but also the loss of the apartment in which they lived, which had been a part of his compensation. The family was forced to move to a smaller home and to take boarders into their quarters. The boarders brought crowded conditions—and disease.

When Marie was nine, her oldest sister died of typhus. Two years later, her mother succumbed to tuberculosis at the age of forty-two.

These two deaths had a dramatic and lasting effect on young Marie. She fell into a profound depression, and for months she would find herself hiding places within the family's small and crowded quarters where she could cry in privacy.[4] She hid this from her family and friends. It was at this point that she began to doubt the existence of God; she was to harbor those doubts throughout her life.

She withdrew within herself and became a very serious child. She did not seek relief in typical youthful pursuits. This was a pattern that was to stay with her throughout the remainder of her life. "From childhood, depression and withdrawal marked Manya and the adult Madame Curie she was to become."[5]

She had already shown herself to be a brilliant child. When she was just four she looked on with wonder as her older sister Bronya struggled to learn to read. Marie picked up Bronya's book and began to read it flawlessly. Everyone looked at her with some wonder, and she became frightened, thinking that she had done something wrong.

As the Russian occupation became more oppressive, additional steps were taken to repress the Poles. Polish teachers such as Marie's father were replaced with Russian teachers. Marie's father fell lower and lower on the academic hierarchy, forcing the family into ever more humble living conditions.

This mistreatment of her father only increased Marie's hatred of the Russian occupiers. On her way to school she and her classmates would pass by an obelisk placed in a prominent spot in Warsaw by the Russian Tzar. The monument was dedicated to those Poles who were "faithful to their sovereign" the Tzar. Frequently, Marie and her friends, after assuring that they were not being watched, would evidence their patriotism by spitting on the obelisk.

As a student, Marie excelled. Such excellence did have its downside, however. The school that Marie attended as a ten-year-old was operated by a Polish patriot. This was known to the Russian agents, and the school was closely monitored. The principal had a secret class schedule. To the Russian secret police the schedule showed Marie's class being taught "Botany," but it was in fact Polish history. "German Studies" was code for the study of Polish literature. If a Russian agent appeared, a bell would ring and the outlawed Polish history and literature books would be collected by designated students and hidden. The botany and German books, in Russian, were then pulled out from the students' desks.

On one occasion, the bell rang. A Russian agent haughtily entered the classroom and demanded to question one of the students. As the class star, Marie was chosen. She was subjected to intense questioning about Russian history and was able to respond in perfect Russian. The last question was, "And who is our beloved Tzar?" to which Marie replied, after a painful hesitation, "Tzar Alexander II." Satisfied, the Russian official left the classroom and Marie burst into tears.[6]

No doubt the obelisk received Marie's attention on her way home from school that day.

When Marie was twelve, her father removed her from the Polish school and enrolled her in a Russian *gymnasium.* Although repulsive to both father and daughter, it was the only means by which Marie could hope to advance beyond a high school education. The Russian teachers treated the Polish students as enemies, but Marie endured it well. At age sixteen she graduated number one in her class.

What to do next?

Marie was not certain what she wanted to do with her life, but at this age she was certain that she wanted to be a "somebody" and to accomplish something that was of importance to the world. To realize that goal, she needed to obtain more education. There were only three universities in all of Europe that allowed women to do graduate work. The University at Warsaw was not one of them.

While contemplating her future, she undertook a bit of seditious education. One of her friends was conducting an illegal "Floating University." This clandestine school was run by Polish teachers and intellectuals. It would meet at night in cellars and attics scattered throughout Warsaw. It was taught in Polish and covered a wide range of subjects. Marie was excited and stimulated by this opportunity—not only because of what she was able to learn but also because it flaunted the Russian prohibition on such institutions. Had they been discovered, both teachers and students ran the risk of being imprisoned or sent off to Siberia. Not only was Marie a dedicated student, she also participated as a teacher of the poorer class of Polish society.

Marie was very close to her sister Bronya, who was two years her senior. Bronya had been instilled with a great desire to become a doctor, as had their only brother. She knew that as a woman her choices were few, but the Sorbonne in Paris was an option. She was struggling to put aside enough to pay for the five-year course of study required to become a physician. At the rate she was able to save, she would be old and worn out before she would dare to leave the haven of family and Warsaw to enroll at the Sorbonne.

Marie and Bronya talked about this frustration often. Eventually, it was the seventeen-year-old Marie who came up with a plan: She, Marie, would go to work as a governess. From the money that she earned she would give as much as possible to Bronya to pay for her education. When Bronya graduated and began to practice medicine, she could then help Marie with her education. With hesitation, Bronya agreed to the plan and was off to Paris.

Marie was off to an adventure of her own. Her first year she served as a governess for a family in Warsaw. The next three years she ventured away from her home and close-knit family to serve as the governess of a family in a distant village.

Here, she was well received and given much freedom. She took advantage of that freedom to again engage in subversive activities, teaching the illiterate children of the local peasants several hours a day. She did so in Polish and insisted on teaching Polish history despite the risk of being arrested for doing so.

During the first summer, the older son of her employer returned from university. He and Marie fell in love. Although they loved Marie, his parents rejected the idea that their son be allowed to marry the governess. Marie's heart was broken. She fell into a state of depression, a black melancholy that possessed her. She convinced herself that she had no future and vested all of her hopes on Bronya and their older brother.

But she survived. Out of desperation, she turned her attention to education.

In the evenings she studied. Her father engaged her in a correspondence course in mathematics. She borrowed books from the local library to learn of science. She had begun to generate her strongly held view that science was a gift for mankind. She focused on chemistry and decided that it was chemistry she wanted to study when she finally made it to the Sorbonne.

When her contract was up she returned to Warsaw and worked as governess for another family. In her spare time she pursued her study of chemistry with a cousin.

By1891, Bronya had graduated from the Sorbonne, one of only three women among a student body of a thousand. She wrote to Marie and told her that it was now her turn.[7]

The Sorbonne

The Sorbonne had existed as a place of higher education for over six hundred years. Its liberality was in stark contrast to what Marie had endured with the Russian education system in Warsaw. "At the Sorbonne, students could attend whatever classes they wanted, whenever they wanted. Exams were voluntary and could be taken at any time. And all this, with some of the best professors in the world, was free."[8]

Marie was now twenty-four years old. It had been eight years since she had graduated from high school. She was pursuing a master's degree in science at one of the great universities in the world. She immediately found that her self-taught mathematics skills were totally inadequate. She also struggled to understand the lectures delivered in French. It was quite a challenge for this young Polish woman!

Her personality was now fixed to a large degree. She was not focused on people. Not that they were unimportant, but her experiences with an adored but distant mother, the early death of that mother and older sister, the rejection by her first love interest, and constant resistance to the Russian occupiers of her beloved nation made her far less concerned with people and relationships and more obsessed with accomplishing something of import. She was a very tough and disciplined woman, traits that allowed her to succeed as a student.

Although the tuition was free, living in Paris was not. Her first year she lived with Bronya and her new husband. This proved to be too distracting to Marie, for Bronya and her husband, Casimir, were the focus of Polish émigrés' Paris social life. The coming and going of her sister's friends was very distracting to Marie.

The bargain that she and Bronya had agreed to many years before was that in return for Marie's help, Bronya would reciprocate. Providing room and board for Marie was Bronya's only way of keeping her part of the bargain. Marie had very little money to fall back on. But she was not going to have her opportunity to succeed as a student impeded in any way. A few months after arriving in Paris she moved out of Bronya's home and into the first of four garret rooms she was to occupy for the next two and a half years of student life.

This chapter in Marie's life is one of the most noteworthy.

The four succeeding quarters that Marie chose to live in were almost identical—the top floor of a tenement house, often the sixth floor. The room was not heated in the winter and it was bitterly cold. In the summer it was boiling hot. Her quarters and living conditions were spartan, to say the least:

> She brought with her a small table, one kitchen chair, a washbasin and a pitcher for water, a coal scuttle, an oil lamp, as well as an iron folding bed, her mattress and bedding from Warsaw, and her old trunk, which doubled as an extra chair. She bought coal in lumps from a dealer nearby but she lit her small stove only on the coldest days and nights. For water she filled a jug from a tap on one of the lower landings. Kerosene for one lamp, which she needed to read by in those dingy quarters, and alcohol for a tiny heater about the size of a saucer for cooking rounded out the small list of monthly necessities.[9]

It was not that Marie lived in such austere housing so that she could splurge on food. To the contrary, her meals were even more meager. "By and large she lived on tea, radishes, and buttered bread, and on rare occasions she treated herself to two boiled eggs or stopped to sip a cup of hot chocolate in a nearby creamery."[10] It was said of Marie that she never learned how to make soup, not because it was beyond her ability but because to do so would have been a waste of valuable time that could be spent in studying physics.

Toward the end of her first year, Marie's self-imposed deprivation almost took her life. She collapsed on the street and Bronya and Casimir were called to the rescue. She was literally starving to death. Bronya kept her at their home long enough to restore her energy, and then Marie was back to her garret.

There was only one thing that Marie luxuriated in: the study of science. She did that and little else. She would sit on the front row of every lecture to make certain that nothing said was unheard. She was obsessed. That summer, instead of returning to her family in Warsaw, as she had promised, she stayed in Paris to work on her mathematics and French.

After two and a half years of an incredibly focused academic life, in July of 1893, Marie received her master's degree in physics. She was number one in her class.

Further, in what was to become a common attribution for Marie, she was the first woman in history to receive such a degree from the Sorbonne.

The significance of that appellation cannot be ignored. The conditions for women in this era, not only in Poland and France but throughout most of the Western world, make Marie's accomplishments more striking. Women could own property and pay taxes on it, but they had no voice in how those taxes would be spent. They did not have the right to vote; that right would not be given to French women until 1944.

For those rare women who attempted to lend their minds to science, it was impossible for them to receive credit for what they accomplished. At best, they would be characterized as good assistants to superior-minded husbands or scientific partners.

In sum, there was much resistance to a woman with Marie's ambition—a desire to do something significant in science. But Marie did not obsess over such mistreatment. She was never motivated by a desire to be a champion of women's rights. Her subsequent involvement in the suffragette movement was always at the periphery and usually forced upon her.

Marie desired only one thing, and that was to be recognized for what she personally accomplished—nothing more and nothing less. Throughout her life, gaining that recognition for her accomplishments was a battle that she had to fight over and over again.

From the beginning, Marie had planned to receive an education for a single purpose: to return to Poland to teach others and to work for Polish independence. After her first degree, Marie became convinced that one more degree was necessary in order for her to truly accomplish that goal—an advanced degree in mathematics. The next fall she was back at the Sorbonne in pursuit of that second master's degree. By now her academic abilities were recognized and she received a scholarship to assist her. But her spartan life continued.

The following summer she received that second master's in mathematics. Much to her disgust, she was second in her class.

Shortly thereafter, the life of the twenty-six-year-old Marie Sklodowska was about to take a turn that would alter not only her own course but that of the world of science. The team of Marie and Pierre Curie was about to be formed.[11]

Pierre

> Marie had ruled love and marriage out of her life's program. There was nothing original in that. The poor girl, disappointed and humiliated in the failure of her first idyll, swore to love no more; still more, the Slavic student exalted by intellectual ambitions easily decided to renounce the things that make the servitude, happiness and unhappiness of other women, in order to follow her vocation . . .
>
> Marie had built for herself a secret universe of implacable rigor, dominated by the passion for science. Family affection and the attachment to an oppressed fatherland also had their place in it: but this was all. Nothing else counted, nothing else existed.[12]

The preceding description of Marie was written by her youngest daughter, Eve. Fortunately for both Eve and the world, Marie's secret universe was about to be invaded.

Following the award of her second master's degree, Marie was hired to conduct a study on the magnetic qualities of steel. To do so she needed a laboratory. She also needed access to precise measurement tools. A common friend suggested that a scientist of some renown,

Pierre Curie, might be able to assist her with both. A dinner meeting was arranged.

Pierre was eight years older than Marie. He was a brilliant man who obtained the equivalent of his bachelor's degree at the age of sixteen. Like Marie, he was renowned for being very private, and little is known about his youth. What we do know is that he was fully dedicated to his science: "By 1880, when Pierre was twenty-two, science had already become his demanding mistress and life in a laboratory was the epitome of his desire. "[13] He had become the laboratory chief at the Paris School of Industrial Physics and Chemistry. This school was not considered to be an elite institution but rather a technical school, a training ground for students who desired to fill the engineering and technical needs of emerging French industries.

Pierre clearly was a superior scientist. His love for the laboratory and experimentation led him to pursue a wide variety of scientific lines, and he had excelled in many. For example, his research into crystals led to advances that were important to the development of the telephone, telegraph, radio, and television. One of his inventions was the Curie Scale, a means of measuring the most minute amounts of electricity generated by different elements. This tool was to be invaluable to the work that he and Marie would eventually embark upon.

At this point in his life, Pierre too had no desire for marriage. He was shy and uncomfortable around women (for that matter, men as well) and detested competition.

Upon their first meeting, Pierre and Marie found themselves remarkably comfortable with each other. Although they came from different countries, they learned that they had much in common. Both came from families of highly intelligent people but very modest means. Both had been influenced by their fathers' love of science. Both of their fathers were patriots and were committed to the betterment of humanity. They both had suffered ill-fated love affairs in their youth and were equally uncommitted to marriage. They both thrived in isolation and limited social contact.

They were both bright, and it did not take Pierre long to realize that his previous assessment that women of genius were rare might still be true, but before him was the exception.

Of most import, they both loved science. They could converse about science, even if uncomfortable in talking about anything else.

They also found that they both loved science for its own sake and not as a means of obtaining personal glory or wealth. They quickly learned that they shared this great passion, a desire to make science work for people. In a letter, Pierre summarized their common interests:

> It would be a beautiful thing, in which I hardly dare hope, to pass through life together hypnotized in our dreams: your dream for your country, our dream for humanity, our dream for science. Of all these dreams, I believe the last, alone is legitimate. I mean to say by this that we are powerless to change the social order. . . . From the scientific point of view, on the contrary, we can hope to accomplish something; the territory here is more solid and every discovery, no matter how small, lives on.[14]

Pierre fell in love immediately. He asked Marie to marry him soon after their first dinner together. Marie, on the other hand, was a bit more committed to her noncommitment pledge. But eventually he won her heart. In July of 1895 they were married. They honeymooned by riding their bikes exploring the French countryside.

Theirs was a marriage that was to become a true love story. Each learned to love the other deeply. "Marie always succeeded in her undertakings. It was thus with her marriage. She had hesitated for more than a year before marrying Pierre Curie. Now that she was his wife, she organized their conjugal life with such farsighted tenderness that she was to make a wonderful thing of it."[15]

And, of great importance, they were to become equal partners in their scientific endeavors, and those endeavors were to shake the world of science.[16]

The Science

By the end of the nineteenth century, the two questions that had intrigued natural philosophers for thousands of years—that is, what are things (matter or mass) actually made of, and what makes things move (energy)—had been answered with more certainty than in the days of Sir Isaac Newton.

By this time, natural philosophers were known as scientists. In addition, the study of matter was known as chemistry and the study of energy was known as physics.

In the field of physics, dramatic advances had been made in the ability to measure the expenditure of energy. From this it became possible to measure how much of one type of energy was needed to produce another type of energy, and this had led to the discovery of the Law of Conservation of Energy. This Law states that energy can be neither created nor destroyed, it can only be transformed from one type of energy to another. For example, the form of energy known as sound can be used to make something move (vibration); the energy source known as heat can produce motion (think of a steam-driven railroad engine); and the source of energy we call electricity can do it all—it can make things move as well as generate heat, light, and sound.

In the field of chemistry, by the beginning of the nineteenth century, chemists had discovered that there were certain substances or materials that could not be broken down any further through the use of chemistry. These most basic of substances were now called elements.

The question that then followed naturally was, "What are elements made of?"

The answer to this question had intrigued natural philosophers and now scientists for a very long time. In the fifth century before Christ, a Greek philosopher named Democritus had proposed the idea that everything was composed of tiny, indivisible units that he called "atoms." Such a notion had been considered and accepted by some and rejected by others through the centuries that followed. Its final acceptance as a scientific truth came about in the first decade of the nineteenth century when John Dalton, an English natural philosopher, proposed that each element was made up of unique atoms. He further suggested that in chemical reactions these atoms are not destroyed, nor are new atoms made, but rather they are simply rearranged. This was to become known as the Law of Conservation of Matter.

It was also presumed that the atom was a solid mass, with no parts, and could not be split or divided. A model of an atom typically displayed in the classroom was a solid, metal ball.

Of course, all of this discussion was theoretical in that no one had ever isolated an atom, thus no one had ever seen an atom per se.

Just as the ability to measure the output of energy had led to significant understanding of energy, improvements in the ability to measure the weight of elements made further advancements in chemistry possible. It was discovered that every element had its own unique weight—that is, a volume of one element would weigh a different amount than an equal volume of every other element.

In order to organize the elements, hydrogen became the baseline. Because hydrogen is the lightest known element, it was given an "atomic weight" of one. Every other element was then compared to hydrogen and awarded an atomic weight based upon that comparison. For example, if you take a certain volume of oxygen and compare it to the same volume of hydrogen, it turns out that the oxygen weighs sixteen times more. Oxygen is thus given an atomic weight of 16.

After this discovery, over the ensuing decades, every then-known element was identified and assigned an atomic weight. Because each element possesses a different atomic weight than all other elements, determining the atomic weight became a means for determining whether in fact a newly discovered material was a new element.

By the time that Marie and Pierre began their work together, there were seventy-nine known elements. It was felt by many that the discovery of new elements was becoming less and less likely—and to make such a discovery was deemed to be a major achievement.[17]

Just a few months after Marie and Pierre were married, two scientific discoveries were made that were to have a major impact on our world. These discoveries were also going to dictate the nature of the scientific path that the Curies were destined to follow. Strangely, both discoveries were purely accidental in nature.

A German scientist by the name of Wilhelm Roentgen was experimenting with a Crookes cathode-ray tube. Named after a British scientist named William Crookes, the cathode-ray tube was the result of one of Crookes's experiments in electricity. Crookes constructed a tube with a piece of metal that had a positive charge on one end and a piece of metal with a negative charge on the other end. When electricity was applied, a huge yellow spark, similar to lightning, occurred between the metal poles. However, Crookes learned that when the tube had all of its air removed, the result was a quiet, green-glowing ray between the two poles, which he called a cathode ray.

This discovery proved to be a source of much interest in the scientific community. Many scientists conducted research into the nature and characteristics of the cathode ray. Roentgen was one of them.

Fortuitously, Roentgen was simultaneously conducting research into the nature of fluorescent materials (those that glow when light hits them), and for a separate experiment he had painted a screen in his laboratory with a fluorescent material.

While conducting his experiment with the Crookes tube, Roentgen was shocked to see that the screen with the fluorescent material would light up. Naturally intrigued by this surprising phenomenon, Roentgen determined to learn whether it was something coming from the cathode tube that was energizing the fluorescent material. To determine it, he cut off all outside sources of light. He also attempted to cut off the source of whatever was coming from the tube, so he covered it with black cardboard. When the current in the tube was activated, the screen still turned fluorescent. He moved the screen as far away as possible. It still glowed. He turned the screen around—the same result. Something was coming from the cathode tube—something no one had ever observed before.

More experiments—for eight weeks he did nothing else. He ate and slept but little. In his experiments, he attempted to cut off the rays (which he called X-rays because they were so mysterious that he could not explain them and he had no way of identifying them other than "X" for unknown) with other materials and discovered that the rays would penetrate everything except the most heavy of metals, such as lead.

But most astounding, and of such great importance for mankind, Roentgen discovered that when he tried to stop the rays emanating from the cathode tube with his hand, an outline of his hand appeared on the fluorescent screen with the bones clearly visible. The bones were casting a shadow on the screen!

Roentgen tried one last experiment. Using his wife's hand as a sample, he learned that the invisible X-rays could expose photographic plates, and he was able to take a photograph of his wife's hand with the bones and her ring clearly photographed. This image was transmitted around the world. (It might be noted that Mrs. Roentgen was not amused by this event—in fact, she was quite terrified to see the bones in her hand thus exposed.)

This was something new—very new!

In early 1896, Roentgen made the world aware of what he had discovered.

X-rays became a worldwide phenomenon. "Within a year fifty books and some thousand papers on X-rays were published worldwide. One curious outcome was a proposed law by the Purity League in the United States to prevent theatergoers from using X-rays in their opera glasses. And clothing stores did a brisk business in X-ray-proof corsets and so-called modesty gowns."[18]

The use of X-rays for medical purposes was obvious. The rays could pass through the soft body tissue, but a shattered bone would show up as a shadow. A foreign object such as a bullet would also cast a discernible shadow. However, many medical practitioners were slow to adopt this new technology, at least in part because the source and true nature of the rays was unknown and so mysterious.

In 1901 Roentgen was to become the recipient of the very first Nobel Prize in Physics. But, as a believer in science as a tool for mankind and not as a source of personal benefit, he donated the prize money to charity and refused to patent his discovery. He was to die in poverty.[19]

The second discovery was equally fortuitous in nature. Enticed by what he believed to be a possible link between X-rays and phosphorescent materials, a French scientist by the name of Henri Becquerel began his own experiments. His father had done research on phosphorescence—the phenomenon in which certain materials retain a glow after they have been exposed to a light source. Becquerel wanted to see if phosphorescent materials would emit X-rays.

Eventually, he experimented with a phosphorescent rock that contained some uranium. Becquerel exposed the rock to sunlight, and when it began to glow, he put it on top of photographic plates. Yes, the plates were exposed below the rock. X-rays were coming from the rock.

He then wanted to see if the rays were powerful enough to pass through copper. He put a copper cross on top of a photographic plate with the rock on top. But when he attempted to expose the rock to the sun to activate the phosphorescence, he was defeated by the fact that it was a rainy day and there was no sunlight. The next day was the same. Distracted, Becquerel put the rock, cross, and plate into a drawer and promised himself that he would get back to it when the rain had stopped.

Returning to the experiment a few days later, he was shocked to see that the cross had been exposed on the photo paper. The rock was sending out X-rays without being "excited" by the sun.

Where did *these* rays come from?

Becquerel continued on. He remained convinced that the phosphorescent materials were the source of the rays. He was to learn that his rays came from any rock that contained uranium. The more pure the uranium in the rock, the stronger the rays. The rays could penetrate thin metal. They were steady. They seemingly would emanate for years. They also gave off a small electric current.

The Law of Conservation of Energy dictated that this energy had to come from somewhere. The fact that he had discovered spontaneous radiation, a nonsolar source of energy, was something that Becquerel thought was impossible. He assumed that the uranium rock must have been exposed to some other form of energy, but what, he did not know.

By 1897, Becquerel had published six papers on his "Becquerel Rays." But he was discouraged when it was noted by some critics that a scientist working in Becquerel's father's laboratory forty years before had noted the same phenomenon. Further, Becquerel never produced rays that were strong enough to match the power (clarity of image) of Roentgen's X-rays.

Believing there was nothing further of value to be discovered in his rays, Becquerel moved on to other things.

As has been noted, the discovery of both X-rays and Becquerel rays had come about by pure accident. But it did not matter, for those discoveries were to prove to be of prodigious significance to humanity.[20]

Marie's Quest

Pierre and Marie settled into married life. They were determined to keep their life as a couple as simple as had been their lives apart. They refused furniture offered by Pierre's family because it would require too much upkeep. "They had what they needed: two chairs, a white wooden table to work on and eat at, plenty of bookshelves and a bed . . . the walls were bare. This was decorating 'a la Marie,' a style with no concession to true comfort or gracious living—which she would never modify but adhere to as long as she lived."[21]

Pierre continued his work at the Paris School of Industrial Physics and Chemistry, earning a meager salary. Marie took the examination that would allow her to teach at a girls school (of course, receiving the highest grade on the exam), but she continued her work on the magnetic qualities of steel. She still needed a laboratory. Out of respect for her husband, she was offered a space to conduct her research in a corridor alongside her husband's own makeshift laboratory.

Then Marie learned that she was pregnant. Letters exchanged

between her and Pierre during this time show how much in love they now were. The brilliant Mr. Curie referred to Marie as his "dear little child whom I love so much." He discussed in detail the type of baby accessories that would be necessary and the baby clothes that were preferred. Marie, in turn, wrote, "My dear husband. Come quickly. I am awaiting you from dawn to dusk . . . I love you with all my heart."[22]

In September 1897, Marie gave birth to their first child, a daughter named Irene. Marie was a devoted mother. She immediately began a new journal in which she recorded every incident in the growth and development of her daughter: her first tooth, her first words, her every indication of superior intelligence. She referred to Irene in letters to Poland as her "little Queen."[23]

Even while she was working, Irene was always on her mind. When she returned to her experiments, a nurse was hired to care for the baby, "though that didn't shield Marie from the occasional, irrational fear that her baby was sick or missing, a fear that would send her hurrying in a panic from the School of Physics and Chemistry to a nearby park or to her home to check that Irene was safe in her nurse's care."[24] The motherly instincts of Marie Curie were real and pronounced and dominated the rest of her life.

When Pierre's mother passed away, Pierre's father moved into the Curies' home and assumed responsibility for the care of Irene while Marie was in the laboratory. He became a dearly loved member of the household.

Despite marriage and motherhood, Marie remained a committed scientist. She could not abandon her decade-long desire to become a "somebody" in science. She knew that in order to accomplish that goal, she had to do something that no other woman in European history had every done—receive her PhD in science.

Marie and Pierre cast about for a subject for her doctoral thesis. They both agreed that she needed to explore an area that was untouched—something new and original. Marie knew that she would never be given respect by the all-male scientific community if she pursued research in something safe.

However, there was also considerable risk in pursuing something entirely new. Yes, pursuing a scientific line completely original could lead to the discovery of something exciting and of great benefit to humanity; on the other hand, the risk in such an endeavor was complete failure—the expenditure of years in pursuit of something that meant nothing.

There was another consideration. One of the preeminent scientists of the age, James Clerk Maxwell,[25] had declared that all of the discoveries in physics had been made. He contended that existing laws could explain everything that needed to be explained. Brilliant though he was, he was very wrong.[26] Marie may not have set out to prove Maxwell mistaken, but had she thought it possible, she would have done so gladly.

By 1897, Marie and Pierre were well aware of both X-rays and Becquerel rays. The first was fascinating, but the second was more so. Even though the actual makeup of X-rays was still a mystery, the source of the energy creating X-rays was easily known—electricity. On the other hand, there was no known explanation for the rays emitted from uranium. The prospect of discovering this source was very enticing to both Marie and Pierre.

Marie decided to undertake a doctoral thesis that explored the nature of uranium and the mysterious rays that it emitted.

> Her decision to work on the Becquerel rays was to be one of the most important of her entire life. It was to govern the rest of her career, intimately link the Curie "clan" to the development of nuclear physics and also affect the life of the entire world. For what the cell is to biology, what the molecule is to chemistry, the atom is to physics. Until the discovery of X rays, few people were interested in studying atoms. Little was known about them, and there seemed no way of finding out anything, for it was considered impossible to analyze what could not be seen. Roentgen's and Becquerel's discoveries changed all this. [27]

For over 100 years, scientists and historians have debated the relative contributions of Marie and Becquerel in the discoveries that were to be made by Marie after her decision to study Becquerel rays. True it is that Becquerel, purely by accident, had discovered the existence of the rays. But it was Marie who made the conscious decision—and, most important, possessed the scientific insight and the tenacity born of a life of overcoming hardship—to investigate and to find the answer to the question of where the rays originated. It was this combination of acumen and tenacity that altered not only her own personal history but that of all science.

To begin her quest, Marie first had to find a place to conduct her experiments. Pierre's supervisor at the School of Physics and Chemistry agreed to allow her to use a small, glass-paneled workshop that had been used primarily as a storage place for old equipment. It was damp and cold and the roof leaked. It was also unheated, and in the winter months that were to follow, Marie would be forced to labor in conditions that were severe. She began her work in December 1897.

She immediately faced her first challenge. Marie knew that she needed a way to measure the rays emitted from uranium. She had decided by this time to also seek an answer to the question of whether there were other substances that emitted similar rays. By what means could she take that measurement and make that determination?

Becquerel had discovered that the rays emitted from uranium caused the air around uranium to become ionized—that is, the air would conduct electricity. If Marie could measure the amount of that very weak electrical current, she could discern the existence of rays from both uranium and other sources, as well as the strength of such rays.

Her challenge was finding an instrument to measure this minute electrical charge.

As fortune would have it, her husband just so happened to have invented a device for making such measurements some years before—the piezoelectric scale. This device came about as part of Pierre's study of quartz. He knew that when quartz is squeezed, it emits electricity.

The more it is squeezed (by applying weights to a plate), the more the electrical discharge. The amount of electricity generated had been calculated and was known. Using this device, the amount of electrical charge from a specimen of uranium or any other element that was placed in a nearby chamber could be compared to the charge from the quartz and thus calculated.

This device was ingenious, but very delicate. In fact, Becquerel had attempted to master it but had given up.

Not Marie. It took her three weeks, but she conquered the scale:

> This was no easy task. Even a fingerprint could change the reading, so the weights had to be placed very carefully on the little tray. She had to sit ramrod straight, with her eyes focused on a glass plate, where a spot of light shifted position based on how much the charge produced by the weights differed from the charge produced by her specimen. With her right hand, she placed the weights on the scale, one by one, without looking at what her hand was doing, similar to a pianist reading music.
>
> She did this until the spot of light stayed in the center of the plate, indicating that the charges were equal. Since the charge from the uranium built up over the course of the session, time was also involved in her measurements. In her left hand she held a stopwatch to keep track of it. All this required intense concentration and dexterity. Perhaps no other scientist could have done as well.[28]

She now had the place and the means, and she began her work in earnest. Over the ensuing weeks she made important discoveries: She learned that the strength of the rays was in direct proportion to the purity of the specimen being tested (the more uranium it had, the stronger the rays). She learned that the rays were not affected in any way by the surrounding environment, that is, the amount of heat or light acting upon the uranium specimen. She also learned that one other element, thorium, produced rays similar to the uranium rays.

She was very careful. She repeated her experiments as many times as she felt necessary to insure that her results were accurate. Her obsessive effort was exacting a physical toll.

Sometime in this period Marie came up with a new name for the rays that she was discovering, measuring, and analyzing: radioactivity.

> Up to this point, Marie's work had been unexceptional, but suddenly she made a leap of genius with the disarmingly simple surmise that the emission of the rays must be a phenomenon occurring with the atom of uranium itself. Since thorium also gave off rays, this was not the property of a single element—that is to say, of uranium and its compounds—and, therefore, it had to be given a name of its own. So Marie coined the word "radioactivity." . . . From this stark hypothesis, which was to be Marie's most important single contribution to science, the mysteries of the structure of the atom were to be exposed as the twentieth century unfolded. The Nobel physicist Frederick Soddy would express it differently: "Pierre Curie's greatest discovery was Marie Sklodowska. Her greatest discovery was that radioactivity was atomic."[29]

Another biographer explained the significance of this discovery in this way:

> She had shown that "the radiation energy has a different origin and must come from the atom itself, irrespective of what the atom is joined up with or how it is behaving; radiation must be an atomic property. From this simple discovery twentieth century science was able to elucidate the structure of the atom, and from it sprang all the practical consequences of a knowledge of atomic structure."[30]

The importance of this discovery was not immediately apparent to Marie. Besides, she had made another observation that intrigued her.

In analyzing pitchblende, a black ore that contains uranium along with other elements, she was amazed to find that it generated radioactivity far in excess of what its uranium content would dictate. Was it possible that there was some other element within pitchblende that could account for this amount of radioactivity—perhaps even another element as yet unknown?

To this point Pierre had been the adviser, the outside consultant to Marie's experiments. But the prospect of discovering a new element was just too tantalizing. He abandoned his work on crystals, never to return to it.

Pitchblende had already been examined by scientists quite thoroughly. Ninety-nine percent of its makeup was already known, and it was understood to contain up to thirty different elements. If there was something new in pitchblende, it was to be found in the uncatalogued one percent. As Marie and Pierre began to search for the source of the excessive radiation, they presumed that the element might be as little as that one-hundredth part of pitchblende. If they had known at the outset what they were to learn, that the unknown element was in fact a one-millionth part of the dark ore, they might not have begun. "In pursuit of material for Marie's Ph.D. thesis, they were about to undertake the most arduous and physically demanding task in the recorded history of scientific research. For both, this would be a dangerous but passionate labor of love."[31]

The hunt was demanding. Marie had to grind the pitchblende into a fine powder and then dissolve the powder in an acid. She would then remove those elements or materials that were not radioactive and kept that which was. The step was then repeated, over and over again, each specimen more "pure" than the one before.

During this time, Marie did not abandon her duties as a wife and mother. Her journals record not only every fact about the development of Irene but also how many jars of jam she was able to make from eight pounds of gooseberries.

But pitchblende was always on her mind.

The three notebooks kept by the Curies during this period show that they would take turns, one manipulating the piezoelectric scale while the other recorded the readings, and then trading and the roles being reversed.

In their notes, a specimen 150 times more active than uranium was noted in bold and underlined. A few weeks later, a specimen 330 times more active was reported.

By July 1898, the Curies knew that they had in fact discovered a new element. They made their finding public when they had isolated the element, which they named polonium in honor of Marie's beloved homeland, and reported that it was 400 times more radioactive than the same volume of uranium. The fact that polonium was an element never before known was also confirmed by spectography. Every element has its own unique rainbow pattern of colors, the "spectra," when an electrical current is applied to it. By July, Marie was able to supply their friend, a renowned expert in spectography, a sufficiently large and pure specimen of polonium for him to examine the spectra and declare it to be something never before seen.

Every significant scientific discovery by French scientists in this age was first reported to the French Academy of Science. Days after confirming the existence of polonium, the Curies asked Henri Becquerel, a member of the Academy, to report on their discovery. (Only members of the Academy were allowed to report to the body.) The Curies included in their report the observation that their discovery was made possible because of the detection of Becquerel rays by the man presenting their discovery.

The Academy was impressed, enough so that they awarded Marie a cash prize. However, according to the standards of the day, they told only Pierre and asked him to announce it to his wife.

The Curies' inquiry was not complete by any means. Upon their return from a summer break they continued to work with the pitchblende. To their surprise, when polonium was removed they detected a substance that was 900 times more radioactive than the same volume of uranium. There was something else in there!

Again they began the arduous process of elimination, one specimen at a time. By December 1898, the Curies announced the possession of a particle of another new element, which they named "radium," the most radioactive element ever discovered. It would eventually prove to be one million times more radioactive than uranium.

The scientific community was fascinated by all of the discoveries made by the Curies, but remained terribly skeptical. They were especially hesitant about Marie's suggestion for the source of radioactivity. If Marie was correct—if radioactivity was the result of spontaneous activity in the atom itself—scientific principles that had been accepted for centuries were undone.

> As the century neared its end, man's knowledge of the structure of the atom and its incredible attributes would be pieced together, not unlike a jigsaw puzzle, by the contributions of a number of scientists around the world. It was Becquerel and the Curies, in their crudely equipped laboratories, who took the first steps into this amazing new world . . . it was Becquerel's detection of radioactivity—the first new property of matter to have been revealed since Newton established the laws of gravity—followed by Marie's revolutionary hypothesis, which upset the centuries' old, natural law that the atom was indestructible and indivisible. And it was the Curies' subsequent discovery of radium, which opened the doors to twentieth-century physics. Scientists now had a powerful source of radiation. Its study would enable them to witness for the first time the manifestation of atomic energy. Radium was the key to unlock the mystery of the composition of the universe, for it would help them explore and understand the structure of the atom, the base of all matter on earth.[32]

The skeptics, justifiably, demanded more evidence. That evidence had to consist of sufficiently large specimens of polonium and radium to award an atomic weight to each. To recover specimens of sufficient size would require the processing of tons of pitchblende. Besides the prodigious physical and mental effort required to conduct such extraction and isolation, there was the question of how the Curies could afford to buy the pitchblende to process. And if they *could* acquire the pitchblende, the Curies would also require a larger facility to process the tons required.

The latter challenge was overcome when the Sorbonne was persuaded to make available to the Curies a ramshackle shed that had most recently been used by medical students for dissecting corpses. It had a dirt floor, broken windows and skylights, and a single stove for heat. Like the little shed they were moving from, the new one was terribly hot in the summer and very cold in the winter. It was ironic that the Curies were to make their most significant scientific discoveries in the most primitive of laboratories and workplaces. Marie once suggested that what had taken them five years to accomplish could have been accomplished in two years if they would have had access to a suitable laboratory.[33]

The challenge of finding tons of affordable pitchblende to process was more difficult. Pierre made inquiries in France, Norway, England, Portugal, and the United States. No success.

Eventually they were alerted to the existence of slag heaps from uranium mines in Bohemia (now Jachymov in the Czech Republic). Uranium had been mined in Bohemia for years. The uranium had been used to add color to ceramics, especially to create the brilliant, yellow-green glass known as "Vaseline glass." The material left over after the uranium had been removed was dumped in the forest. A ton was offered for free. An anonymous donor helped the Curies buy a few additional tons. The material was delivered to the new "laboratory" in sacks, complete with pine needles, early in 1899.

Marie got to work—and work it was.

> This, and subsequent loads, she would sort, grind, dissolve, filter, precipitate, collect, redissolve, crystallize and recrystallize, over and over again. Visitors were astonished to see the apparently fragile young woman wielding a hefty iron bar almost as tall as herself to stir a vat of the boiling

> solutions for hours on end—unprotected from the poisonous hydrogen-sulphide used in the purification process.[34]

Month in and month out the processing continued. Besides the hydrogen sulfide, both Marie and Pierre were being exposed to radon gas, unbeknownst to them.[35]

Marie relished the work. It would leave her completely exhausted at the end of the day, but she persisted. When it was too hot in the summer to work in the shed, the Curies would move the vats outside to the courtyard. In the winter, they tried to keep warm standing by the little stove.

Eventually, the physical part of the processing became too much for Marie and Pierre alone. They accepted the assistance of volunteers, young teachers at the School of Physics and Chemistry or the Sorbonne. Ultimately Pierre was forced to hire an assistant for Marie.

Spending money that they did not have and accepting the help of friends was a matter of simple necessity. Both of the Curies were afflicted with health problems. Pierre was suffering from what they thought was a severe case of rheumatism. He suffered terrible pains in his legs that often kept him from sleeping. Marie had fits of coughing that always led to concern that she was going to suffer the same fate as her mother, an early death from tuberculosis.

Always in need of additional money for both their research and their personal needs, Marie was finally able to take advantage of the teaching degree that she had earned in 1896 when she secured a position teaching physics at a teaching college for girls, the Sevres. This was another first to add to Marie's list—she was the first woman to ever be a lecturer at the Sevres. Marie was to become a very popular teacher, and her students remained her fans and supporters for life. For his part, Pierre took a position teaching at the Sorbonne.

The Curies were asked to prepare a report on radium for an International Congress of Physics to be held in Paris in the summer of 1900. The Congress was to be a part of a scientific exhibition that would attract tens of millions of visitors. In this report, Marie and Pierre acknowledged that their conclusions about the nature of radioactivity seemed to violate the Law of Conservation of Energy, which held that energy could be converted from one form to another but could not be either created or destroyed. "Radium just emitted energy without seeming to undergo any change."[36]

Slowly but surely they were beginning to isolate their new elements. On one occasion, anticipating what radium might actually look like, Pierre had expressed the hope that it might have a lovely color. Their daughter, Eve, recounts the evening when, sitting at home after a long day in the "miserable old shed," Marie suggested that they take an evening walk back to the laboratory for a brief look. Marie and Pierre strolled back to their laboratory and entered the shed in the dark, just to observe the specimens of radium extract, scattered around on table and shelves, with a wonderful, luminous, bluish glow that was bright enough to read by.[37]

Despite the beauty of it, the task was very difficult. As the specimens became more and more pure, Marie's enthusiasm increased. Pierre, on the other hand, did not have her persistence. He was disturbed that all of their effort was resulting in such paltry increases in specimen purity. He suggested that they put off the project and work on some other research for a little while.

But Marie was not to be distracted. "He counted without his wife's character. Marie wanted to isolate radium and she would isolate it. She scorned fatigue and other difficulties and even the gaps in her own knowledge which complicated her task. After all, she was only a very young scientist."[38]

Finally, on March 28, 1902, some forty-five months after they had announced the possible existence of radium, Marie proved it. She had managed to isolate a tiny sample, one-tenth of a gram, approximately 1/50th of a teaspoon. To segregate this minute sample, she had processed ten tons of pitchblende.

When she took the sample to her chemist friend to weigh it, the sample was so radioactive that it made his electrical instruments go crazy. Several efforts were required to accomplish the task, but in the end an atomic weight was obtained: 225.93. (Today the atomic weight of radium is listed at 226.)

The skeptics were silenced. The existence of radium had been proven. A process that the Curies had expected to take a few weeks, perhaps at worst a few months, had taken almost four years. They had expected radium to be a hundredth part of pitchblende; it turned out to be a millionth.

"The incredulous chemists—of whom there were still a few—could only bow before the superhuman obstinacy of a woman. Radium officially existed."[39]

The Miracle of Radium

Immediately upon calculating the atomic weight of radium, Marie notified her father. He had been seriously injured when hit by a train and was soon to pass away. His reply was a sincere expression of congratulations, but he added that he was disappointed that the years of work might have no practical application. He did not understand, as was suggested some forty years later, that his daughter's discovery might be comparable to the discovery of fire.[40]

The impact that radium had on opening the door to understanding the atom has already been mentioned. That benefit is most easily recognizable looking backward. There were, however, long catalogs of benefits that were to be revealed almost immediately.

The pure radium isolated by Marie Curie had unique characteristics. It was one million times as radioactive as uranium. It was luminous in the dark. The radioactive rays emitted could penetrate everything except for a thick-walled lead container. The rays made certain fluorescent chemicals glow in the dark (like X-rays). Radium made genuine diamonds luminous. Radium emitted heat spontaneously. Certain materials that were not themselves radioactive became so when exposed to radium. That included the contents of the Curies' laboratory, their clothes, and their notes.

The Curies' clothes and notes, which have been preserved, are still radioactive 100 years after they were exposed.

The many benefits to mankind that were to follow from Marie's discovery of radium were to flow largely from the subsequent work of a variety of scientists on several continents. This happened because of the generosity of the Curies. Steeped in the belief that science was never to be used for personal gain, but rather was for the advancement and improvement of the human condition, the Curies were very willing to share the product of their prodigious effort with other scientists. In response to requests they supplied radioactive samples to scientists in England, Canada, Iceland, Poland, Germany, Austria, and Denmark. Many of these scientists were competitors of the Curies on the international scientific stage, but the Curies did not care.

Among those blessings was an immediate increase in an understanding of the atom. Marie had early on suggested that radiation was the result of the disintegration of the atom. Her hypothesis was rejected by both Pierre and Becquerel, the latter still convinced that radioactivity was a form of phosphorescence, while Pierre viewed it as the result of some outside force. Marie held fast to the hypothesis that it was, in fact, the result of something happening within the atom.

In the end Marie was proven to be right. Using a radium sample donated by the Curies, two scientists working at McGill University in Montreal, Rutherford and Soddy, proved that radioelements slowly and spontaneously transmute, or change, from one element to another. They observed thorium transmute into helium. This happened because radioactivity is the emission of charged particles and thus the breakup of the atom, just as Marie had suggested years before. This disintegration theory "became the foundation for all future discoveries relevant to the nature and behavior of the atom."[41] It also "contradicted one of the best-established laws in physics—the immutability of chemical elements."[42]

Rutherford and Soddy published their initial observations in the fall of 1902. They finalized their work the following year, proving that other radioactive elements also transmuted. They were able to make their remarkable findings only because they had Marie's radium sample to work with.

> Not more than five years before, scientists had believed our universe to be composed of defined substances, elements fixed forever. Now it was seen that with every second of passing time radium particles were expelling atoms of helium gas from themselves and were hurling them forth with enormous force. The residue of this tiny, terrifying explosion, which Marie was to call "the cataclysm of atomic transformation," was a gaseous atom of emanation which, itself, was transformed into another radioactive body which was transformed in its turn . . . radium was a "descendant" of uranium, polonium a descendant of radium. These bodies, created at every instant, destroyed themselves according to eternal laws.[43]

The Curies had shown that radioactive elements also generated heat. It was for other scientists to establish the extent of that generation. In 1903, the Laborde brothers published their findings that just one gram of radium spontaneously heated a gram of water from freezing to boiling in one hour. This was an amazing display of spontaneous energy!

It was up to Albert Einstein to explain how radium emitted this enormous amount of energy. For several years he had been working on his famous theory that all matter in the universe was a storehouse of energy. In 1905, he penned his famous equation, "$E=mc^2$." He acknowledged that this theory—that mass contained energy and that converting even a tiny portion of that mass could release a tremendous amount of energy—was not provable until Marie's discovery of radium. Einstein's theory is evidenced today in the form of nuclear-generated electricity and the atomic bomb. It is also the basis for our understanding how the sun and other stars can generate heat for billions of years.[44]

One of the most immediate and direct benefits of the discovery of radium was in the treatment of cancer. The discovery of this use for radiation came about as the result of an accident. Ironically enough, that accident, once again, involved Becquerel.

Marie had given a small vial of radioactive barium to Becquerel, who carried it in his jacket for six hours. To his dismay, he received a burn on his skin in the shape of the vial, although he did not feel any burning sensation. One of the German scientists that the Curies had shared a sample with wrote and shared his personal experience with the burning of his skin by radioactivity. Pierre experimented by burning himself. His burn took almost two months to heal.

From these observations, the Curies and others were motivated to experiment with radium as a means of attacking cancerous growths. The results were miraculous. It was shown that radium could kill certain forms of cancer, and when the wound healed, it healed with normal cells. The treatment of cancer by radium became known as Curie-therapy. This was the first step that led to today's use of radiation as a treatment for cancer.[45]

Recognition that radium might be a cure for cancer, as well as public acknowledgment of its other wondrous properties, set the world afire. Radium replaced X-rays as the scientific story of the new century. The Curies found themselves the subject of intense and totally undesired media attention. The human interest side of the discovery of radium was just too much for the press to resist:

> Imagine! The miraculous remedy for cancer had been found by a slender blond foreigner, working against tremendous odds. A wife and mother, this frail creature had been doing a day laborer's job, with longer hours and more abominable conditions than any self-respecting workman would tolerate—all for no pay.[46]

Besides the legitimate benefits of radium, it became the haven of seemingly every crank in the world. Radium became a multimillion-dollar industry when it was found that radium could be diluted with zinc sulfide up to 600,000 to one and still retain most of its remarkable qualities. For the next forty years radium was touted as a cure for multiple diseases. It was added to tea, face creams, lipsticks, and bath salts. Health tonics containing radium were marketed. Costumes that would glow in the dark became popular. Hair tonics containing radium promised to stop hair loss. It was asserted that radium could restore virility, cure arthritis, whiten teeth, and cure mental illness.

Tiny vials of radium bromide became the status symbol of high society. The salons of the rich and famous were not legitimately so unless that salon had been the setting where an expert had lectured on radium at least once.[47]

From the exploitation of radium, both the legitimate and the bogus, Marie and Pierre could have become wealthy. They could have patented radium and licensed its use. They could have protected the secrets of how it had been extracted from pitchblende. In Marie's four laborious years of isolating the radium she had invented a technique and process for its manufacture. At a minimum they could have required payment, a very steep payment, for the radium specimens that they so readily handed out to scientists throughout the world. Until the production of radium was fully commercialized, it was an incredibly expensive product. In 1904, a gram of radium cost in excess of $100,000 U.S. dollars today.[48] A quarter of a century later, despite the commercialization of the production of radium, there were still only 300 grams in the entire world.[49]

But Marie and Pierre did not exploit their discovery. They both recognized that an immense fortune was available to them. They were still very poor and had no reason to believe that their financial situation would ever improve. They already had one daughter, and perhaps more children would be born to their marriage. Financial security for their children was of no small importance to both of them.

But, "it would be contrary to the scientific spirit," they both agreed:

> In agreement with me [Marie was to write twenty years later] Pierre Curie decided to take no material profit from our discovery; in consequence we took out no patent and

> we have published the results of our research without reserve, as well as the processes of preparation of radium. Moreover, we gave interested persons all the information they requested. This was a great benefit to the radium industry, which was enabled to develop in full liberty, first in France and then abroad, furnishing to scientists and doctors the products they needed. As a matter of fact this industry, is still using today, almost without modification, the processes which we pointed out. [50]

Perhaps the greatest miracle attached to radium was that the two people who were responsible for bringing it into the world were so truly noble and high-minded.

PhD, a Nobel Prize, and Fame

In June of 1903, thirty-six-year-old Marie Curie defended her doctoral thesis: the account of how, over a period of six years, she, with her husband and their assistants, had isolated two new radioactive elements. She did so in front of a large and somewhat boisterous audience, including adoring students from her classes at the Sevres.

At the insistence of Bronya she wore a new dress. She did, however, demand that it be a plain black dress so that she could wear it in her laboratory thereafter.

The three questioners were all distinguished members of the scientific community, two of whom were subsequently to earn Nobel Prizes. They engaged Marie in a conversation of which she was obviously the master.

At the end of her defense, she was awarded her degree, the first woman in the history of France to receive a PhD. One of the members of the panel declared that her doctoral dissertation "represented the greatest scientific contribution ever made in a doctoral thesis."[51]

It was a day of great triumph for both of the Curies.

By this time, however, a great irony was becoming apparent to friends and associates of the Curies. In the course of having discovered an element that was already beginning to show great promise for improving the health of society, the Curies had destroyed their own health. Exposure to the chemicals needed to process pitchblende as well as the radon gas emitted by radium, coupled with the radioactivity that they were exposed to every day, was taking its toll. A significant deterioration in the physical condition of both Marie and Pierre was obvious. Pierre continued to suffer intense pain in his legs, which were most inflamed at night and kept him from sleeping. Marie had become a sleepwalker. Both frequently complained of being tired. Marie had lost fifteen pounds from an already small frame since she began her work on radium. She was also anemic. Their fingers were incessantly red, deeply cracked, and as hard as concrete from handling radioactive materials.

Two months after receiving her doctorate, five months pregnant, Marie lost her second child to a miscarriage. She was devastated by the loss.

Following a visit with the Curies, a friend wrote Pierre a ten-page letter urging that both of the Curies improve their eating habits, slow down their pace, and temper their obsession with science, suggesting specifically that they quit discussing it at every meal. He appealed to their love of Irene for reinforcement of his arguments.

There is little evidence that either Marie or Pierre was willing to accept the sincere advice offered by this or others of their many friends.

One man who had not been too principled to make a fortune from his invention was Alfred Nobel. When he died in 1896, the fortune that this Swedish industrialist had amassed from his discovery of dynamite was immense. He used some of that fortune to create a fund to honor those who made major contributions to mankind in the fields of physics, chemistry, physiology or medicine, literature, and peace. The first prizes were awarded in 1901.

In November of 1903, Marie and Pierre were informed that they were to share that year's Nobel Prize for physics with Becquerel. This honor was one that they both cherished, for it did not violate their sense of the "scientific spirit." The prize was for the discovery of radioactivity and for the knowledge obtained regarding it.

Little did Marie appreciate, however, that she had almost been excluded from being recognized. The four Frenchmen who had made the nomination mentioned only Pierre and Becquerel. All four of these men knew that Marie was responsible for most of the effort that had resulted in the discovery of polonium and radium, but they could not bring themselves to mention her name because she was a woman. It required machinations within the Nobel Prize committee itself to have her contribution recognized.

She was the first woman to receive the award.

But Marie was still a woman in a man's world.

The Nobel Prize was a great boon to the Curies. The cash award was significant, and the Curies would never again suffer from financial hardship. Marie was very generous with the award money, giving gifts to family members, friends, Polish students in financial need, lab assistants, and a large sum to her sister, Bronya, so that she and Casimir could establish a tuberculosis sanitarium. Most thoughtful, perhaps, was a gift to her childhood French teacher, who was given enough to travel to her hometown one last time before her death.

But the prize also brought something that they did not desire—additional public exposure and acclaim. Pierre was to declare that receiving the award was "the disaster of our lives."[52]

The media descended upon the Curies. For two people who had long wished to be left alone, this was a terrible price to pay. Strangers stopped them on the street, and visitors called at their door. They were inundated by letters from all over the world. Both Pierre and Marie met their public duties stoically and as politely as they could.

The Nobel Prize also led to other honors: the Davy Medal of the Royal Society of London, honorary doctorates, invitations to lecture, and, for Pierre, membership in the French Academy of Science. Of greatest import, France finally decided that it was time to award its most famous scientists with a fully equipped and staffed laboratory at the Sorbonne.

Some of the press ignored or minimized the role that Marie had played in the discovery and analysis of radioactivity, but most reporters presented her role accurately.

Marie Curie became the most famous woman scientist in the world, and one of the most recognizable of all scientists.

Tragedy and Survival

In December of 1904, Pierre and Marie welcomed a healthy baby girl into their home and named her Eve. Marie was beginning to surrender her obsession with science. She started to find great pleasure in the time she spent with her family. Eve was an unusually beautiful baby, and when Marie received compliments about her beauty, she smiled and displayed her sense of humor by advising that Eve was just a little orphan. Marie began to spend her mornings at home to care for her two daughters and the household. She was most comfortable with her family and the small circle of friends that she and Pierre had cultivated.

Earlier that fall Pierre had become a professor of physics at the Sorbonne. He was finally receiving recognition for his brilliance. He was to receive his laboratory and Marie was to become a member of his staff. She was finally going to receive some compensation for the research that she was undertaking.

Marie and Pierre's love was growing deeper. In a letter to her sister, Marie said of Pierre, "I have the best husband one could dream of. . . . He is a true gift of heaven, and the more we live together the more we love each other."[53]

In April 1906, the family took an Easter vacation in the French countryside. It was an idyllic few days. Marie felt that she now had everything a woman could desire and in the future "nothing was going to trouble us. . . . We were happy."[54]

But it was not to be. Just a few days after returning from their Easter break, on a rainy day in Paris, Pierre was killed when he accidentally walked into the path of a horse-drawn heavy wagon and was run over by the rear wheel. He died instantly.

The death was a crushing blow to Marie. She could not be consoled and for a long time refused any visitors except for her brother, Bronya, and Pierre's brother.

A few days after her husband's death, Marie started a new journal in which she wrote to Pierre directly. She and Pierre had experimented with spiritualism, and Marie believed that she had the ability to communicate with her deceased husband and did so in writing. She continued to write in the journal for months.

As a widow and the mother of two children, Marie received much public sympathy. Some notables suggested that France ought to take responsibility for her financial future, but Marie refused. She was still young and healthy, and she fully intended to care for herself and her two children on her own.

But she was forever after a very lonely woman. Her depression was deep and long lasting. She had a firm rule that no one was to mention Pierre's name in her presence ever again. When she finally returned to the laboratory, she suffered from despondency even there.

She focused her attention on her daughters, doing everything she could to see that they received the best education and that they developed their talents. The oldest, Irene, was to follow in her mother's footsteps in science. In all of the letters that Marie was to write to Irene through the years, she always included math questions to challenge her skills in mathematics.

Eve was an extrovert, an accomplished musician and an author. She was to write a best-selling biography of her mother's life. In that biography she paid the following tribute to her mother:

> Several things, nevertheless, were permanently imprinted upon us: the taste for work—a thousand times more victorious in my sister than in me!—a certain indifference toward money, and an instinct of independence which convinced us both that in any combination of circumstances we should know how to get along without help. . . .

> It is not without apprehension that I have striven to grasp the principles that inspired Marie Curie in her first contacts with us. I fear that they suggest only a dry and methodical being, stiffened by prejudice. The reality is different. The creature who wanted us to be invulnerable was herself too tender, too delicate, too much gifted for suffering. . . .
>
> Like a great many children, we were probably selfish and inattentive to shades of feeling. Just the same we perceived the charm, the restrained tenderness and the hidden grace of her we called—in the first line of our letters spotted with ink, stupid little letters which tied up with confectioners ribbons, Marie kept until her death—'Darling Me' . . . who, along with the years, neglected completely to apprise us that she was not a mother like every other mother, not a professor crushed under daily tasks, but an exceptional human being, an illustrious woman.[55]

Those traits were to prove to be invaluable to her two daughters. Irene, along with her husband, Fred, would win the Nobel Prize in 1935 for the discovery of artificial radioactivity. Eve was to become a French resistance fighter during World War II. After the war she married a man, Henri Labouisse, who was to receive the Nobel Prize for his leadership of the United Nations International Children's Emergency Fund (UNICEF) in 1965.

Marie's life as a scientist and an educator were not over by any means. Shortly after Pierre's death, the Sorbonne offered her the position of professor. She was the first woman to receive a post in higher education in the history of France. She also inherited Pierre's laboratory. In the ensuing years she became a great influence in the education of an entirely new generation of students, both male and female. Many went on to great success in the sciences.

She proposed that an institute devoted to the research of radium be established. She spent many of her remaining years bringing the Radium Institute to life and seeing that it was properly funded. She also assisted in the creation of a similar institute in her beloved Warsaw. These two facilities became training grounds for many scientists in the arena of atomic physics, including Irene.

Marie continued with her great love—the laboratory. She soon had a reason for spending many hours in that laboratory.

Just four months after Pierre's death, a notable scientific figure, Lord Kelvin of Great Britain, published a letter in a London newspaper in which he asserted that radium was not, in fact, a separate element but rather a compound made up of helium and lead. Kelvin was no small-time figure, for he was acknowledged to be one of Britain's most accomplished physicists.

His letter was a challenge to Marie, perhaps one that saved her life. Her response was to prove Lord Kelvin wrong. For four years she labored in her laboratory and finally produced a few grams of pure, silvery, radium metal. Lord Kelvin was not around to apologize, unfortunately, having passed away three years before.

In 1911, she received her second Nobel Prize in chemistry for her work in discovering radium and polonium and for isolating radium in its pure metallic state. She was to remain the only woman to receive the Nobel Prize until Irene in 1935, and is to this day the only one to ever receive the Nobel Prize in two different areas of science.[56]

Despite this honor, her nomination was rejected when she attempted to join the French Academy of Science in 1911. The vote took place in a meeting in which, by tradition, women were excluded from the room. Although she was not only the most famous scientist in France and according to some the most famous scientist in the world, and a two-time Nobel Prize winner, she was never allowed to present her own papers before France's most distinguished scientific body. The Academy of Science finally admitted its first woman member in 1962. She was a former doctoral student of Marie's.

World War I provided Marie an opportunity to further demonstrate her great humanity. At the beginning of the war she was astounded to learn that the military medical community was not prepared to use X-rays in the treatment of its hundreds of thousands of wounded soldiers. It frustrated her to deal with army doctors who could not see the value of an X-ray to find shrapnel or bullets, or to detect broken bones. She immediately abandoned all of her other public duties and set about to correct this.

She began by setting up X-ray units in hospitals. She soon realized that it was at the battlefront that the need was most urgent. Using her fame, her contacts, and her stubborn personality, she bullied her way until she was able to supply the military with twenty mobile X-ray vehicles, complete with generators for electricity, X-ray equipment, and trained personnel to operate them.

Irene, now in her late teens, joined Marie in running these "little Curies" just behind the battle front. Here the two of them lived like soldiers, sleeping in tents in the mud and dust. It is estimated that over one million soldiers in the last two years of the war were X-rayed. Countless lives were saved and many of the badly injured were helped.

Marie also organized training programs for X-ray technicians, and after the war many Americans were trained by her in the science of X-rays before returning home.

It is accepted that both Marie and Irene were physically harmed by their heroic work during World War I. Irene's husband, Fred, believed that Irene died of leukemia at an early age because of her overexposure to radiation during the war effort.[57]

Following the war, Marie continued in her laboratory, focusing primarily on an effort to isolate polonium. She also continued to educate and train young scientists.

During her lifetime Marie Curie received eight major prizes, including her two Nobel Prizes, sixteen medals and decorations, and more than 100 honorary degrees and doctorates.[58] During a 1921 visit to the United States, she was characterized by the American press as "The Greatest Woman in the World."[59]

Marie died on July 4, 1934. Her death was undoubtedly hastened by her years of exposure to the materials to which she gave scientific birth—radium and radioactivity.[60]

What Madame Curie Meant to the World

Her fellow scientists were the most credible reviewers of Marie's place in history. Professor Colt Bloodgood of Johns Hopkins University praised the fact that "Countless lives are being saved and the ravages of cancer are being controlled by the use of the X-ray and radium." Ernest Rutherford acknowledged that it was her work "which played a most important part in the origination of an entirely new science."

Albert Einstein had been a friend of Marie's for twenty years. This most distinguished scientist noted that it was not just what she had accomplished but the sacrifice required to accomplish it that set Marie apart: "The greatest scientific deed of her life—proving the existence of radioactive elements and isolating them—owes its accomplishment not merely to bold intuition but to a devotion and tenacity in execution under the most extreme hardships imaginable, such as the history of experimental science has not often witnessed."[61]

Arguably, the twentieth century was dominated by the atom, the first forty years in learning its structure and its potential, and the last sixty years putting that potential to the benefit of mankind. The latter would not have happened but for the former, and the former could not have happened but for Marie Curie and her discoveries of radiation and radium.

For good or bad, man's ability to split the atom to generate the enormous amount of energy predicted by Einstein in the form of nuclear weapons was the single most dominating consideration of man from 1945 on through the remainder of the last century.

Even today the world remains gripped by the issue of which rogue nations may or may not be able to develop nuclear weapons. The world also remains fixated on avoiding the catastrophe that could result if terrorists became capable of obtaining and using nuclear weapons.

Mankind's reliance on inexpensive energy is a key to the economic prosperity of the world. Nuclear energy has been shown to be one of the least expensive and most environmentally sound sources of energy.

According to the Nuclear Energy Institute, there are thirty countries that rely on some amount of electrical generation by nuclear reactors. It is only fitting that France is the most dependent, receiving almost three-fourths of its total electrical generation from nuclear reaction.[62] Many experts assert that mankind must continue to develop additional nuclear energy to avoid the negative environmental consequences of fossil-fuel sources.

Was Marie the only one who could have discovered the nature of radioactivity and the element radium? Clearly, the answer is no.

However, considering the fact that it took five years of the most incredible intellectual focus and physical labor to unlock those two secrets, who else could have duplicated it, or would have duplicated it, and when would they have done so?

Becquerel didn't.

Even Pierre wanted to give up midway through the journey.

Only Marie had the tenacity to extract that one-millionth part of pitchblende from ten tons of rock over those long, physically demanding, four years.

A further question: What if Marie and Pierre had not been possessed of the true "scientific spirit" that led them to eschew the wealth they could have possessed had they kept their method and product secret and controlled? It was their generosity that allowed the entire scientific community to make the discoveries that it did in relatively short order.

Finally, it was Marie Curie who opened the door for the world to accept the contributions of one-half of the population of the world, women, in the field of science—and perhaps many other fields.

Marie never asked to be treated differently from a man, only the same: "She had survived because she had made men believe that they were not just dealing with an equal, but with an intensive equal."[63]

There is no doubt that Marie Curie bore the mark of a giant in world history.

Notes

1. Felder, *100 Women,* 8.
2. Ibid. Felder assigns Marie Curie the position of being the second most influential woman to ever live, behind only Eleanor Roosevelt.
3. Her given name in Polish was Marya, but she was always called Manya. When she moved to France to obtain her education, she changed her name to the French version, Marie. To avoid confusion, she will be referred to as Marie throughout.
4. Cobb, *Marie,* 15.
5. Goldsmith, *Genius.*
6. The incident is related in most of the biographies of Marie; see, for example, Goldsmith, *Genius,* 27; Pflaum, *Grand,* 3–5.
7. For more information about Marie's early years, see Brian, *Curies,* 16–33; Cobb, *Marie,* 10–31; Curie, *Madame,* 3–90; Goldsmith, *Genius,* 20–44; Pflaum, *Grand,* 3–22.
8. Goldsmith, *Genius,* 46.
9. Pflaum, *Grand,* 28–29.
10. Ibid., 29.
11. For more information about Marie's years as a student at the Sorbonne, see Brian, *Curies,* 33–39; Cobb, *Marie,* 31–35; Curie, *Madame,* 93–118; Goldsmith, *Genius,* 44–52; Pflaum, *Grand,* 23–33.
12. Curie, *Madame,* 119.
13. Pflaum, *Grand,* 40.
14. Cobb, *Marie,* 51–52.
15. Curie, *Madame,* 138.
16. For more information about Pierre and his pursuit of Marie, see Brian, *Curies,* 1–15, 40–46; Cobb, *Marie,* 46–55; Curie, *Madame,* 119–37; Goldsmith, *Genius,* 53–60; Pflaum, *Grand,* 35–53.
17. This description of the state of the science at the end of the nineteenth century comes from Cobb, *Marie,* 36–45.
18. Brian, *Curies,* 54.
19. The amount of the Nobel Prize money was substantial—70,000 gold francs, a large sum for any man, especially a poor one such as Roentgen.
20. For more information about the discovery of Roentgen's X-rays and Becquerel's uranium rays, see Brian, *Curies,* 52–55; Cobb, *Marie,* 59–64; Goldsmith, *Genius,* 61–67; Pflaum, *Grand,* 57–60.
21. Pflaum, *Grand,* 55–56.
22. Ibid., 61.
23. Ibid., 69.
24. Brian, *Curies,* 50–51.
25. A Scottish physicist and mathematician who lived from 1831–1879 and was

deemed to be the most significant physicist of the nineteenth century, and behind only Newton and Einstein among all physicists in history.

26. See Pflaum, *Grand*, 58.
27. Ibid., 63.
28. Cobb, *Marie,* 65.
29. Pflaum, *Grand*, 65–66.
30. Brian, *Curies,* 57–58, quoting biographer Robert Reid.
31. Ibid., 58.
32. Pflaum, *Grand*, 72.
33. Ibid., 63.
34. Brian, *Curies*, 64.
35. Radon gas was discovered by a New Zealand physicist, Ernest Rutherford, while studying radioactivity at Cambridge University in 1899.
36. Brian, *Curies,* 69.
37. Curie, *Madame,* 175–77.
38. Ibid., 174.
39. Ibid., 175. For a full account of the four-year effort to isolate radium, see Brian, *Curies,* 55–70; Cobb, *Marie,* 63–78; Curie, *Madame*, 152–77; Goldsmith, *Genius,* 68–100; Pflaum, *Grand,* 62–94.
40. Brian, *Curies,* 70.
41. Pflaum, *Grand*, 98.
42. Ibid.
43. Curie, *Madame*, 197.
44. See Brian, *Curies*, 72.
45. For the account of the recognition of radium as a cancer cure, see Brian, *Curies,* 65–66; Curie, *Madame*, 195–96; Pflaum, *Grand*, 91–92.
46. Pflaum, *Grand,* 93.
47. See Goldsmith, *Genius,* 118–21.
48. Ibid., 121.
49. Pflaum, *Grand*, 276.
50. Curie, *Madame*, 204–5. See pages 202–5 for Eve Curie's full account of the conversation that Marie and Pierre had to make this decision to forgo wealth from their discovery.
51. Brian, *Curies*, 75.
52. Goldsmith, *Genius*, 115.
53. Pflaum, *Grand*, 79.
54. Goldsmith, *Genius*, 132.
55. Curie, *Madame,* 272–73.
56. Linus Pauling has also received two Nobel Prizes, but only one in science—chemistry—and the other in peace.

57. For a brief account of this great effort, see Cobb, *Marie*, 109–11; Pflaum, *Grand*, 195–211.
58. Cobb, *Marie*, 120.
59. Pflaum, *Grand*, 224.
60. For information about the life of Marie Curie generally, see Brian, *Curies*; Cobb, *Marie*; Curie, *Madame*; Felder, *100 Women;* Goldsmith, *Genius;* Pflaum, *Grand.*
61. Brian, *Curies*, 252–53.
62. See www.nei.org for more details about the nuclear energy industry.
63. Felder, *100 Women*, 10.

Chapter 6

Dr. Martin Luther King Jr.

I still have a dream. It is a dream deeply rooted in the American dream that one day this nation will rise up and live out the true meaning of its creed.

DR. MARTIN LUTHER KING JR., 1963

Midway through the twentieth century, the citizens of the United States of America were feeling very good about themselves and their country. True, the so-called Cold War was taking shape: the contest between the free nations of the earth and the communist powers of the Union of Soviet Socialist Republics and its allies. But for the moment it was the United States that was the undeniable superpower in the world.

Economic good times were at hand. The soldiers who returned home from fighting in World War II had ignited an economic boom that was sweeping the nation along to new heights of prosperity.

Most important, the United States and its allies had just disposed of two great menaces to mankind—Nazi Germany and Imperial Japan. Until defeated by Allied military might, the regimes of those two nations had distinguished themselves for their racist hatred. The leaders of both had retained their power in large part by engendering attitudes of racial superiority among their people. Hitler was consumed with a passion for exterminating the Jews. The Japanese were infamous for their cruelty toward those they deemed to be inferior races in the lands that they had conquered, in particular Korea and China. Both regimes had been brought to an abrupt end by the bravery and doggedness of American soldiers.

The problem was that when they returned home, those same soldiers were returning to a nation that was itself rife with a racism that permeated its soul. Black Americans were the victims of that racism—a racism that was the official policy of the Southern states of America but was to be found in all regions. This was a racism that not only resulted in horrific examples of violence against innocent citizens of this country, but diminished the quality of life—in fact devalued the life—of 10 percent of our citizens. It was a racism that destroyed the moral authority of the United States.

It Did Not Have to Be

As was the case with most nations on the earth, the United States had a history of slavery. Unlike other nations, however, our slavery was an act of obscene hypocrisy, for we were a nation whose founding document, the Declaration of Independence, proclaimed that "all men are created equal" and that "all men" are endowed by God with the inalienable right of "Life, Liberty and the pursuit of Happiness." Equality under the law was denied the slaves of African descent, as was the right to liberty and the power to possess that which they earned by the sweat of their brow (which the Founders meant by "pursuit of Happiness.") Not only that, but the very life of a slave was deemed to be of little worth—unless one was considering that slave's worth in the field or value at the auction.

But we fought a bloody Civil War and ended slavery.

Following that war, a door swung open that could have led to an acceptance of all Americans, regardless of their race or color, into full citizenship. There were many citizens—in the North to be sure, but also in the South—who joined the effort to assimilate the newly freed slaves into American society.

To assure that there would never again be any ambiguity about our nation's position on slavery, and to assure the former slaves' rights in society, our nation passed three amendments to our Constitution. The first, in the same year that the Civil War ended, abolished slavery (Thirteenth Amendment, 1865). Three years later, the Fourteenth Amendment was ratified. This amendment provided that all slaves born in America were citizens of the United States as well as their states of residence. Further, it prohibited any state from denying any citizen the "privileges or immunities" enjoyed by any other citizen, nor was anyone to be denied by a state the right of due process under the law, nor could any state deny any person the equal protection of the law. Finally, the Fifteenth Amendment, passed in 1870, provided the right to all citizens to vote regardless of race, color, or previous servitude.

This was not all. The Congress of the United States realized that more was needed to guarantee that the former slaves be assimilated into the mainstream of American life. In 1866, civil rights legislation was passed guaranteeing to all citizens of every race and color the same right as white citizens to make and enforce contracts, to sue in court, to own property, and to receive the protection under the law of their person and property. Nine years later Congress passed the Civil Rights Act of 1875, which outlawed discrimination based upon race in inns, theaters, common carriers (such as railroads), and other places and forms of "public accommodation."

Stretching its constitutional authority to the limit, by these pieces of legislation the post–Civil War Congress sought to bring equality under the law in the treatment of black Americans.

For a short while the door was opened to making America true to the truths contained in the Declaration of Independence.

But that door shut—slowly but most assuredly. Southern states passed laws to circumvent the federal legislation. The United States Department of Justice failed to properly implement the laws. Courts were slow to enforce the new laws because of questions about their constitutionality.

In 1883, the 1875 Civil Rights Act was declared unconstitutional by the United States Supreme Court.

All of the efforts to bring America into conformity with its expressed ideals were foiled.

And then, the coup de grace. In 1896, the United States Supreme Court issued its decision in the case of *Plessy v. Ferguson.* This decision, one of the most infamous in Court history, upheld as constitutional a Louisiana law that demanded that railroad companies segregate their passengers by race. The Supreme Court endorsed the concept that "separate but equal" railroad cars were legal.

Over time, this state-sanctioned segregation became the norm in Southern states, not only in transportation but in schools, parks, hospitals, churches, swimming pools, graveyards, restaurants, restrooms, and every other place where the races might possibly mingle. "Jim Crow" laws were passed to assure the separation of the races.

State-endorsed segregation in the persona of Jim Crow was the norm for the next six decades.[1]

The Black Experience in Mid-Twentieth-Century America

What were the consequences of those sixty-plus years of Jim Crow laws and institutionalized racism in America? What impact did they have in the everyday lives of those fifteen million Americans of African descent, roughly 10 percent of our country's population?[2]

How were those men, women, and children who descended from African slaves treated by those whose forefathers had enslaved them and profited from their forced labor?

In sum, what was it like to be black in America before Martin Luther King Jr.?

To fully appreciate the significance of Martin Luther King Jr. in the history of this great nation, it is necessary that those questions be answered with absolute candor—even though the answers reveal an ugly stain on the history of the United States.

The summary response is that black Americans were second-class citizens. They were both separated and denigrated. They were the object of conscientious efforts to "keep them in their place" by every means necessary. They were informed by both the actions of their government and the everyday treatment by whites that they were inferior. Pride in race was extinguished whenever it displayed itself. Whites in America, particularly in the Southern states, could not (out of fear of their numbers) or would not (out of plain racism) allow black Americans the simple luxury of self-respect.

An instrument of this American version of apartheid was violence. From the end of the American Civil War through the Civil Rights era wrought by Martin Luther King Jr., black citizens of America were too often the victims of irrational violence.

It is difficult to explain fully the motivation of those white Americans who imposed Jim Crow laws in the South and demanded segregation in housing and schools in the North. Racism, except to the racist, is somewhat inexplicable. Preserving white superiority was their objective. To retain superiority, white Americans had to keep blacks in their "correct" position of inferiority to the whites. Any suggestion that black Americans were threatening the superiority of whites would be met with retaliation and often violence.

Efforts to keep the blacks "in their place" permeated society and were reflected in the customs and traditions of Southern culture. Certain behavior was demanded of blacks. For example, if you were black, you were required to tip your hat when you walked past a white person. In conversation, it was demanded that you call the white man "sir" and the white lady "ma'am." (If you were a male, you had to be very careful about talking to a white woman at all, especially a young white woman!)

If you were a black man or woman strolling down the sidewalk and a white man or woman approached and the sidewalk was too narrow for the two of you to pass, you were the one who was to step into the street.

If you attended school in Florida, you had to be certain to never be found using a "white" textbook—those were only for whites—you had your own "black" textbooks. If you worked in a factory in South Carolina, you must never get caught looking out the windows of the factory that were reserved for just white workers.

Most definitely, you would never dare to use a drinking fountain that had been designated for the whites—or, heaven forbid, a "Whites Only" restroom!

Propagating the idea of black inferiority began at birth but was most effectively ingrained in the elementary school years. *Plessy v. Ferguson* said that the separate facilities for blacks had to be equal to the facilities provided to the whites. But that was almost never the case for public schools. For example, a study by the National Association for the Advancement of Colored People (NAACP) found that in South Carolina in the 1930s, white students were funded at ten times the level of black students. Twenty years later, one county in South Carolina spent $179 per year on white students compared to $43 for black students. In that same county, the teacher-to-pupil ratio for white students was 1:28 while for black students it was 1:47.

The school buildings provided for black students were far from equal with the schools where white students attended. Just one example: in a school district in Virginia, one black high school had twice as many students as the school was built for. It had no cafeteria to provide a lunch and no gymnasium for indoor sports. When petitioned for help, the all-white school board reluctantly authorized the construction of tar-paper and wood shacks for new classrooms.

The combination of Jim Crow laws, everyday patterns of relationships between whites and blacks, and separate but unequal schools had its impact on the children.

Dr. Kenneth Clark, a graduate of Harvard who earned his PhD from Columbia University, devised an ingenious test for assessing the harm to black children from segregation: He used dolls—one white and one black. He would then question black children to test their perceptions of themselves by having them identify themselves with one of the dolls.

In one such test, Dr. Clark showed the two dolls to sixteen black children ranging in age from six to nine. The children were asked which of the two dolls they liked the best. Ten of the sixteen black children said that they liked the white doll the best. Eleven of the children said that the black doll looked bad to them, while nine of them said that the white doll looked nice. Seven of the children identified themselves as the white doll.

> Clark recalls, "The most disturbing question—and the one that really made me, even as a scientist, upset—was the final question: 'Now show me the doll that's most like you.' Many of the children became emotionally upset when they had to identify with the doll they had rejected. These children saw themselves as inferior, and they accepted the inferiority as part of reality."[3]

The vestiges of segregation followed the black student beyond the public schools. Only a few colleges were available to any but the most brilliant of black high school graduates. Even upon graduation from college or a professional school, the opportunities for utilizing an education were limited.

> The future of the Negro college student has long been locked within the narrow walls of limited opportunity. Only a few professions could be practiced by Negroes and, but for a few exceptions, behind barriers of segregation in the North as well as the South. Few frustrations can compare with the experience of struggling with complex academic subjects, straining to absorb concepts which may never be used, or only half-utilized under conditions insulting to the trained mind.[4]

Beyond the years of a black person's youth, into adulthood, the sense of inferiority that was so firmly imbedded into their psyche inevitably led to a sense of being "less than human."[5]

Most blacks calmly and patiently accepted the imposition of "insult, injustice and exploitation."[6]

Segregation resulted in economic deprivation. Blacks were discriminated against in hiring. Blacks who *were* hired were paid less than whites. Black families required government assistance in numbers three to four times that of whites. This was true not just in the South but in the North as well.

> Of the good things in life, the Negro has approximately one half those of whites. Of the bad things of life, he has twice those of whites. Thus half of all Negroes live in substandard housing. And Negroes have half the income of whites. When we view the negative experiences of life, the Negro has a double share. There are twice as many unemployed. The rate of infant mortality among Negroes is double that of whites.[7]

Among the great indignities inflicted on black Americans was the denial of the suffrage—the right to vote. The right to vote was denied by poll taxes, literacy tests, or simply ignoring a black person's request to register. If they were registered, they were often refused access to the ballot box. This refusal was often accompanied by either threats or actual violence. The deprivation of the suffrage was noted in *The Report of the President's Committee on Civil Rights (1947).* In that document, President Truman's Committee reported:

> The fact that Negroes and many whites have not been allowed to vote in some states has actually sapped the morality underlying universal suffrage. Many men in public and private life do not believe that those who have been kept from voting are capable of self rule. They finally convince themselves that disfranchised people do not really have the right to vote.[8]

If the blacks had no vote, they had no voice. No voice meant no political power or influence. To assure white supremacy, it was imperative that blacks not ever be allowed to vote—they must never achieve any political power or influence.

As Jim Crow took hold in the South, many blacks thought the only answer was to escape. Their destinations were the cities to the North. Between 1910 and 1930, more than one million blacks headed to Northern cities.[9] Although they did not face official, state-sanctioned segregation there, they still found themselves forced into ghettos. More often than not their children would attend schools just as segregated as those they had fled from in the South. Usually they were forced to live in crowded housing in totally segregated neighborhoods.

As these migrating blacks attempted to enter the workforce and demanded housing, they posed a threat to whites. The reaction was sometimes violent. There were numerous race riots following World War I, and they were to continue for several decades. In 1919, race riots erupted in twenty-six cities as widespread as Chicago, Illinois; Washington, D.C.; and Omaha, Nebraska. Unlike those that were to occur in the 1960s, these riots were not initiated by blacks. To the contrary, they normally involved mobs of whites attacking black neighborhoods to wreak havoc on both persons and property. Many lives were lost in these assaults. The last such race riot occurred in Detroit, Michigan, in 1943, where thirty-four people were killed and property loss was estimated at $2 million.[10]

Back in the South, violence against blacks was common and usually aimed at individuals. Such violence is often connected with the term *lynching.* When defined as the killing of someone by a mob, most often by hanging or shooting, as punishment for an accused or suspected crime, lynching has occurred far too frequently in American history. It has been common enough that three organizations have monitored the occurrence of lynchings and have kept track of the number of lynchings for over 100 years: the *Chicago Tribune* newspaper (since 1882), the Tuskegee Institute (now Tuskegee University located in Tuskegee, Alabama; since 1892) and the NAACP (since 1912). The numbers vary among these three sources and are not precise because the primary source of information has always been news reports. Further, the definition of *lynching* is subjective, and whether any given death met the definition was subjective. Those caveats notwithstanding, the facts are still somewhat staggering.

According to the Tuskegee calculations, in the sixty-nine years between 1882 and 1951, 4,730 people were lynched in the United States; 3,437 of them were black. Lynchings occurred in every section of the country, although most took place in the states of the South. The suspected or alleged crimes for which people were lynched (again, usually by hanging and shooting, although death was also inflicted by burning at the stake, dismemberment, and other forms of physical brutalization) included assault, rape or attempted rape, robbery, and theft. Many were lynched for no suspected crime at all. Some blacks were lynched for offenses such as attempting to vote, asking a white woman for marriage, or disputing with a white man.

Lynchings usually took place in small towns in rural areas. Studies have shown that local law enforcement often joined in the lynching or stood back and allowed a lynching to occur without interference.

Lynching was a tool—a tool to assure that no black man or woman individually, nor the blacks as a race, would become too assertive, too disrespectful, too much a threat to white superiority.[11]

Much to the distress of whites in the South, the end of World War II witnessed a dramatic increase in the manifestation of unacceptable assertiveness. That manifestation emanated from a potent force: those black soldiers who returned home from service in World War II.

For a moment, try to imagine yourself as one of those black American soldiers returning from honorable service to your country in 1945 or 1946. Like every soldier, you wore your uniform proudly as a symbol of your service. Like every soldier who had served and survived combat, you had developed a high level of self-confidence and carried yourself accordingly. Like every soldier who had helped to defeat Nazism in Europe, or the empire of Japan in the Pacific, you were justifiably pleased with what you and your brother soldiers had accomplished. You might have even been foolhardy enough to expect an occasional expression of gratitude from those Americans, both white and black, who were beneficiaries of your service.

But when you were discharged from active duty and returned to your home in the South, you were now the enemy. Your pride and self-respect were viewed as a genuine threat to the entire system. Your wearing of the uniform of the United States was deemed to be treasonous. You had to be reminded of your proper place as quickly as possible.

This was the reality in the South after World War II. The result was a remarkable show of disrespect toward black veterans—particularly from police officers. Systematic acts of violence against black soldiers upon their return home became common.

Sergeant Isaac Woodard, United States Army, serves as a striking and tragic illustration. Isaac had worn the uniform of his country for four years. He had served in the Pacific and had won medals for his bravery and honorable service.

Early in 1946, he was honorably discharged and mustered out from Camp Gordon in Georgia. He climbed on a Greyhound bus anxious to return to his home in North Carolina, excited to see his family after so many years far from home. When the bus stopped outside Augusta, Georgia, Isaac asked the bus driver if he could leave for a moment to go to a restroom. For some reason, this request angered the driver.

Upon Isaac's return to the bus, nothing was said. But at the next stop, Batesburg, South Carolina, the driver called for the local police to remove Isaac from the bus. Everything about Isaac seemed to enrage the police. They took him to a nearby alley and beat him. They continued to beat him with their nightsticks as they hauled him to the police station. They beat him during the night he was in jail.

The next morning, war veteran Isaac Woodard was blind in both eyes and a victim of amnesia. He was never to recover his sight. He was taken to a hospital, where he was given minimal treatment. Isaac was discovered there by his family three weeks later.[12]

As proved to be the case with so many of the actions and reactions of the white community in the decades that were to follow, this single episode backfired badly. Nationwide criticism came down hard on the officers and community of Batesburg.

But that attention was small compared to that which fell on the state of Mississippi nine years later because of violence not against a war veteran but against a child.

In August of 1955, Mamie Bradley of the south side of Chicago put her fourteen-year-old son, Emmett Till, on a train headed for Mississippi. Emmett was going on a summer vacation to visit family members in Mississippi, where his mother was from.

Mamie knew Mississippi. She warned her young son "not to fool with white people down south: 'If you have to get on your knees and bow when a white person goes past, do it willingly.'"[13]

The eighth grader had gone to stay with his cousin Curtis near Money, Mississippi. One evening, Emmett and Curtis had borrowed Curtis's grandfather's 1941 Ford to drive to the local store. There, they joined up with a group of other boys. As the outsider, and brash by nature, Emmett bragged about a white girl who was his friend in Chicago. The local boys egged him on to prove himself by saying something to the white girl in the store. Emmett went inside, and as he left he said to the twenty-one-year-old, married woman, "Bye, Baby."

Three days later, the woman's husband, Roy Bryant, and his brother-in-law, J. W. Milam, showed up at the cabin of Mose Wright, Curtis's grandfather. They demanded Emmett. The grandfather begged that he just be whipped. He told them that the boy was from the North and just didn't know how to act with white people in the South.

The men took Emmett, beat him, wrapped a piece of barbed wire around his neck, tied a seventy-five-pound cotton-gin fan to the wire, shot him in the head, and dropped him in a river.

His body was found three days later.

Less than a month after the murder, the two men were put on trial. In a demonstration of remarkable courage, Mose Wright testified against the white men, telling the all-white jury that Bryant and Milam were the ones who had taken Emmett. Several other blacks who had damning testimony to establish the murderers' guilt also testified. All of them had to flee after the trial—never to return to Mississippi.

The two men were acquitted by the jury.

Several months later, for a hefty price of $4,000, the two were convinced to tell their story to William Huie, a journalist from Alabama. They admitted the murder. Their excuse: the eighth grader just wouldn't play the role of the inferior black—he wouldn't apologize. Milam told the reporter: "What else could we do? . . . He was hopeless. I'm no bully; I never hurt a nigger in my life. I like niggers in their place. I know how to work 'em. But I just decided it was time a few people got put on notice."[14]

Emmett Till was not the first black child to be murdered, nor would he be the last. However, his murder—and the astonishing injustice that his murderers' acquittal entailed—galvanized the nation and energized the infant Civil Rights Movement.

But it also had a devastating impact on young blacks. As one black woman later wrote of its effect on her as an adolescent:

> Before Emmett Till's murder, I had known the fear of hunger, hell and the Devil. But now there was a new fear known to me—the fear of being killed just because I was black. This was the worst of my fears. I knew once I got food, the fear of starving to death would leave. I also was told that if I were a good girl, I wouldn't have to fear the Devil or hell. But I didn't know what one had to do or not do as a Negro not to be killed. Probably just being a Negro period was enough, I thought.[15]

Perhaps the most effective way to summarize the state of the black citizens of America before Martin Luther King Jr. stepped forward to lead the Civil Rights Movement of the 1950s and 1960s is to quote Dr. King from one of his most famous discourses, his *Letter from a Birmingham Jail.* While incarcerated for participating in a civil rights demonstration in Birmingham, Alabama, in 1963, he wrote this letter to respond to a plea from eight ministers who had criticized King for being too aggressive in his efforts to bring justice for the blacks. The letter contains much to be recommended, but the following narrative of the multitude of wrongs that Dr. King was trying to address is invaluable:

> We have waited for more than 340 years for our constitutional and God-given rights . . . and we still creep at horse and buggy pace toward the gaining of a cup of coffee at a lunch counter. I guess it is easy for those who have never felt the stinging darts of segregation to say, "Wait." But when you have seen vicious mobs lynch your mothers and fathers at will and drown your sisters and brothers at whim; when you have seen hate-filled policemen curse, kick, brutalize and even kill your black brothers and sisters with impunity; when you see the vast majority of your twenty million Negro brothers smothering in an airtight cage of poverty in the midst of an affluent society . . . when you are harried by day and haunted by night by the fact that you are a Negro, living constantly at tiptoe stance never quite knowing what to expect next, and plagued with inner fears and outer resentments; when you are forever fighting a degenerating sense of "nobodiness"; then you will understand why we find it difficult to wait. There comes a time when the cup of endurance runs over, and men are no longer willing to be plunged into an abyss of injustice where they experience the blackness of corroding despair.[16]

Those words best answer the question, "What was it like to be black in America before Martin Luther King Jr."?[17]

The Civil Rights Revolution

The term *Civil Rights Movement* refers to those court decisions, legislative enactments, marches and demonstrations, powerful speeches, and the adjustment of societal and personal attitudes that occurred in the decades of the 1950s and 1960s. That movement represents one of the most remarkable crusades in the history of the United States. To attempt to provide detail about all of the actions and events—indeed, to even attempt to reference them all in this chapter—would be impossible.

The fact is that the movement needed the help of powerful people in Washington, D.C., including Supreme Court justices, presidents, and members of Congress. It was energized by national organizations such as the NAACP, the Southern Christian Leadership Conference, Student Nonviolent Coordinating Committee, Congress on Racial Equality, and the National Urban League.

There were many leaders, especially among the black churches of the South, who spoke out and provided key leadership to the movement. There were individuals, ordinary black Americans, who stood up and said to white America: "Enough is enough—I demand the rights that God gave me and that you steal from me!" Further, there were many white Americans in both the North and the South who lent their support to the black community. Again, to make any effort to herald the courage, eloquence, and actions of all of them is impossible.

It is important to understand that the Civil Rights Movement was not monolithic in nature. Some people involved in the effort to bring blacks into the mainstream of American society with full, first-class status argued that a "go slow, don't cause offense" approach was the best. Those who believed in this approach were very anxious that violence be avoided at all cost. In their view, violence could be avoided only by calm persuasion and by appeals to a sense of morality and basic decency to alter the attitudes of white Americans. Followers of this glacial approach to change believed that the only pressure that should be brought was in allowing the blacks to vote, and that by way of the ballot box and electoral victories the rest of the needed changes would follow.

On the other side of the spectrum were those who were furious at the condition of black Americans. They saw with great clarity how truly wrong it was for the United States of America to be the home of rampant racism. They believed that blacks had been patient for too long. They had no faith that persuasion or even passive resistance would succeed. These were the militants—the blacks who demanded "Black Power" now. They had very little patience with either the white supremacists or the blacks who were willing to try to accomplish their goals without violence. They wanted immediate equality and thought that it would be accomplished only by brute force.

There was also a middle ground. These were those blacks who were also angry, clearly saw the gross injustice, and demanded change. But they were tempered by beliefs that abhorred violence. They followed those beliefs and charted out a course of nonviolent but constant pressure against the white power structure.

The Birth of the Movement

Arguably, the United States Supreme Court, that body which had given official sanction to segregation with its 1896 *Plessy* decision and approval of "separate but equal," had to recant that decision in order for the Civil Rights Movement to ever succeed. As long as there was no legal barrier to segregation, the ability to make a moral appeal would have been moot.

In 1954 the Supreme Court did recant. In its unanimous opinion of *Brown v. Board of Education,* the Supreme Court renounced "separate but equal" in public education. *Brown* was actually a decision that consolidated five separate actions brought by a variety of young students or their parents from the states of Kansas, South Carolina, Virginia, Delaware, and Washington, D.C. The opinion specifically referenced the work of Dr. Clark and his dolls as proof that separation inevitably created a feeling of inferiority in black children. It declared that separate educational facilities were inherently unequal.

Among blacks, *Brown* was viewed as a godsend—the great beginning of the end of segregation. Expectations were raised of immediate changes in the education of their youth. The hope was widespread that such changes in public education would immediately result in integration in other areas and eventually the end of segregation. Those feelings of euphoria were quickly dashed, however, for the whites of the South were not about to let nine liberals from up north upend their cherished system. White reaction was fierce and massive in its scope.

"White Citizens Councils" were organized to assure that black and white children would never attend school together. Members of these councils were so intent that they agreed to withdraw their children from the public schools and create their own private school system if necessary. Over time, as the movement unfolded, these same councils would use more sophisticated means of pressuring blacks to stay in line, measures such as firing blacks who supported desegregation, declining to give them mortgages, calling their loans in, denying them credit at the local store, or refusing farmers seed for planting or machinery for working their farms.

Efforts to thwart blacks from registering to vote were stepped up. Some states passed new legislation making it even more difficult for blacks to exercise their constitutional right to vote.

Federal elected officials also followed the lead of their constituents. In March 1956, 101 members of the United States Senate and House of Representatives from eleven Southern states signed a "Declaration of Constitutional Principles: The Southern Manifesto," in which these elected officials declared the *Brown* decision to be an abuse of judicial power and commended those states that had already declared their intention to ignore the ruling.[18]

Following *Brown,* violence against blacks increased. Emmett Till was just one of many victims of that violence. The raised hopes of black Americans were being crushed.

And then, a forty-three-year-old black woman in Montgomery, Alabama, did something extraordinary—and very brave.

Rosa Parks was employed as a tailor's assistant at a downtown department store. She was married, described as quiet but very strong-willed. She had worked with the local NAACP as its secretary and had been an adviser to the Association's Youth Council.

The Montgomery public bus system was racially segregated, in conformance with both city and state ordinances that demanded segregation. On the average day, 40,000 black passengers would pay their fares and get on the bus—three-fourths of all the daily customers. Once black passengers paid their dimes, they were to go to the back of the bus. Sometimes, after paying the fare, they were told to get off the bus and then to reenter through the back door.

Blacks were not permitted to sit in seats reserved for whites. That meant that a black passenger might be forced to stand next to an empty seat designated as a "white" seat. If a white passenger needed a seat, the black passenger was expected to give his or hers up, even if it was in the area of the bus reserved for the blacks.

Segregation touched every aspect of Southern life, but there was something unique about segregation on a bus. It was shared. It was very personal. It was intimate.

It was one thing for blacks and whites to attend separate restaurants, or to play at different playgrounds or parks, or to use separate public restrooms or drinking fountains.

But to be black and forced to crowd into seats or stand in the back of the bus while white passengers sat comfortably in the front—just a matter of a few inches or feet away—there was something more degrading about that. It was an in-your-face reminder that you were considered to be worth less than your fellow white passengers. And the black passengers were confronted with it nearly every day of their lives.

On Thursday, December 1, 1955, Rosa was on her way home from work. She got on the bus and found a seat. At the next stop, a group of white passengers got on. One was left without a seat. When Rosa did not surrender her seat, the bus driver told her to do so.

She refused.

"When he saw me still sitting," Parks recalls, "he asked if I was going to stand up, and I said, 'No, I'm not.' And he said, 'well, if you don't stand up, I'm going to have to call the police and have you arrested.' I said, 'You may do that.'"[19]

She was arrested and taken to the local police station. To add insult to injury, at the station she was refused the right to drink out of the water fountain, it being "Whites Only."

Events unfolded quickly. Parks was bailed out by E.D. Nixon, a former head of the local NAACP, who made a proposal to Mrs. Parks. Would she be willing to let hers be the case that attacked segregation on the bus system? Although both her mother and her husband had warned her that her involvement with the NAACP was going to get her lynched, she agreed.

Nixon turned to the local ministry. The next day, Friday, he called a reverend whom he knew, Ralph Abernathy, and convinced him to call a meeting of ministers for that evening.

In the meantime, another woman of great determination, Jo Ann Robinson, who had herself been driven from a bus for sitting in the nearly empty white section, decided to join the fray. Working all night Friday, she ran off 35,000 handbills calling for a boycott of the Montgomery bus system on Monday, the day of Rosa's court appearance. Through a remarkable system of contacts, she got the handbills filtering throughout the black community on Friday and over the weekend.

Her call to action of the black community was bold. If they did join the boycott, how exactly were the 40,000 daily users of the buses going to get to work, to school, to stores?

Friday evening, nineteen black ministers met. There was no unanimity that it would be wise to support the boycott. Half the ministers left the meeting before it concluded.

But the boycott happened.

Monday, the scene in Montgomery was surreal. It was cloudy and cold. Black-owned taxis ferried black passengers about for minimal fare. Many blacks simply walked—miles, if they had to. On street corners, small groups of blacks would gather and hope for shared rides with those blacks who owned cars. Even mules and buggies were seen on the streets of Montgomery that day.

And passing by this strange scene came bus after bus—all nearly empty.

A mass meeting had been called for that night at the Holt Street Church to decide what to do next. Specifically, the question at hand was whether the boycott should extend beyond one day.

In preparation for that meeting, the ministers met Monday afternoon. It was decided to create a new organization to speak for the black community—the Montgomery Improvement Association—the MIA.

A president had to be chosen. The twenty-six-year-old minister of the Dexter Avenue Baptist Church was elected, even though he had been in the city for just one year.

His name was Martin Luther King Jr.

The Man

Martin Luther King Jr. was born in 1929. He was born to be a preacher. Not only was his father a preacher, but several generations of his family before his father had been as well.

In some respects, Martin Luther King Jr. was an unlikely candidate to lead the Civil Rights Movement. He was raised in Atlanta, Georgia, the son of the very popular and successful minister of the Ebenezer Baptist Church. By his own admission, his was a middle-class upbringing. The people in his neighborhood were of average income, and it was a "wholesome community" with little crime and neighbors who were deeply religious.[20] Martin was to enjoy opportunities for education, including a PhD from Boston University, that were in stark contrast to the disadvantages that the majority of blacks suffered.

But Martin was far from oblivious to segregation. In his youth he learned what it meant to be black. As a very young man he had a friend that was white. For several years they enjoyed a friendship that was typical of any two young boys. But one day the friend told Martin that he could never play with him again. Why? Because Martin was black and his father had told him that it was not right.

Martin also saw his own father, a man of great achievement and held in the highest esteem by his congregation, treated with contempt by whites: the store clerk who would not help Martin and his father buy shoes unless they moved to the fitting chairs in the back of the store; the police officer who called his father "boy"; the ninety-minute bus ride as a young teenager when he had to stand along with an elderly teacher just because they were black.

Yes, Martin understood segregation.

His family life was a happy one, and one that uniquely prepared him for the life work that he would undertake. He described his parents' home as being filled with love. His mother, in particular, tried to help Martin understand what it was like to be black in a segregated America. She taught him that he was somebody. She taught him to not let the system convince him that he was inferior. She told him that he was "as good as anyone."[21]

His father taught him to detest the system. His father resisted segregation and worked within his congregation and as a member of the NAACP to change the system. "With this heritage," Martin wrote, "it is not surprising that I also learned to abhor segregation, considering it to be both rationally inexplicable and morally unjustifiable."[22]

Throughout Martin's years he was given educational opportunities that were to prepare him for a leadership role in the Civil Rights Movement. Upon graduating from high school he attended Morehouse College. There he struggled in the same way that most college-aged students do with his faith, with his political outlook, and with his future. But, in the end, he followed his destiny. Upon graduation, he enrolled at Grozer Seminary in Pennsylvania.

King's introspection continued in the three years that he studied to become a minister. Like so many of his generation, Martin studied and considered communism. Following World War II, communism developed a considerable following in the United States. To many, espousing it was a fashionable thing to do, a way to establish one's sophistication. To others, it appeared to be a legitimate way of addressing the woes of the world's poor and powerless. King was no exception. But while at Grozer he consciously rejected communism after studying it and acknowledging its incompatibility with what he believed—specifically, communism's rejection of God and religion, its ethical relativism, and its totalitarianism. This third point was particularly important to Martin, for his belief that man is a child of God was irreconcilable with communism's basic assertion that man does not matter, that man is simply made for the state.

But King was also troubled by what he saw as the flaws of capitalism. As a youth of the Great Depression, and growing up in the South, he had seen the misery of the unemployed and the underprivileged. King rejected the purely materialistic quality of capitalism, believing that it dehumanized those who lived only for profit and had no time for life's other priorities. That belief would remain with him and motivate him throughout the remainder of his life.

In Martin Luther King Jr.'s philosophical journey, the most important trip was a literal one, to Philadelphia, in the spring of 1950.

Years before, King had been exposed to the teachings of Henry David Thoreau. King had been enticed by Thoreau's example of nonviolent protest. But in the ensuing years, as his heart had been hardened by exposure to segregation, King had all but rejected the idea that nonviolence could be the means to bring about social change. At this point in his life, he had concluded that segregation could be ended only by an armed revolt. This was a conclusion that was shared and preached by many in the black community. It was a conclusion King would be forced to contend with throughout the years that he was the leader of the nonviolent Civil Rights Movement.

For it was in Philadelphia in 1950 that King was exposed to the life and teachings of Mahatma Gandhi. He was to say of that exposure:

> Prior to reading Gandhi, I had about concluded that the ethics of Jesus were only effective in individual relationships. The "turn the other cheek" philosophy and the "love your enemies" philosophy were only valid, I felt, when individuals were in conflict with other individuals; when racial groups and nations were in conflict a more realistic approach seemed necessary. But after reading Gandhi, I saw how utterly mistaken I was.

> Gandhi was probably the first person in history to lift the love ethic of Jesus above mere interaction between individuals to a powerful and effective social force on a large scale. Love for Gandhi was a potent instrument for social and collective transformation. It was in this Gandhian emphasis on love and nonviolence that I discovered the method for social reform that I had been seeking for so many months.[23]

King had been converted. He had discovered the method for bringing about social reform that was not only to be his unique contribution to the American Civil Rights Movement but was to be emulated by others in far-flung places of the world.

Following his graduation from Grozer Seminary, King entered Boston University in pursuit of his PhD.[24] While there, he met Coretta Scott and they were married. They were to become the parents of four children during their fifteen years of marriage.

When approaching the end of his doctoral residency in Boston, Martin and Coretta were faced with other decisions. Yes, he came from a family of ministers. Yes, he had his bachelor in divinity degree from Grozer Seminary. But was his future really in the ministry, or was it in education? He had offers from several colleges in both teaching and administration. If he were to follow in his father's footsteps, where should he seek to become a minister? He had offers from churches in both New York and Massachusetts.

The decision to become a minister came first:

> As a young man with most of my life ahead of me, I decided early to give my life to something eternal and absolute. Not to these little gods that are here today and gone tomorrow. But to God who is the same yesterday, today, and forever.
>
> I'm not going to put my ultimate faith in the little gods that can be destroyed in an atomic age, but the God who has been our help in ages past, and our hope for years to come,

> and our shelter in the time of storm, and our eternal home. That's the God that I'm putting my ultimate faith in.[25]

The decision of *where* to serve God was a more difficult question. In January of 1954 King had been asked to deliver a sermon before the congregation of the Dexter Avenue Baptist Church in Montgomery, Alabama. He did well. Shortly afterward, he was offered the position of pastor of that church.

Coretta was from Alabama. Both she and Martin had been raised in the segregated South. For several years both had lived in the North, where racism existed but, in contrast to the South, was a minor inconvenience. They had both learned to love the freedom of the North. They had grown accustomed to the feeling of approval and the acceptance as equal human beings. They had enjoyed the invitations into the homes and lives of whites. They had been allowed to excel based upon their hard work. They enjoyed self-respect and the respect of others—both white and black.

Now they were being invited back to the South—to Montgomery, Alabama, the city known as the "Cradle of the Confederacy," the first capital of the Confederacy. If they took the position, their children would have to be raised in segregated Alabama.

In the end, Martin and Coretta agreed to return. They did so, after much thought and prayer, out of a belief that it was their moral duty to take the position, at least for a few years.

And that is how Martin Luther King Jr., one year later, found himself the leader of the Montgomery bus boycott.[26]

Montgomery Bus Boycott

The Montgomery bus boycott was to become the seminal event of the Civil Rights Movement. It was not the first example of nonviolent protest that had succeeded, but for several reasons it became the most important. Among those reasons was that it was the platform by which Martin Luther King Jr. rose to the forefront of the movement.

In addition, the boycott was going to confirm that King's theory of nonviolent civil action could succeed.

Martin Luther King Jr. was only twenty-six years old in December 1955. He was one year removed from the rarified world of Boston University. He was a nearly new pastor of a Baptist church. He firmly believed in Christ's teachings about love, yet he also believed in justice. He was about to put those two beliefs to the test.

Following the late afternoon election to head the new Montgomery Improvement Association, there was only one half hour before the mass meeting scheduled at the Holt Street Church. King had about thirty minutes to prepare the most important speech of his young life.

The Monday, December 5, boycott had been a great success. At the meeting where the MIA had been created, some had strongly suggested that they ought to declare the boycott a success and quit. There was considerable doubt about the ability to hold the black community together for a longer time. What if it took days to change the bus system? Or weeks? What would happen if some of the blacks started returning to the buses? How were the 40,000 black passengers going to get where they needed to be? Yes, they had managed for one day, but how could they do it for days or weeks?

King had to walk a fine line. He had to inspire the crowd sufficiently that they would be motivated to continue the boycott as a unified people. But he also had to make certain that he did not encourage any of them to release their latent anger and frustration and turn to violence.

The Holt Street Baptist Church was completely filled. Thousands more stood outside.

King was introduced. Few in the crowd even knew who he was. He spoke:

> We are not wrong in what we are doing. If we are wrong, the Supreme Court of this nation is wrong. If we are wrong, the Constitution of the United States is wrong. If we are wrong, God Almighty is wrong. If we are wrong, Jesus of Nazareth was merely a utopian dreamer that never came

down to earth. And we are determined here in Montgomery to work and to fight until justice runs down like water and righteousness like a mighty stream. . . .

We, the disinherited of this land, we who have been oppressed so long, are tired of going through the long night of captivity. And now we are reaching out for the daybreak of freedom and justice and equality. May I say to you, my friends, . . . that we must keep . . . God in the forefront. Let us be Christian in all of our actions. . . .

Standing beside love is always justice and we are only using the tools of justice. Not only are we using the tools of persuasion but we've come to see that we've got to use the tools of coercion. Not only is this thing a process of education but it is also a process of legislation.

As we stand and sit here this evening and as we prepare ourselves for what lies ahead, let us go out with a grim and bold determination that we are going to stick together, we are going to work together. Right here in Montgomery, when the history books are written in the future, somebody will have to say, "there lived a race of people, a black people, 'fleecy locks and black complexion,' a people who had the moral courage to stand up for their rights. And thereby they injected a new meaning into the veins of history and civilization."[27]

By this speech, prepared in just a matter of minutes, Martin Luther King Jr. presented to the black community of Montgomery, and to the world, the essence of what he had learned from Thoreau and Gandhi—what he had pondered and debated within himself through all the years of gaining his education. This speech became the framework of the strategy that was going to change the United States of America. He was for a moment a prophet: He predicted that the importance of the moment would not be lost on the world—and it has not.

A resolution had been prepared in which the boycotters' demands were stated. First, they insisted that they be treated with respect by the bus drivers; second, passengers were to be seated on a first-come, first-served basis; and third, black bus drivers were to be employed by the bus system. The resolution stated that the black community of Montgomery would boycott the bus system until their demands were met.

So little was asked for—such modest demands—but so much was at stake!

The matter was put to a vote, and the crowd at the Holt Baptist Church, inside and outside, stood in unison as a show of support.

The boycott would continue. But how would the community hold it together? Leadership was the key. King provided that leadership, along with a handful of other men and women.

The first hurdle faced by this small group was pure logistics: how do we get the 40,000 black citizens of Montgomery who regularly ride the buses to where they need to be, day in and day out? The Monday boycott had succeeded in large part because the black-owned taxi companies had subsidized their riders. That continued for a while, until the city threatened the taxi companies with punishment for not demanding full fare.

In the end it came down to two alternatives: the willingness of those who had cars to help those who did not, and walking. Every car owner was needed to assist in the effort, and for the most part they willingly joined in carpooling. The pool of available cars received an unexpected boost from white housewives who found it necessary to keep their black housemaids on the job, even if the housewives had to risk the ire of the city officials by going to their housemaids' homes and picking them up.

But for many, walking was the only way. Some had to walk as far as fourteen miles to and from their work. The spirit shared by the walkers is best illustrated in the anecdote related by one pool driver who noticed an elderly black woman walking with some difficulty. The driver pulled up and invited the woman to get in his car. "Jump in, grandmother," he said. "You don't need to walk." She waved him on.

"I'm not walking for myself," she explained. "I'm walking for my children and my grandchildren."[28]

To keep the community unified, twice-weekly mass meetings were held at various churches around the city. These meetings were essentially pep rallies. They were heavily attended. King would often attempt to make an appearance at all of these meetings, sometimes five in one evening. It took a toll on him personally.

The purpose of these meetings was not just to offer a boost to those whose lives were disrupted by the boycott but to provide King the opportunity to explain why this nonviolent but confrontive approach was necessary. King was able to preach about the blending of Jesus' call for love and Gandhi's method for utilizing that love as a tool.

King's nonviolent strategy was not accepted without opposition, however. As the boycott dragged on, frustration built in the black community. The day in and day out of walking, the standing on street corners hoping that a carpool vehicle might show up, the anger against the recalcitrance of the white leadership of the city, and the unwillingness of the bus company to negotiate an end to the boycott all tested even the most committed black protester. As the months passed, that frustration would be unleashed in the mass meetings. Even some of the ministers would speak out in anger. King feared that such sentiments expressed by the ministers would release the latent rage bubbling in the members of the congregation. He constantly had to beg for forbearance and patience.

Demands for resorting to violence were frequent. On one occasion, a member of King's Dexter Avenue congregation suggested, with some seriousness, that someone needed to "kill off" eight to ten white people. "This is the only language these white folks will understand."[29] That view was held by more than a few of the members of the black community. King constantly had to withstand demands for more aggressive actions. That too wore him down.

At first, few expected the boycott to hold together for more than one week. That week went by, and then it was a month. Months passed. The boycott held.

Through those weeks, and then months, the leadership provided by Dr. King and the others who stepped forward to assist was extraordinary.

On the other hand, the leaders of the city of Montgomery and the bus company did not sit idly by. They were constantly trying to split the black community. False rumors were started to make King and the other leaders look bad, including claims that they were somehow making money from the boycott. The rumor was passed that King was buying expensive new cars. Older ministers within the church community were challenged to do something about the young upstarts, such as King, who were bringing so much contention and discord to the city. Not only was King young, but he was an outsider!

As the winter months passed and the boycott held, more aggressive efforts were applied. The police were ordered to chill the carpoolers by ticketing them at will. Tickets were handed out for minor, sometimes imaginary, infractions of the traffic laws. Some carpool drivers were arrested and taken to jail. The hope was that the threat of losing auto insurance because of too many traffic tickets would end the carpools.

In January, Dr. King himself was arrested. He was accused of going thirty miles an hour in a twenty-five-mile-an-hour zone, even though King knew that he was being followed by the police and was scrupulously following the traffic laws. King was thrown in the back of a police car and hauled off to jail. This was the first of what would be many occasions when Dr. Martin Luther King Jr. would find himself arrested and locked up. For this young man, raised in a genteel environment, holder of a PhD in theology, and a church minister, to be tossed into jail was quite the shock. "For the moment strange gusts of emotion swept through me like cold winds on an open prairie. For the first time in my life, I had been thrown behind bars."[30]

As the city resisted any effort to settle the boycott and began to use more and more aggressive methods to undermine the leadership of the boycott, King came to realize something he felt he should have comprehended before—that the white community was bent on keeping the blacks not just separated from them but oppressed and exploited by them as well. This understanding was driven home by one of King's most ardent opponents, the attorney for the bus company, who said: "If we granted the Negroes these demands, they would go about boasting of a victory that they had won over the white people, and this we will not stand for."[31]

The unity being shown by Montgomery's black community, the sense of purpose, the pride, were all viewed to be a mortal threat to the old system. The white community hunkered down.

The stakes were high on both sides.

From the beginning of the boycott, threats of violence and racist attacks were leveled against King and others of the Montgomery Improvement Association leadership. The threats came by mail, by telephone, and through rumors that rippled through the city. King received dozens of threatening calls and letters daily. Coretta was often the one who answered the telephone to be told that her husband was a dead man.

On January 30th, while home alone with her young daughter and a friend, Coretta heard a noise on the front porch of her home. Instinctively she would have gone to investigate, but fortunately, instinct did not prevail. Instead Coretta led her friend and daughter to the back of the house. Moments later, a bomb exploded on the front porch.

By the time Martin arrived home after hearing of the bombing, an angry crowd had gathered. Some of the blacks were armed. Police were trying to calm the crowd, but tempers were soaring. King addressed the people from the wreckage of his own front porch—again pleading for calm. "We must meet the violence with nonviolence. Remember the words of Jesus: 'He who lives by the sword will perish by the sword. . . . We must love our white brothers . . . no matter what they do to us.'"[32]

Calm was restored. Another teaching opportunity had been offered and taken advantage of by Dr. King.

The white leadership and community made another attempt at breaking the boycott. In February, a grand jury indicted King and a hundred other leaders of the boycott for violating an Alabama law that prohibited the organization of a conspiracy to prevent the operation of a lawful business without just cause.

When the indictments were announced, something remarkable occurred. Instead of cowering in fear of the legal establishment, as had always been the reaction of the blacks before, and which was the reaction expected by the white authorities, those indicted came forward with almost a joyful attitude. Some who had hoped to be indicted, but had not been, expressed disappointment. "A once fear-ridden people had been transformed. Those who had previously trembled before the law were now proud to be arrested for the cause of freedom."[33]

In March, Dr. King was the first to face trial for the conspiracy charge. Over four days, he heard the testimony against him. That evidence was followed by defense witnesses who were called to testify that the boycott was in fact a just cause. There was the widow whose husband had been shot and killed for arguing with a bus driver, the wife of a blind man who testified of how his leg had been caught in the door of a bus and he had been dragged, the woman who had been called an "ugly ape" by a driver.

In the end, King was found guilty. But he received a minimal sentence of a fine, and the other defendants' trials were continued pending appeal of King's conviction. Although now a convicted man, Dr. King rejoiced with his supporters outside the courthouse—another expression of unity—more determination on display.

The winter of 1955–56 passed. Spring came. The boycott held.

Despite the modest nature of the demands of the MIA, the white leadership and the bus company stuck to their guns. Finally, the MIA decided to up the ante.

In the spring a federal lawsuit was filed by the Association. The claim was that the segregation demanded by Alabama and Montgomery laws violated the Constitution, specifically the equal protection clause of the Fourteenth Amendment. Arguments on the lawsuit were heard in May.

The lawyers for the MIA presented a simple argument: In *Brown*, the Supreme Court had overturned *Plessy* in the area of public education. Now *Plessy* should be overturned as the justification for other Jim Crow laws. Segregation of buses was no longer permitted under the Constitution of the United States. Separate but equal was dead.

The three-member federal district court agreed. The city immediately appealed.

Summer came and went. The boycott continued.

In November, the city tried a new line of attack. The boycott had survived because of the carpools. That month, the city filed a lawsuit against the MIA and others asserting that the carpools were an illegal operation because they did not have a license to operate as a business. Again King was in court, this time expecting a loss, and perhaps a fatal loss at that.

But as the trial was under way, suddenly whispers began to spread throughout the courtroom. King was approached by a reporter who handed him a piece of paper. It contained a brief report that the Supreme Court of the United States had sustained the decision of the federal district court. Segregation of buses was unconstitutional!

One jubilant spectator shouted out, "God Almighty has spoken from Washington, D.C.!"[34]

The end of the boycott was not quite yet. The Supreme Court's mandate was not to arrive for several weeks. It was decided that the boycott should continue until it arrived. Again demonstrating great wisdom, King and the MIA used this time to train the black community how to conduct themselves on integrated buses. The training included stressing the underlying theme that their victory *was not* a victory over the white man, but rather a victory *for* justice and democracy. King knew that the road ahead to full equality was going to be a long one, and any evidence of gloating or boasting by blacks would only harden the resolve of the entire South.

The MIA sponsored training sessions for the black community. These sessions included role playing of what to do, or not to do, if insulted or assaulted by a white passenger. Written guidelines were prepared with specific instructions, including:

General Suggestions:

. . . 6. Remember that this is not a victory for Negroes alone, but for all Montgomery and the South. Do not boast! Do not brag!

7. Be quiet but friendly; proud, but not arrogant; joyous, but not boisterous.

Specific Suggestions:

. . . 4. If cursed, do not curse back. If pushed, do not push back. If struck, do not strike back, but evidence love and goodwill at all times.

. . . 7. If another person is being molested, do not arise to go to his defense, but pray for the oppressor and use moral and spiritual force to carry on the struggle for justice. . . . [35]

Unfortunately, in the weeks leading up to the court-ordered integration of buses, no white leaders or organization showed the courage or the foresight to provide the same type of training for white passengers. To the contrary, just a matter of days before the mandate was issued and the blacks returned to the buses, the Montgomery City Commission issued a statement in which it asserted:

> The City Commission, and we know our people are with us in this determination, will not yield one inch, but will do all in its power to oppose the integration of the Negro race with the white race in Montgomery, and will stand like a rock against social equality, inter-marriage, and mixing of the races under God's creation and plan.[36]

Other white leaders predicted that violence was inevitable. That prediction was to become a self-fulfilling prophecy. The threats against Dr. King and other black leaders continued. One letter threatened that if the blacks went back on the buses, fifty homes would be burned. The danger seemed very genuine.

On December 20, 1956, the Supreme Court ruling mandating

the end of segregated buses reached Montgomery. The next day, more than one year after it began, the boycott ended. Black passengers returned to the Montgomery City buses.

Violence accompanied them. Verbal assaults were common. One teenage girl was beaten severely by white men. Buses were fired upon by snipers. One pregnant black woman was shot in the leg.

Bombings returned. Homes were targeted, including the home of King's right-hand man, the Reverend Ralph Abernathy. Black churches and businesses were also bombed. A package of dynamite containing ten sticks was discovered on the porch of the King home.

Again and again King and others begged for calm, pleaded for no revenge, reminded the angry blacks of Christ's teachings. The black community remained composed.

The bombings finally prompted some in the white community to rise up in condemnation of the violence. Some men were arrested for the bombings, and, although those men were acquitted, the bombings stopped.

Calm descended on Montgomery.

Dr. Martin Luther King Jr. had won—not just the right to sit where he wanted on a bus, but, most important, he had won the battle for the hearts and minds of the black community.

The Significance of Montgomery

The victory of the black community in Montgomery was the beginning of the end of Jim Crow in America. True, segregation in public education had been declared unconstitutional two years before in the *Brown* case. But the fact was that very little had been done to accomplish desegregation in schools by 1956. Also, *Brown* spoke only to "separate but equal" in public schools; it did not affect the host of other Jim Crow laws that required the separation of the races in every other setting.

It was the one-year bus boycott in Montgomery that gave life to the Civil Rights Movement. The boycott was covered by both the national and international press. Throughout the world, millions watched in either hope or fear that it would succeed.

Montgomery mattered for many reasons.

First, it established Dr. Martin Luther King Jr. as the voice and face of the Civil Rights Movement. His name became synonymous with the movement, and he was to be its dominant figure for the next twelve years. In that role, he performed with great dignity and courage. It is highly doubtful that any other black leader could have accomplished what Dr. King did.

Second, because King was the recognized leader of the Civil Rights Movement, his overarching strategy of relying on Christian love and nonviolence became the accepted tactic for accomplishing the goals of the movement. That strategy was acknowledged to be not only the morally correct strategy but also an effective one. Although black anger erupted into violence from time to time, the success of Montgomery proved that violence was not necessary for the triumph of the movement.

Third, after the nonviolent strategy had been shown to work in Montgomery, similar boycotts began in other cities in the South. Black leaders from throughout the South came together to form a permanent organization. In January of 1957, a hundred ministers from eleven Southern states met in Atlanta, Georgia, and formed the Southern Christian Leadership Conference. Dr. King was elected its president. That organization became the major force in the emerging Civil Rights Movement—deriving much of its influence from the fact that its membership consisted of ministers of the Christian faith.

Fourth, Dr. King and others recognized that a template had been created for future protests. That template was, in its simplest form, this: Rely on nonviolence and strive to show Christian love. If then unity can be achieved, if tenacity can be demonstrated, if public sympathy can be generated, all you have to do is to hold on until either the local or the state government caves or some action is undertaken by the federal government (be it a court decision, legislation, or executive branch action) that gives you victory. This template was to be followed in coming years in many different settings.

Finally, and most important, Montgomery was the birthplace of a new black confidence—in fact, an entirely new view for black Americans to hold of themselves. As Dr. King described it:

> Once plagued with a tragic sense of inferiority resulting from the crippling effects of slavery and segregation, the Negro has now been driven to reevaluate himself. He has come to feel that he is somebody. His religion reveals to him that God loves all His children and that the important thing about a man is not "his specificity but his fundamentum"—not the texture of his hair or the color of his skin but his eternal worth to God.
>
> This growing self-respect has inspired the Negro with a new determination to struggle and sacrifice until first-class citizenship becomes a reality. This is the true meaning of the Montgomery story. One can never understand the bus protest in Montgomery without understanding that there is a new Negro in the South, with a new sense of dignity and destiny.[37]

Yes, Montgomery was the beginning of the end of Jim Crow in the South and the emergence of a nationwide awareness of the racism that existed throughout the country and had to be erased.[38]

The Movement Grows

The rest of the story of the Civil Rights Movement is a story that needs to be told, although it is impossible to do it justice in an abbreviated form.

It is a story of demonstrations and protests to focus the nation's attention on the evil of segregation—some that succeeded and some that did not. It was Little Rock, Arkansas, in September 1957, and nine young black students under the protection of federal troops and federalized national guardsmen who integrated Central High School. It was Albany, Georgia, in 1961 and 1962, where a series of nonviolent protests against job discrimination, segregated bus and train terminals, and police brutality resulted in the arrest of more than 1,000 blacks. Martin Luther King Jr. was himself arrested three times. In the end, little was accomplished, primarily because the federal government was unwilling to support the protests. It was Birmingham, Alabama, "the most segregated city in America,"[39] in the spring of 1963, and King's confrontation with the infamous Police Commissioner "Bull" Connor and his snarling police dogs, high-pressure hoses, horse-mounted police, jails filled with nonviolent protestors (again, including Dr. King), protesting children suffering at the hands of police, and finally federal intervention to mediate the end of the violence against the protestors. It was the August 1963 March on Washington where a quarter of a million people heard Martin Luther King Jr. deliver his stirring "I Have a Dream" address. It was the Selma to Montgomery March in the spring of 1965 to demand greater access to the voting booth, fifty miles of marching protestors, three of whom were killed by segregationists. It was Dr. King in Chicago in 1966 to demand the end of segregated housing and education.

Dr. King did not lead or participate in every one of these events. However, he was the leader of the most important of them. Most significant, his strategy of nonviolence proved to be indispensable in those incidents where the movement's goals were achieved.

It is a story of how Washington, D.C.—presidents, members of Congress, and the Supreme Court—acted to remove roadblocks to progress. It is the story of federal courts that stepped in repeatedly to strike down Jim Crow laws and demand enforcement of new federal legislation and Supreme Court decisions. It is the story of the 1957 Civil Rights Act, the first civil rights legislation in eighty years, which allowed federal lawsuits against voting registrars who denied blacks the right to vote. It was the Civil Rights Act of 1964, which gave the federal government powers to enforce laws against school segregation (which was lagging a full decade after *Brown*) and discrimination in employment and in restaurants, motels, and other areas of public accommodation. To assure its success, the federal government was given the power to cut off federal funds to any state or local government that still practiced Jim Crow. It is the story of the Voting Rights Act of 1965, which eliminated the ability of Southern states to block blacks from voting. It is the story of the Housing Act of 1968, which prohibited discrimination in housing.

All of this federal legislation followed on the heels of some protest or demonstration orchestrated by Martin Luther King Jr. "This legislation was first written in the streets."[40]

It is a story of young people, both black and white, who took up the cause. In February 1960, four college students in Greensboro, North Carolina, decided it was time that they be allowed to sit down at a lunch counter and enjoy a cup of coffee at the local Woolworths. They were refused by the white waitress, "I'm sorry, but we don't serve colored here."[41] Thus began the "sit-in" movement, where black students would go to segregated lunch counters and ask to be served and, when refused, sit in silence. Soon white students joined the movement by sharing their food with the black "sitters." It is the story of how, over the next year, the "sit-in" movement spread to more than two hundred cities and involved thousands of young blacks who demanded the right to be served at lunch counters and restaurants.

These young people were sitting down where they were not allowed to sit because they were inspired by Martin Luther King Jr.

It is the story of young "Freedom Riders" who rode buses from the North to the South to force desegregation of bus terminals, even when faced with firebombing of the buses and assaults on the young riders. It was the hundreds of young students from the North who descended on Mississippi in the summer of 1964—the Freedom Summer—to encourage blacks to register to vote.

It is a story of recalcitrance. It is a story of segregationists who would not accept the changes taking place in their world. It is a story of closing not only schools but entire school districts to avoid the possibility that a black student would be allowed to attend school with white children. It is a story of shutting down city parks so that the whites would not have to share the park with a black family. It is a story of city-sponsored sports being eliminated to avoid integration.

It is a story of state legislatures passing laws making it more difficult to vote. It is a story of the jailing of thousands of men and women for simply exercising their constitutional rights. It is a story of threats and intimidation by those who had sworn to uphold the Constitution of the United States.

Sadly, it is a story of violence and tragedy. When all other efforts at resistance failed, there were those who resorted to bloodshed to preserve the tradition of white supremacy. It is the story of countless murders of civil rights activists, activists such as Medgar Evers in Jackson, Mississippi. It is the story of three young men killed in Mississippi early in the Freedom Summer. It is the story of four young girls killed by a bomb as they attended Sunday school in Birmingham, Alabama, in September 1963. It is the story of bombings and burnings, riots by angry mobs of whites, and Ku Klux Klan rallies and raids and displays of power.

It is the story of presidents confronting segregationist governors: Dwight Eisenhower facing down Orval Faubus in Arkansas when he tried to block black students from attending Central High School; John Kennedy facing down Ross Barnett in Mississippi when Barnett blocked the entrance of James Meredith at Ole Miss; and Kennedy again, facing down George Wallace when he attempted to prevent black students from entering the University of Alabama—the same George Wallace who had declared in his inaugural address, "segregation now, segregation tomorrow, segregation forever!"[42]

It is a story of outstanding oratory—stirring oratory by Martin Luther King Jr. He was justifiably celebrated for his speech making. His speeches were intended to give inspiration, hope, and direction for the new black personality emerging in the country.

> In the new age, we will be forced to compete with people of all races and nationalities. Therefore, we cannot aim merely to be good Negro teachers, good Negro doctors, good Negro ministers, good Negro skilled laborers. We must set out to do a good job, irrespective of race, and do it so well that nobody could do it better.[43]

He spoke to make the case for nonviolence:

> There is more power in socially organized masses on the march than there is in guns in the hands of a few desperate men. Our enemies would prefer to deal with a small armed group rather than with a huge, unarmed but resolute mass of people. . . . All history teaches us that like a turbulent ocean beating great cliffs into fragments of rock, the determined movement of people incessantly demanding their rights always disintegrates the old order.[44]

He spoke to reinforce that he believed that his cause was God's cause:

> In recent months, I have also become more and more convinced of the reality of a personal God. . . . Now it is a living reality that has been validated in the experiences of everyday life. Perhaps the suffering, frustration and agonizing moments which I have had to undergo occasionally as a result of my involvement in a difficult struggle have drawn me closer to God. Whatever the cause, God has been profoundly real to me in recent months. In the midst of outer dangers, I have felt an inner calm and known resources of strength that only God could give. In many instances I have felt the power of God transforming the fatigue of despair into the buoyancy of hope. I am convinced that the universe is under the control of a loving purpose and that in the struggle for righteousness man has cosmic companionship.[45]

He used his gift to define what the future of America should be:

> I still have a dream. It is a dream deeply rooted in the American dream that one day this nation will rise up and live out the true meaning of its creed—we hold these truths to be self-evident, that all men are created equal. . . .

> I have a dream my four little children will one day live in a nation where they will not be judged by the color of their skin but by the content of their character. I have a dream today![46]

He used his speaking skill to calm those who feared for the future—his future and theirs:

> Well, I don't know what will happen now. We've got some difficult days ahead. But it doesn't matter with me now. Because I've been to the mountaintop. And I don't mind. Like anybody, I would like to live a long life. Longevity has its place. But I'm not concerned about that now. I just want to do God's will. And He's allowed me to go up to the mountain. And I've looked over. And I've seen the promised land. I may not get there with you. But I want you to know tonight, that we, as a people, will get to the promised land. And I'm happy, tonight. I'm not worried about anything. I'm not fearing any man. Mine eyes have seen the glory of the coming of the Lord.[47]

It is a story with victory at the end, but Martin did not live to see that end. He was murdered the day after he spoke the words just quoted, in Memphis, Tennessee on April 4, 1968.[48]

What If?

As with all of our giants, it must be noted that Martin Luther King Jr. was not a perfect man. Dr. King had his weaknesses and his failures. He often lamented the fact that his activities kept him from being home to be the type of husband and father to Coretta and their children that he would have liked. There are other aspects of his personal life that have been the subject of criticism.

Unfortunately, many also remember Dr. King more for the last two years of his life than for the first decade of his leading the Civil

Rights Movement. In those last two years, Dr. King became a more polarizing figure as he spoke out against the Vietnam war. Further, as the Civil Rights Movement wound down—as segregation was eliminated and federal legislation cemented the rights obtained "in the streets"—Dr. King also began to shift his attention to economic injustice. He was engaged in the creation of a "Poor People's Campaign" at the time of his assassination in 1968. He was undertaking this expanded focus at least partly in response to riots by blacks in Northern cities, such as Watts in 1965 and Chicago the next year. Such riots clearly distressed many throughout the nation. As riots later erupted in other Northern cities, including Newark and Detroit in 1967 and Washington, D.C., in 1968, the memory of the nonviolent protests and demonstrations of the prior decade faded.

The combination of the refocus of King's efforts, along with the riots, affected the popularity and influence of Dr. King. Although he remained much admired within the black community,[49] he lost his relationship with President Lyndon B. Johnson because of his outspoken opposition to the war in Vietnam. Criticism of Dr. King emerged from many of his former supporters and allies.

He was always haunted with rumors of his being a secret communist. Since his death those rumors have persisted, despite the fact that he consciously rejected communism as a young man. Others have focused on his socialist leanings. These characterizations have emanated from his most bitter foes as well as those who have looked favorably on his later efforts to bring about economic justice.

To the extent that any of this may have diminished the reputation of Dr. King, it ignores a most important reality—Dr. Martin Luther King Jr. changed the course of the history of the United States of America in a most positive way.

What if Dr. Martin Luther King Jr. had decided to take one of the positions in higher education that had been offered him as he finished up his doctorate at Boston University? What if had chosen to become a minister in a Northern city instead of deciding, as he and Coretta did, to spend a "few years" as a minister in Montgomery, Alabama?

In September 1958, a woman who was subsequently determined to be mentally deranged assaulted King with a knife while he was signing books in Harlem, New York. The blade of the knife came within a fraction of his aorta. What if he had died in that incident?

What if Dr. King had never been the voice and the face of the Civil Rights Movement?

The answer is simple: If not for Martin Luther King Jr., the history of the United States of America over the last half of the twentieth century would likely have unfolded very differently than it did.

The oppression of black America could not have gone on unabated. The building rage and frustration of black Americans would have been unleashed sometime, somehow.

The American Civil Rights Movement has to be viewed in some context. At the same time that black Americans were first beginning to stir—to demand their constitutional rights—most of the world's people of color in Africa and Asia were emerging from the era of European colonialism. Black Americans were witnessing the retreat of European colonial control of nation after nation. The American black community was seeing freedom delivered to the peoples of Africa and Asia and asking, "Why not here?"[50]

Additionally, in America segregation and racism were resulting in a widening economic gulf between white Americans, who were seeing incomes rise and prosperity grow in the postwar economic boom, and black Americans, who were being left ever further behind. The disparity in living conditions that had always existed was becoming too wide to not incite greater anger.

It was inevitable that the injustice and deprivation of basic rights could not continue in this nation. It had to end sometime.

So the only question was, How? In bloody conflict, or peacefully?

Some have suggested that segregation would have eventually just faded away, given enough time. Among the most vocal of Dr. King's critics were those who contended that a rising sense of morality among white Americans would have eventually worked things out. The argument was that the whole world was changing; America would have changed too. These critics complained that Dr. King and his supporters were pushing too hard and too fast.

It is true, segregation and racism might have eventually died a natural death. But if our nation had let things just run their course, suffered through decades of slow progress, how many more innocent lives would have been lost, how much additional economic deprivation would have been suffered, how many blacks would have lived their entire lives as second-class citizens, deprived not only of their constitutional rights but also of their self-respect.

How many generations would it have taken? Would our nation's black community have been content to let changes happen gradually?

The suggestion that segregation might have died a natural death also ignores the condition of the black personality at the outset of the movement, as Dr. King described it. The Civil Rights Movement succeeded because it enjoyed early successes such as Montgomery. Such successes were necessary for the mind-set of the black community to change, to gain self-respect, to rise above the feelings of inferiority inculcated by hundreds of years of slavery and Jim Crow.

How would that change of mind have ever been triggered if not for those protests and demonstrations generated by Dr. King and his followers that showed that the blacks could, in fact, win!

It is arguable that the more likely alternative to Dr. King's nonviolent approach would have been a truly violent and nationwide revolution—a revolution that erupted to a limited degree in many cities in our nation in the late 1960s.

Martin Luther King Jr. was constantly being berated from two extremes. On the one hand, there were the racist whites who hated him for everything that he was doing to end segregation. On the other hand, there were those black extremists who thought that he was nothing more than a sell-out of the black cause. In August 1966, while marching in Chicago to protest housing discrimination, he was hit by a rock thrown by hate-filled whites.[51] Not long before, while visiting New York, Black Nationalists at the urging of Malcolm X had thrown eggs at him because they considered him a "polished Uncle Tom."[52]

It was Dr. King's aim to defeat the former. But to do that, he had to defeat the latter as well. He wisely understood that if the Civil Rights Movement had become violent, it would have failed. He constantly reminded the advocates for violence—and they were everywhere, including among those who were close to him—that the blacks of America were a distinct minority and that if it came to war, they would lose. "We are 10 percent of the population of this nation and it would be foolish for me to stand up and tell you we are going to get our freedom by ourselves. There's going to have to be a coalition of conscience and we aren't going to be free . . . until there is a committed empathy on the part of the white man of this country."[53]

Even the most insignificant forceful reply to white violence, justifiable as it might have been, was deplored by Dr. King. He had witnessed how it emboldened the segregationists and offended the movement's allies in the white community. That is why in Selma, anticipating police violence, King instructed those who were going to march with him, "I say to you, when we march, don't panic and remember that we must remain true to nonviolence. I'm asking everybody in the line, if you can't be nonviolent, don't get in here. If you can't accept blows without retaliating, don't get in the line. If you can accept it out of your commitment to nonviolence, you will somehow do something for this nation that may well save it."[54]

Is it conceivable that any other man could have stayed so true to his beliefs? Is it conceivable that any other man would have been able to exact the discipline of tens of thousands of his supporters as Dr. King did?

Martin Luther King Jr. was a man who had access to the highest leaders in our land. He met with every president who sat during his years of activity: Eisenhower, Kennedy, and Johnson. He had access to their vice presidents and their attorneys general. Yet he would subject himself to beatings, stoning, bombings, egging, arrest, and illegal incarceration over and over again at the hands of brutal and hate-filled law enforcement from North to South. He did so because he believed in his cause and in the means to accomplish it. He believed in the morality of his message and was able to convince millions to agree with him.

Who else could have done the same?

The answer is that no one did before, and no one did after him. In the four decades since Dr. King's murder, there has been no leader in the black community who has even come close to possessing the influence that Dr. King achieved.

If there had been no Martin Luther King Jr., the Cold War, that life-or-death struggle between the world's free nations and the tyrants of the communist bloc, may well have turned out very differently. Had America remained a segregated and racist nation, we would have had no moral authority to encourage the world, especially those nations just removed from colonialism, to side with us. The communists were always viewed as the friends of the emerging third-world nations. If we had remained an openly racist nation, would our system have ever appealed to those nations? The fact that we worked to overcome our racist past gave us the ability to reach out to the rest of the world and to say, "We are a beacon of freedom!" and to so say without having to apologize for the fact that 10 percent of our population was not free.

Martin Luther King Jr.'s influence was felt worldwide. The changes that were affected by his actions were watched closely by the entire world. In 1964, he was awarded the Nobel Peace Prize. In making the presentation, the chairman of the Nobel Committee observed:

> Though Martin Luther King has not personally committed himself to the international conflict, his own struggle is a clarion call to all who work for peace.
>
> He is the first person in the Western world to have shown us that a struggle can be waged without violence. He is the first to make the message of brotherly love a reality in the course of his struggle, and he has brought this message to all men, to all nations and races.
>
> Today we pay tribute to Martin Luther King, the man who has never abandoned his faith in the unarmed struggle he is waging, who has suffered for his faith, who has been

> imprisoned on many occasions, whose home has been subject to bomb attacks, whose life and the lives of his family have been threatened, and who nevertheless has never faltered.[55]

If Martin Luther King Jr. had not been in Montgomery in 1955, if he had not been elected the head of the Montgomery Improvement Association, if the bus boycott had failed, if he had not been the leader of the Civil Rights Movement over the next decade, the dark stain on America of segregation and institutionalized racism might have endured for decades, perhaps even still.

Martin Luther King Jr. removed that dark stain. This sin of America was brought to an end.

He was a giant!

Notes

1. For information concerning the post–Civil War efforts to integrate the former slaves into mainstream society and to protect their rights of citizenship through constitutional amendment and federal law, see McConnell, *Originalism.*
2. Per United States Census Bureau figures, there were 15 million black Americans in 1950.
3. Williams, *Eyes,* 20.
4. King, *Dream,* 77.
5. Ibid., 17.
6. Ibid.
7. Ibid., 170.
8. Lawson, *Debating,* 50.
9. Landau, *Civil Rights,* 11. Another four million were to migrate north between 1940 and 1970.
10. *The Negro Holocaust: Lynching and Race Riots in the United States, 1880–1950,* at www.yale.edu/ynhtl/cirriculum/units/1979/2/79.02.04x.html.
11. Ibid. See also *Lynchings: By Year and Race* at http://law2.umkc.edu/faculty/projects/ftrials/shipp/lynchingyear.html, a chart prepared by the University of Missouri-Kansas City School of Law.
12. For information about Isaac Woodard, see Landau, *Civil Rights,* 3–5; also http://en.wikipedia.org/wiki/IsaacWoodard.
13. Williams, *Eyes,* 41.

14. Ibid., 43. For more information about the murder of Emmett Till, see ibid., 39–57 and Landau, *Civil Rights,* 14–17.
15. The words of writer Anne Moody, found in her book *Coming of Age in Mississippi,* as contained in Williams, *Eyes,* 56.
16. King, *Dream,* 88–89.
17. For more information about segregation and its effect on the black citizens of the United States, see King, *Dreams;* Landau, *Civil Rights;* Lawson, *Debating;* and Williams, *Eyes.*
18. For information about the *Brown* decision and the reaction to it, see Lawson, *Debating*, 10–12, 59–62, and Williams, *Eyes,* 11–39.
19. Ibid., 66.
20. King, *Autobiography*, 2.
21. Ibid., 4.
22. Ibid., 5.
23. King, *Stride,* 84–85.
24. He was to receive his doctorate in systematic theology in 1955.
25. King, *Autobiography*, 33.
26. For information about King's early life, see King, *Autobiography*, 1–49.
27. Ibid., 60–61.
28. King, *Stride*, 63–64.
29. Ibid., 74–75.
30. Ibid., 119.
31. Williams, *Eyes*, 77.
32. King, *Stride*, 128.
33. Ibid., 138.
34. Ibid., 153.
35. Ibid., 157–58.
36. Ibid., 160.
37. Ibid., 183.
38. For more information about the Montgomery bus boycott, see King, *Dream,* 50–99; King, *Stride*; Landau, *Civil Rights,* 17–20; Lawson, *Debating*, 13–14; Williams, *Eyes*, 60–89.
39. King, *Dream,* 173.
40. Ibid., 245.
41. Williams, *Eyes*, 127.
42. King, *Dream*, 173.
43. Ibid., 20.
44. Ibid., 52.
45. Ibid., 61.
46. Ibid., 104.
47. Ibid., 203.

48. For information about the Civil Rights Movement generally, see Jackson, *Human Rights*; King, *Dream*; King, *Stride*; Landau, *Civil Rights;* Lawson, *Debating*; Williams, *Eyes*.
49. He had an approval rating of 88 percent with blacks in 1966. See Jackson, *Human Rights*, 24.
50. King mentioned this often in his speeches, for example, his speech from May 17, 1957, entitled "Facing the Challenge of a New Age," found at King, *Dream*, 14–28.
51. www.chicagotribune.com/news/politics/chi-chicagodays-martinlutherking-story,0,4515735.story (January 2012).
52. King, *Dream*, 266.
53. Ibid., 320.
54. Ibid., 281.
55. See http://www.nobelprize.org/noble_prizes/peace/laureates/1964/press .html?print=1.

Chapter 7

Mother Teresa

Where there is love, there is God.

Mother Teresa

Just a few days before Christmas in 1948, a little woman, just five feet tall, entered the dusty streets of one of the most miserable places on earth—the slums of Calcutta, India. She was alone, dressed in a white sari with blue trim and wearing sandals. She had only a handful of rupees to her name. She was a European in the midst of brown faces. She was entering this forsaken place in response to a call from God. Her name was Mother Teresa.

The slum, ironically enough possessing the beautiful name of *Moti Jihl*—Pearl Lake—was one of many to be found in India. These slums were a collection of makeshift homes constructed out of whatever materials could be scrounged: plastic, pieces of tin, cardboard, mud bricks, pieces of scrap wood. The floors were dirt. Those who had such shelter paid rent for it. Those who could not afford the rent simply lived on the streets.

The slums had always been crowded. In 1948, however, they were more so because one year earlier India had won its independence from

Great Britain. Under the Raj of Great Britain the Muslim and Hindu populations had been forced to live together in relative peace. Under independence, this was no longer the case. Of necessity, two nations had been created from what had been the India of the British Empire—India for the Hindus and Pakistan for the Muslims. Because both nations contained a mixture of Hindus and Muslims, a great shifting was under way. Sixteen million people had been or were migrating from India into Pakistan or Pakistan into India. Many of those moving into India found themselves in the slums of great cities. Some of the resulting slums now had a population density of 200,000 people per square mile. Calcutta alone had two million slum dwellers.

A famine had also struck India, forcing many from the countryside into the cities. This desperate population also swarmed into the streets and slums of the already teeming cities.

Few slum areas had sewers or running water. Most families had no place to go to wash their bodies or to relieve themselves. Open sewers ran filthy and reeking. Garbage was everywhere. Disease was rampant. The air was putrid and deadly—filled with dust and smoke from the cooking fires burning indiscriminately on the streets.

In the slums, the average life expectancy was among the lowest in the world.

Under such conditions human life was devalued. Newborn babies were often left in the streets to die. Old people would be abandoned by their children. Later, Mother Teresa would tell the story of an aged woman, left by her family in the streets of the city, whom she found being eaten by rats. She would also tell of an old man covered with maggots who was taken into one of her homes and cleaned up so that he could die with dignity.

There were no trees, bushes, or flowers. There were no hospitals or schools.

In the summer the heat killed and magnified the stench. For four months of the year the monsoon rains turned the streets into a collection of mud and human waste.[1]

What did this petite woman, thirty-eight years old, possessing no wealth, with but a few weeks of training in basic medical treatment, hope to accomplish in this sludge pool of poverty, disease, and death?

The answer was simple: She wanted to bring God's love to those who did not feel it. She wanted to quench the thirst and hunger of as many of God's children as she could. She wanted to serve the poorest of the poor in every way possible.

How did she come to undertake this most remarkable mission?

Agnes Gonxha Bojaxhiu

The woman whom the world knows as Mother Teresa was born August 26, 1910, in the city of Skopje, Serbia.[2] Her name was Agnes Gonxha Bojaxhiu. Her parents were both from Albania. They were devout Catholics—a minority religion among the predominantly Muslim population of Skopje—and they clung to their religion and raised their children to understand the importance of their Catholic faith. Agnes was the youngest of the three Bojaxhiu children.

Agnes's father, Nikola, was a prominent citizen of the city. A merchant and a trader, he traveled throughout Europe on business and delighted his children with accounts of the wonderful places that he visited. He possessed the gift of learning languages easily, a gift that his youngest daughter was to inherit, and he spoke five languages fluently. He was progressive, a supporter of the arts, and was responsible for financing the construction of the first movie theater in Skopje.

He was also a political activist. As an Albanian, he was a leader in the movement to create an independent Albanian nation and to attach to it lands then considered part of Serbia. Because of these activities, he had many enemies. In 1919, while attending a political conference to discuss the issue of Albanian borders, he was taken ill. He died shortly after his return to Skopje. Many of his friends as well as family members believed that the forty-five-year-old man, previously a picture of health, had been poisoned.

From this great tragedy in their young lives, Agnes and her older brother and sister learned a painful lesson—that on occasion there was a price to be paid for standing up for one's beliefs.

Agnes's mother, Drana, found herself not only a young widow but an impoverished one at that. Nikola's business partner laid claim to all of his business assets. Drana confronted the situation with resolve and undertook to provide for her young family. Agnes was then eight years old.

Despite her own struggles, Drana was an extraordinarily generous and compassionate woman. She believed that her Christian faith demanded that she care for the poor and the needy. If a family needed food, she took it to them or invited them into her home and fed them. One elderly woman came recurrently to their home to share their food. A neighbor was an alcoholic and covered with sores—Drana visited her every week to feed and minister to her. A mother of six was dying—Drana spent what time she could to comfort her children and see to their needs. An elderly woman had been abandoned by her family—Drana visited her weekly to clean her house.

Drana often took young Agnes to help in these acts of charity. She also taught her daughter the important lesson that such charity must be performed without drawing attention to oneself. "When you do good, do it quietly, as if you were throwing a stone into the sea."[3]

This was just one of many axioms Agnes heard from her parents that stuck with her and that, as Mother Teresa, she would later teach. Examples included her father's adage, "My child, never eat a single mouthful unless you are sharing it with others,"[4] and her mother's, "The family that prays together stays together."[5]

Drana also taught her children an invaluable lesson about complaining. Whenever any of the Bojaxhiu siblings would criticize—about a teacher, for example—their mother would turn off the electricity to the house, saying, "I'm not going to pay for electricity for children who bad-mouth people."[6]

Later in life, Mother Teresa was hesitant to talk about her childhood. But she always declared it to be a very happy time in her life, despite her father's tragic death. Perhaps her youthful happiness derived in part from the acts of compassion and kindness that her mother allowed her to participate in.

Agnes had her first inkling that she was destined for a life of devoted religious service when she was just twelve. But she went on to live the life of a normal teenager. She was very active in the activities sponsored by her family's Catholic priest. She was a good student, and as she grew into a lovely young woman she became much accomplished in music. She was known for her skill in writing and published articles in a local newspaper. Her many friends admired her for her joyful personality and sense of humor. She was a born leader and was turned to for organizing community and church events.

It was during these teenage years that Agnes was first exposed to the tragic human conditions to be found in India and to the efforts of Catholic missionaries working there to alleviate such conditions. Her parish priest was the first to inform his young parishioners of those missionary efforts. Agnes was intrigued enough that she followed up by reading in Catholic magazines about the missionary exploits among India's population. A missionary from India visited Skopje and spoke of the country's needs; Agnes helped to raise money to contribute to this missionary.

Young Agnes Bojaxhiu had much going for her. She clearly had a future in either music or writing. She had every reason to believe that she would one day marry and have children. She had nothing to escape from except a normal, happy life.

At the age of eighteen, she decided to escape from that life. She decided to become a nun.

Her mother did not consent to her daughter's wishes at first. She wanted to test Agnes to see if her decision was a firm one. Agnes' oldest brother, Lazar, who was then serving in the Albanian army, wrote and challenged her decision. Agnes, displaying some of the fire that the world was going to see in her in future years, replied, "You think you are important because you are an officer serving a king with two million subjects. But I am serving the King of the whole world."[7]

Eventually, her mother gave her consent. She did so by challenging her daughter to be "only, all for God and Jesus." Drana told Agnes that one day she would be asked by her mother, "My child, have you lived only, all for God?"[8]

With that charge from her widowed mother, Agnes left Skopje, never to see Drana again.

To follow her dream of serving the poor of India, Agnes joined the Sisters of Loreto, an order with its headquarters in Ireland. This Catholic order had its origins in 1609 when its founder, an Englishwoman named Mary Ward, suggested that nuns should not live cloistered lives of prayer and meditation but rather should be out in the world doing good and serving the needy. The Sisters of Loreto followed that principle by sending nuns to serve the poor of India as early as 1841.

Agnes was to spend a brief six weeks in Ireland. There, she was required to learn English, the common language of India. In order to assure that she absorbed that language quickly, she was told to never speak her native tongue again. She obeyed that instruction. Fortunately for her, she had inherited her father's gift for languages, and she mastered English quickly.

On December 1, 1928, Agnes began a five-week voyage to India, the place where she was to spend the remainder of her life.

Mother Teresa of the Child Jesus

As a new member of the Sisters of Loreto, Agnes Bojaxhiu was required to assume a new identity, one committed to poverty, chastity, and obedience. She also needed to adopt a new name. She chose the name "Sister Mary Teresa of the Child Jesus" after Teresa of Lisieux, a Catholic saint who was known for believing that one could obtain holiness through many small deeds instead of great actions. This name, which was later to be shortened to "Mother Teresa," was a most fitting choice for the young Albanian woman who would ultimately achieve sainthood through a multitude of small deeds.

Mother Teresa arrived in India in January 1929. She was

immediately assailed by the poverty and needs of the people. However, her personal work among those people was not to begin quite yet.

After a few days in Calcutta, Teresa made the long railroad journey to Darjeeling in the foothills of the Himalayas. Here in the Loreto convent, which was a world apart from the worst of India, she worked on her English. She also began to master the two major languages of India, Bengali and Hindi.

As a younger teenager Teresa had displayed her gift for teaching. At Darjeeling she was given the opportunity to share that gift by teaching local children in a one-room schoolhouse. Her training as a Sisters of Loreto nun also included working with nurses in the local clinic. Her exposure to the people suffering so horribly from disease and starvation haunted her. She was to write:

> Many have come from a distance, walking for as much as three hours. What a state they are in! Their ears and feet are covered in sores. They have lumps and lesions on their backs, among the numerous ulcers. Many stay at home because they are too debilitated by tropical fever to come. One is in the terminal stage of tuberculosis. Some need medicine.

On another occasion, a man handed her a bundle that turned out to contain a starving child. The man demanded that the nuns keep the boy:

> The man is afraid we will not take the child, and says, "If you do not want him, I will throw him into the grass. The jackals will not turn up their noses at him." My heart freezes. The poor child! Weak, and blind—totally blind. With much pity and love I take the little one into my arms, and fold him in my apron. The child has found a second mother.[9]

In 1931, Teresa was assigned to be a teacher at the Sisters of Loreto convent in Calcutta known as Loreto Entally. At this school Teresa was to become a popular teacher of geography and history. Her students were a mixture of young women from wealthy Indian families, the daughters of foreigners living in India, and orphans who lived at the school. They grew to love their teacher. She did display one odd habit, however. Every day before class, Teresa would sweep and wash the floor of her classroom. The young women from wealthy families were amused that such a chore was performed by their teacher and not by a servant from one of India's poorer castes.

In 1937, Teresa took her final vows as a nun of the Sisters of Loreto, pledging herself to a lifetime of poverty, chastity, and obedience. From that point forward, she was to be known as "Mother Teresa."

The nuns of Loreto Entally were generally kept apart from the streets and slums that were so close at hand. But Mother Teresa managed to gain approval to visit the slums every Sunday. She there learned a lesson that was to become of great significance to her: she came to realize that one could have nothing, no material belongings at all, and still find joy. She saw how much happiness her simple presence brought to the most impoverished of the slum dwellers.

Eventually, Mother Teresa became the headmistress of her school. When she wrote to her mother to announce that fact, a letter that contained perhaps a hint of pride, her mother replied with a not-so-subtle reminder of what Agnes had gone to India to do: "Dear child, Do not forget that you went to India for the sake of the poor."[10]

The Sisters of Loreto were, indeed, in India to help the poor. But they believed that the way to do so was through educating the people. In that respect they were successful. Many of their students went on to become teachers or social workers. However, the Sisters did not believe their primary mission was to minister directly to the poor.

For almost twenty years, Mother Teresa obediently fulfilled her vows in the way of the Sisters. However, during World War II the Sisters of Loreto at Entally were forced to extend themselves to help victims of the war as well as those who suffered from two years of famine that befell India during the war years. Mother Teresa joyfully joined her fellow Sisters in ministering to the growing numbers of the dispossessed and destitute that were crowding the streets of Calcutta.

After the war, as India moved toward independence, violence

between the Hindus and the Muslims increased dramatically. Chaos reigned. Normal channels of food delivery fell apart. During one major outbreak of violence, Mother Teresa set out to find food for the nuns and students at Entally. She was forced to pick her way among the dead and dying who littered the streets of Calcutta. It was a gruesome setting for the tenderhearted, cloistered nun to find herself in. She succeeded in convincing a group of British soldiers to help her and was able to return to Entally with a truckload of rice. This bit of scrounging was an early display of her indomitable spirit that was far out of proportion to her small frame. Her willingness to beg for assistance was a trait that was going to prove invaluable in just a few years.

Mother Teresa had always been sickly. Even as a young woman her mother had worried about her frailty and often commented that she did not expect her youngest daughter to live long. Following World War II, Mother Teresa became seriously ill. Her ailment was in part a reaction to the pressures that she had endured as she was forced to accept responsibility to provide for the basic needs of her fellow Sisters and their young charges during the war and throughout the interminable religious violence that followed. Her Sisters of the convent were deeply concerned for her well-being. She was eventually ordered to leave Calcutta for the convent at Darjeeling. She was told to rest, to refrain from work, to seek spiritual guidance.

In September 1946, Mother Teresa boarded the train for Darjeeling. What happened on that train ride was to alter the future of Mother Teresa—and in many respects the world.

"I Thirst"

The day was September 10, 1946. Somewhere along the noisy and meandering journey to Darjeeling, Mother Teresa heard a voice:

> I was sure it was God's voice. I was certain that He was calling me. The message was clear: I must leave the convent to help the poor by living among them. This was a

> command, something to be done, something definite. I knew where I had to be. But I did not know how to get there.[11]

Mother Teresa received what she deemed to be a "call within a call."[12] She was later to explain that she distinctly heard the words, "I thirst." She knew that those were among the last words spoken by Christ while he hung on the cross at Calvary. Mother Teresa understood these immortal words to mean much more than the cry of a man asking for something to quench his craving for drink:

> On that train journey to Darjeeling, Mother Teresa realized deep in her heart that God does not just love us in a general way, but that His words "I thirst" are the ultimate and supreme expression of His love, an expression of His longing for the love of His creation and for the salvation of their souls. Jesus spoke these words on the Cross, for the Cross is the "act" by which He tries to convince us of God's love, which is limitless and extends beyond death.[13]

The words "I thirst" had an additional meaning. Mother Teresa understood that:

> In the hungry, thirsty, broken bodies of the poor, the Missionaries of Charity would also see the Christ who in St. Matthew's Gospel (25:35) had so specifically identified himself with those in need: "For I was hungry and you gave me food; I was thirsty and you gave me to drink."[14]

Later, Mother Teresa would remind people that Christ also taught that "Inasmuch as ye have done it unto one of the least of these my brethren, ye have done it unto me."[15] She would assert, "The whole Gospel . . . could be counted on five fingers: You-did-it-to-me!"[16]

Her call was clear. How she was to accomplish that call remained a bit of a mystery. Over the next few days, as she undertook her recovery at Darjeeling, she sought further guidance and began to keep notes of the inspiration that she received.

Upon her return to Calcutta, she shared the outline of what she believed was the means to accomplish her "call within a call" with a dear friend, Father Celeste Van Exem, a Belgian Jesuit priest who was to become her mentor and spiritual adviser. Under her plan, she was to leave the Sisters of Loreto but to keep her vows as a nun. She would begin her own organization. She, and those who might choose to join her, were to work among the poorest of the poor in the slums. They were not to run large institutions such as hospitals. Eventually, they would, however, operate small dwellings that they would call homes.

All nuns made vows to undertake lives of poverty, chastity, and obedience. But Mother Teresa and those who were to become part of her distinct group were also to make a vow of "wholehearted free service to the poorest of the poor."[17] In order to serve in this way, Mother Teresa "resolved to live a life of poverty among the poor, to possess nothing, and to trust entirely in God's providence and guidance."[18]

This was the means by which Mother Teresa believed she could help to quench Christ's thirst. Ultimately, all of the chapels in all of the homes operated by the "Missionaries of Charity," as Mother Teresa's group was to become known, would have inscribed in them the words, "I thirst."

Her mind was settled. But the path forward was not without obstacles. In order to proceed, she needed permission from both the Sisters of Loreto and the Catholic hierarchy. Eventually, the former was granted. The latter, however, was harder to obtain. Permission had to come from Rome. Permission to petition Rome had to be granted by the Archbishop of Calcutta, Ferdinand Perier. Archbishop Perier was apprehensive, and with good reason. The thought of granting permission to a young European nun to go into the slums to live and to serve, with no resources—in fact, one who had taken a solemn oath of poverty and was committed to living based solely upon what God would provide—was disconcerting, to say the least. He hesitated.

It was nearly two years after Mother Teresa had received her call, in the summer of 1948, that permission was finally obtained from Rome.

When it became known by her fellow Sisters of Loreto what Mother Teresa had requested and been granted permission to do, the Sisters were shocked and saddened. One did not leave their order! But they were instructed, "Do not criticize. Do not praise. Pray."[19]

Teresa began to prepare for her departure. She purchased three white saris of the cheapest fabric, each lined with blue. On August 16, she set aside the habit of the Sisters of Loreto, the habit she had worn for almost two decades, and put on one of the white saris. She left Entally at night to avoid a scene with her Sisters.

Leaving Entally, leaving the Sisters of Loreto, "was my greatest sacrifice, the most difficult thing I have ever done. It was much more difficult than to leave my family and country to enter religious life. Loreto, my spiritual training, my work there, meant everything to me."[20]

Father Van Exem had arranged for Mother Teresa to spend some time receiving basic medical training. She was also trained in proper nutrition. Mother Teresa had initially thought that her vow of poverty required her to eat just what the poorest of the poor ate. She was, reluctantly, convinced that she would soon suffer from the same debilitating weakness that afflicted those she was to serve if she and her future followers did not eat nutritious meals.

On December 21, 1948, the tiny Albanian nun entered the slum of Moti Jihl and began her new life.[21]

Among the Poorest of the Poor

With Father Van Exem's assistance, Mother Teresa found herself a temporary place to sleep at a home for the elderly operated by a Catholic order called the Little Sisters of the Poor. Her days were to be spent in the streets.

On her first day in Moti Jihl, Mother Teresa passed the word that she would be starting a new school the next day. Her second day, she was greeted by twenty-one students at her school, a plot of ground near a pond where families would go to gather water. Her first blackboard was dirt and her chalk was a stick. The first subject to be taught was the Bengali alphabet.

Each day thereafter, the number of students increased.

After daily class she would spend her time ministering to the poor. Among her first efforts was helping a man who came to her to be treated for a thumb that was gangrenous. She had nothing but a pair of scissors. With what she had, she cut. Her patient fainted and fell to the ground—to be quickly joined by Mother Teresa.

The presence of the little woman in white soon became widely known. Some of the residents of the slums were mistrustful. They suspected that her true motivation was to convert slum dwellers to Christianity.

She was also viewed with scorn by other missionaries operating in the slums. One Jesuit priest confessed that, at first, "We thought she was cracked."[22] Another priest suggested that Mother Teresa's work was the "wiles of the devil."[23]

On occasion, even Mother Teresa doubted herself. The incredible poverty and suffering that she observed every day drained her emotionally. The enormity of the task of serving such a huge mass of afflicted humanity was overwhelming. She confessed to being tempted many times to return to the friendly confines of Loreto Entally. But she harbored no doubt about her call, and she persevered.

Soon, help began to arrive in small doses. Some gave money. Some gave food. Others gave medical supplies. Another teacher volunteered to help.

When there was no help volunteered, Mother Teresa went begging. She confessed to not being very good at it at first, but again, she persisted.

A local priest gave her 100 rupees with which she was able to rent two small huts in Moti Jihl. The first she turned into a school. She even had enough money to buy milk for her students, and as she taught basic hygiene, she rewarded students with bars of soap. Within two weeks, Mother Teresa's little school had fifty students and three other teachers to assist.

The second hut was dedicated to a different purpose. Mother Teresa had been profoundly touched by an incident in which she had found a woman, obviously near death, outside a local hospital. She carried the woman into the hospital but was refused admission because she had no money. The woman died on the street. Mother Teresa was most affected by the fact that this woman was dying alone, with no family to comfort her.

The second hut was thus converted into a place where the dying could go to depart this life with dignity and with someone nearby to provide companionship and compassion.

Eventually, a permanent home was found for Mother Teresa. The second floor of a large home owned by a Catholic, Alfred Gomes, was offered her. She moved in. Her furniture consisted of a chair, some wooden boxes, and a bed given her by the Sisters of Loreto. This was to become her first convent.

On occasion, Mother Teresa had no food for herself. When she got hungry enough, and no one else would respond to her begging, she would write a note to Alfred Gomes and ask him for a bit of food.

Besides being hungry from time to time, she was also very lonely. For the first three months of her ministry, she was all alone. Finally, in March, a former student arrived at her door and volunteered to help. She was the first of what would become the Missionary Sisters of Charity. Others were to join in ensuing months, and by the summer Mother Teresa had ten young Sisters. The youngest was only sixteen. All were former students.

Their task was simple. They would go from door to door begging for food or money. What they were given they would take to the very poor. They would also go among the streets of the slum comforting the sick and those who were dying. They would teach the children. They would work in the home for the dying.

All of them lived together on the second floor of the Gomes home.

In 1950, Mother Teresa sought official recognition for her

congregation. With Father Van Exem's assistance, a constitution was drafted for the Missionaries of Charity. It was approved by Pope Pius XII. In October, the eleven young Sisters who had joined with Mother Teresa began their "postulancy"—their application and apprenticeship to join the Missionaries of Charity. These young Sisters undertook a life of "loving trust," "total surrender," and "cheerfulness."[24] They were required to cut their hair short, a great sacrifice for young Bengali women.

They were true to the vow of poverty. They washed themselves and their saris in buckets. They brushed their teeth with ashes from the fireplace. Often they would share sandals. They wore the distinctive-for-their-simplicity white saris. Some were forced to make their saris from bags previously used to ship wheat. They were allowed but few possessions aside from their personal clothing: rosary beads, an umbrella, a bucket, and a thin mattress. Mother Teresa would say:

> Our rigorous poverty is our safeguard. We do not want to do what other religious orders have done throughout history, and begin by serving the poor only to end up unconsciously serving the rich. In order to understand and help those who have nothing, we must live like them.[25]

Mother Teresa expected nothing from her young nuns that she was not willing to do herself. She shared the same room with her postulants on the Gomes's second floor. She owned nothing more than they did. She would go to the streets to beg and to administer to the people. One new Sister had found the toilet to be disgusting and turned away from it. She soon saw Sister Teresa pass by, observe the dirty toilet, and set about to clean it.

Exactness in performing their duty and total obedience was required of the young Sisters of the Missionaries of Charity.

The small amount of money that the Sisters kept for their own needs was set aside by Mother Teresa in a small tin box. Sometimes it was empty. Often, when it was, and there was nothing for the Sisters to eat, small miracles occurred and random gifts of food were provided at just the right time. On one occasion, a new mattress was needed for a new Sister and there was no material to make it. That very day, a man who was leaving Calcutta to return to England showed up at the door to donate his.

As their numbers grew, the Gomes's house became too small. A prominent Muslim member of the community who had decided to move to Pakistan had built a home for himself on one of Calcutta's main thoroughfares. He agreed to sell the property to the Catholic church for far less than it was worth. The sale was made quickly. The Missionaries of Charity moved into the three-story building in the late winter of 1953. It was to become the "Motherhouse" for Mother Teresa's growing organization and remains so today.

The hut devoted to the dying was growing too small. The city of Calcutta offered the Missionaries of Charity a large building that became the new center for the dying. On one of the walls of this new home was posted the sign, "I Am Going to Heaven Today." It was widely broadcast that the home was open to all: Hindu, Muslim, Protestant, or Catholic. None were turned away. Those who found their own way there, or were brought by others, were cleaned and given a bed. Typical was the old man who had never lain in a bed his entire life who held on to the metal frame and said, "Now I can die like a human being."[26]

Soon, Mother Teresa opened another home for discarded babies and small children. It was not uncommon for babies to be abandoned in the slums. When word spread that a new shelter had been opened, babies began to arrive from hospitals and police stations. Mother Teresa refused to turn any infant away. Some died soon after being delivered to the home, but they at least died with someone caring for them. The home was often overwhelmed with children. If necessary, they were placed two or three in a bed. As the city's population learned of this remarkable effort to aid the abandoned infants of Calcutta, donations flowed to the Missionaries of Charity to assist in the operation of the home.

Mother Teresa knew that helping the children to merely survive was not enough. Those who could be were put up for adoption. Those who were not adopted were taught a skill or a simple profession so that they could provide for themselves.

If Mother Teresa had simply passed the rest of her life operating the homes for the dying and the abandoned infants, and had remained engaged in her daily ministering to the sick and dying and lonely of Calcutta, her life would have been truly remarkable. But she was not content. There were too many others whose thirst needed to be quenched.

A Mission to the World

As the years passed, the Missionaries of Charity organization grew. More Sisters joined. Greater recognition of the good works being performed resulted in additional assistance, including substantial financial assistance. Doctors and nurses volunteered to help. More homes for children were opened in Calcutta. Greater opportunities for adoption of the abandoned children in India as well as Europe and North America were made available.

Typical of the extension of Mother Teresa's desire to serve the "poorest of the poor" was the attention focused on the lepers of Calcutta. It was estimated that the city was the home for 30,000 people who suffered from leprosy. That disease thrived in areas where poverty, cramped living conditions, and malnutrition were found—and those were an apt description of Calcutta's slums. Many of the victims of leprosy suffered from a type that was not infectious, but that did not matter. Once people were diagnosed, they were shunned. They lost their jobs, their friends, often their families. Because leprosy was such a devastating disease, many hid their condition until it was too late to treat it.

From the beginning, lepers were welcomed at the facilities operated by the Missionaries of Charity. Mother Teresa and her Sisters treated them with great tenderness and respect. On one occasion, Mother Teresa was treating an ailing leper who had putrid-smelling sores. A reporter who was watching stated that he would not do the same for a million dollars. Mother Teresa replied that neither would she, for a million dollars, but that she would for Jesus.[27]

Foiled in an effort to establish a fixed leprosy treatment clinic, the type of disappointment that Mother Teresa always assumed was God's will, she decided instead to establish a mobile clinic. She received a substantial gift from Philips Electric Light Company, and an ambulance was gifted from the United States. A retired doctor who was a specialist in skin diseases came to Mother Teresa and offered to spend the rest of his life serving with her. In 1957, the first mobile leprosy clinic began its operation.

The next year, a permanent fixed clinic opened its doors. This clinic was the result of a financial bequest from a large corporation to fund the building following a gift of the land by the local municipal government. The speaker at the grand opening was a high government official, and he was introduced by a wealthy British expatriate who had become an active supporter of Mother Teresa. The grand opening was attended by the social elite of Calcutta.

Mother Teresa had come a long way in ten years.

But she was not yet satisfied when it came to her desire to serve the lepers of Calcutta. She organized programs to train them in vocations. She knew that restoring their self-respect was almost as important as treating or curing their disease.

Her ultimate dream, however, was a place where lepers could live, and die, with dignity. The Indian government donated thirty-four acres of land, and an entire community was planned. Money was raised from Germany for houses and a convent and chapel. Pope Paul VI visited India in 1964. A white Lincoln Continental was provided for his use during his trip. Upon leaving, he donated the car to Mother Teresa. She had the car raffled off, raising enough money to build a hospital for the little village.

As the community was being planned, a well was dug, ponds were constructed and stocked with fish, and banana and palm trees were planted. By the time the first residents arrived, the community was ready.

The residents learned to make bricks to help construct houses for those yet to come. The villagers ran their own cattle and raised their own rice. The self-sufficient little town became the home for four hundred families who were able to live relatively normal lives despite being victims of a disease that would otherwise have forced them into loneliness and isolation.

This is just one example of Mother Teresa's incredible fortitude, her growing circle of influence, and her ability to perform her mission inside India. She had progressed from renting a hut for a school to building cities.

By 1959, the Missionaries of Charity had increased their reach into other major cities in India. There were now 119 nuns who were part of the order and many hundreds of volunteers at Mother Teresa's various homes. Her reputation had grown to the point that at the opening of her home for children in the nation's capital, New Delhi, the event was attended by India's prime minister.

In their first fifteen years of existence, the Missionaries of Charity became involved in an impressive number of endeavors:

> "Our discernment of aid is only ever the necessity," Mother Teresa would claim on more than one occasion. The necessity always perceived as that of the thirsting Christ seemed to call for an expanding range of responses: clinics for those suffering from tuberculosis, ante-natal clinics, general dispensaries, mobile leprosy clinics, night shelters for homeless men, homes for abandoned children, homes for the dying and the destitute, nursery classes and crèches, primary schools, secondary schools, provision for further education, feeding progammes, villages for lepers, commercial schools, training in carpentry, metal work, embroidery, needlework or other skills, child-care and home management, and aid in the event of emergencies and disasters arising from riots, epidemics, famine and flooding.[28]

The Missionaries of Charity became famous for their ability to respond quickly in emergency and disaster situations. One reason they were so efficient was because of their vow of obedience. If Mother

Teresa saw a need for her Sisters, she would dispatch them forthwith and, regardless of the danger or risks, the nuns would obey. It was not uncommon for Mother Teresa to make a decision in the morning and have one or more of her nuns dispatched by the afternoon. Since the nuns had no personal belongings, travel was simple.

By 1960, Mother Teresa had not been out of India for thirty years. But the moment had arrived for her to make an appearance on the world stage.

In that year she traveled to the United States and Europe. She addressed a huge convention of Catholic women in Las Vegas, Nevada, and left the convention hall with literally bags of cash donated by the three thousand women in attendance who swarmed her following her speech. Perhaps Las Vegas was a most fitting place for bags of cash to be handled by the little Albanian nun.

After visiting other cities in the United States and meeting with Catholic leaders and United Nations officials, she ventured on to England, Germany, Switzerland, and finally Rome. In Germany, Mother Teresa was faced with a dilemma. A German Catholic charity offered to finance a new home for the dying in New Delhi if she would agree to provide a financial report as to how the money had been spent. She refused. She countered that neither she nor her other nuns had the time or the ability to generate such a report. This refusal remained a sticking point for Mother Teresa as her organization expanded in future years.

And expand it did. In 1965, Pope Paul VI granted permission for the Missionaries of Charity to begin operations outside of India.

The first request came from Venezuela. There, local Catholic leaders saw a great need for the presence of the Missionaries of Charity. Mother Teresa was at first hesitant to dispatch Sisters so far from the Motherhouse. But when it became clear that the Catholic hierarchy supported the request, she obeyed.

In July, Mother Teresa and five Sisters flew to Venezuela. An entirely new chapter was opening in the life of this giant of a woman and the Missionaries of Charity.

The operation in Venezuela posed fresh challenges for them. The culture was different. She was astounded at the number of couples living together who were not married. The Sisters were required to fill the role of religious educators necessitated by the absence of priests in many areas. They were also expected to perform duties that had traditionally been handled exclusively by priests in India, such as taking Holy Communion to the sick and conducting funerals.

But, as the needs arose and the challenges were confronted, Mother Teresa found a way to adapt. Soon her order was asked to open a home in Rome, and then Tanzania. Other requests quickly followed.

It became apparent that more workers were needed. A male order that mirrored the Sisters of Charity was created in the 1960s and called the Missionary Brothers of Charity. An organization of volunteers, called Co-Workers, was also organized. Membership in both the Missionary Brothers and Co-Workers increased quickly. Over time, Mother Teresa's Missionaries of Charity expanded to include a presence on every continent except Antarctica.

By the time of their leader's death in 1997, the Sisters of Charity numbered over 3,800 and they were working in 594 facilities (called houses or tabernacles) in 120 countries; the Brothers of Charity numbered 363 and they were operating 68 facilities in 19 countries. There were approximately 30,000 Co-Workers in England alone and another 10,000 in other areas of Europe and the United States. Many of these Co-Workers spent their efforts in raising money to fund the various worldwide operations.[29]

By 2010, the number of Sisters had increased to 5,000 and there were more than 750 facilities.[30]

There is no way to estimate the number of lives that were saved, enriched, or dignified by the efforts of Mother Teresa and her Sisters and Brothers. That accounting is for heaven alone to do.[31]

Her Teachings and Philosophy

In addition to the countless good deeds that Mother Teresa performed, she must also be acknowledged for being a wonderful teacher—a teacher who displayed great wisdom and sagacity. She was in many respects a philosopher. She taught through her spoken words and writings. She instructed her nuns regularly and gave many public speeches, although reluctantly. She was to author a number of books.[32] Perhaps most important, she taught through the life she lived—by her example.

It is impossible to provide an adequate summary of all that she taught, but the following is a representative sample.

In Her Own Words

> If the poor die of hunger, it is not because God does not care for them. Rather, it is because neither you nor I are generous enough. It is because we are not instruments of love in the hands of God. We do not recognize Christ when once again He appears to us in the hungry man, in the lonely woman, in the child who is looking for a place to get warm.[33]

> We have no right to judge the rich. For our part, what we desire is not a class struggle but a class encounter, in which the rich save the poor and the poor save the rich.[34]

> I believe that the cry of the children, those who are never born because they are killed before they see the light of day, must offend God greatly.[35]

> In every country there are poor. On certain continents poverty is more spiritual than material, a poverty that consists of loneliness, discouragement, and the lack of meaning in life. . . .
>
> You in the West have the spiritually poorest of the poor much more than you have the physically poor. Often among the rich are very spiritually poor people. I find it is easy to give a plate of rice to a hungry person, to furnish a bed to a person who has no bed, but to console or to remove

> the bitterness, anger, and loneliness that comes from being spiritually deprived, that takes a long time.[36]

> Peace and war start within one's own home. If we really want peace for the world, let us start by loving one another within our families. Sometimes it is hard for us to smile at one another. It is often difficult for the husband to smile at his wife or for the wife to smile at her husband.[37]

> If someone feels that God wants from him a transformation of social structures, that's an issue between him and his God. We all have the duty to serve God where we feel called. I feel called to help individuals, to love each human being. I never think in terms of crowds in general but in terms of persons. Were I to think about crowds, I would never begin anything. It is the person that matters. I believe in person-to-person encounters.[38]

Stories from Others

On one occasion a Catholic priest arrived at the Motherhouse in Calcutta with his arm red and swollen, covered with bedbug bites. Mother Teresa immediately sought him out and asked, "Father, what do you have there?" He replied that it was insect bites, to which she replied, "A gift of God!" He was at first surprised. But, "Later I understood that for her any adversity, pain or suffering could be a 'gift of God.' Anything, in fact, through a little act of the will, could be transformed into a 'gift to God.'"[39]

This same man once accompanied Mother Teresa to her village of lepers. He expressed some discomfort at the thought of finding himself among an entire community of people suffering from leprosy. Mother Teresa taught him:

> Father, you will meet Jesus there in His distressing disguise as the poorest of the poor. Our visit will bring joy,

> for the most terrible poverty is loneliness and the feeling of being unloved. The worst disease today is not leprosy or tuberculosis, but the feeling of being unwanted. . . . There is more hunger in the world for love and appreciation than for bread.[40]

Despite the unbelievable amount of good that Mother Teresa was responsible for, she was often subjected to criticism, sometimes severe criticism. One line of criticism was that she should have been teaching people "how to fish," instead of simply "giving them a fish to eat." To this condemnation she replied, "My poor people are too weak to hold the fishing rod themselves." Then, with a twinkle in her eye, she added, "But if they are ever well enough to hold a fishing rod, then our critics can go ahead and teach them how to fish."[41]

Mother Teresa lived among much evil, but she was not willing to condemn those who might be responsible for it. She also refused to denounce her critics. Her nuns would often joke that she would make excuses for the devil. This woman, whose mother would turn the electricity off to the house if young Agnes or her brother or sister spoke ill of others, had learned that lesson well. "One sin that I have never had to confess is that I judged someone,"[42] she said.

Mother Teresa loved those she served. She often talked about how wonderful the poor were. She referred to the example of the family she visited whose members were suffering from severe hunger. When she gave food to the mother, she was surprised to see her immediately take some of the food and leave the home. Upon her return, she explained that her neighbors needed the food more than she did.

Mother Teresa taught that for giving to really matter, we must "give until it hurts." She would use as an example the experience she had when she was preparing to undertake a mission to serve the starving in Ethiopia. She was approached by little children in India who had been told by the Sisters about the terrible conditions of the children in Ethiopia. The Indian children were there to offer up small amounts of money or whatever else they had to give. She told of one little boy who explained that he had no money, but he did have one piece of chocolate. He said to Mother Teresa:

> "And you give that, take that with you and give it to the children in Ethiopia." That little child loved with great love, because I think that was the first time that he had a piece of chocolate in his hand. And he gave it. He gave it with joy to be able to share, to remove a little [of] the suffering of someone in far Ethiopia. This is the joy of loving: to give until it hurts.[43]

Mother Teresa was always aware of the need to set a proper example. On one occasion, a Catholic priest accompanied her on a several-day trip around India. They were assisted by a high-ranking police officer who was very imperious—in fact, rude. He made it clear to both the priest and Mother Teresa that he was there to perform his duty and wanted none of the religious stuff. By the second day, the officer was beginning to soften. At the end of the trip, he had been so touched by what he had witnessed that with tears in his eyes he asked Mother Teresa for a blessing. Afterward, she told her traveling companion, "Father, our witness for Christ must always be of such a kind that people cannot decide against Him by mistake!"[44]

Mother Teresa was admired for her grace under pressure and also for her sense of humor. Considering how much misery she found herself immersed in, and how much her worldwide ministry demanded of her, she was a remarkably calm and cheerful person. However, she once admitted, "I know that God will not impose on me anything that I cannot bear. But sometimes I wish that He did not have such great confidence in me."[45]

The later decades of her life were incredibly busy. Travel and demands upon her time were intense. Sometimes her traveling companions became exasperated at the frequent changes in schedules, people to be met, demands for decisions to be made. At the end of one particularly busy day, one commented to Mother Teresa that "traveling with a saint is really not at all easy," to which Mother Teresa smiled and replied, "You know, Father, who is a saint? A saint is someone who lives with a saint."[46]

Example in the Life She Lived

Mother Teresa was, first and foremost, a living example of what she taught. She did not preach something that she did not herself live. She did not ask her nuns and brothers to do something that she had not done or was not doing.

She rejected every effort to amend or weaken one of her first and most firmly held beliefs, that in order to serve those who were in poverty, one had to live in poverty oneself.

Often, a building would be donated to the Missionaries of Charity in order to entice the organization to open a house in a given country or city. If that building was deemed by Mother Teresa to be too elegant, she would insist that it be remodeled—for example, the carpeting removed, expensive mattresses replaced, or air conditioning dismantled. She did not want herself, or her nuns, to live and work in facilities that were more comfortable than the living conditions of those they served.

She traveled extensively. In the last thirty-five years of her life, she was visiting one of her houses, or attending to some fund-raising event, or meeting with another dignitary, an average of every third day.[47] She could be on the road for up to ten months of every year.[48] She would travel by economy class on the airlines or by train—no special treatment was requested for her. However, because she traveled so much, she became familiar to many airlines. Although she would have purchased a ticket in the economy section of the plane, from time to time she would receive a complimentary upgrade to first class. Mother Teresa would take advantage of such an opportunity and would request of the crew that all the food left over from the flight be donated to the poor. She was known to leave an airport with bags of leftover airline food. Sometimes she would also leave with large sums of cash solicited by friendly flight attendants from among the crew and passengers.

She never wasted time. A prolific letter writer, she would utilize travel time to pen letters and notes. She was responsible for writing thousands of letters and notes to supporters, world leaders, organizations, and children.

In 1979, Mother Teresa was awarded the Nobel Peace Prize. When she attended the ceremony to receive the prize at Oslo, Norway, she requested that the $5,000 allocated for the traditional banquet be donated to the hungry instead. Her request resulted in an additional $64,000 in volunteer contributions for the hungry from the citizens of Norway.

From the beginning of her mission to the "poorest of the poor," she lived by faith. She did not engage in strategic planning. She did not have a master plan for fund-raising. She believed that she was on God's errand and God would provide. Her faith was rewarded time and again.

Once she gave her last rupee to a priest without any way of knowing what she herself would do, but that very night a stranger knocked at her door and gave her 50 rupees in an envelope.

Later, when the Missionaries of Charity were feeding thousands of people in Calcutta, they ran out of food. The Sisters were about to send a message to the hungry that they would not be fed that next day, but Mother Teresa asked them to give her the chance to pray. The next day, schools were unexpectedly closed and the government delivered all of the unused school lunch food to the Sisters for distribution to the hungry.

A Sister on kitchen duty at the convent came to Mother Teresa and informed her that they had no more flour. She was told to go pray about it. While the Sister was praying, a stranger rang the doorbell and handed over a large sack of flour.

Mother Teresa taught the people to have faith in God, and she lived her life in full compliance with that teaching.

She demanded no privilege because of her fame. In October 1985, she was invited to address the United Nations General Assembly. She began the day as any other, personally washing her own sari and then washing the floors and cleaning the toilets in the Missionaries of Charity house in New York. At the appointed time, she was driven to the headquarters of the United Nations by a volunteer in a nondescript vehicle. At the United Nations, she was greeted by the delegates and heads of state with a standing ovation. She proceeded to deliver a powerful message about love and prayer and the evils of abortion. She was then driven back to the local Sisters' house by the volunteer to continue with the day's routine.

She had an obsession for cleaning toilets. Cleaning toilets was one way of keeping herself humble. She said of herself, "I am a specialist in that, probably the world's best specialist in cleaning toilets."[49] She was even observed cleaning the toilets of the aircraft flying her to Washington, D.C., for a meeting with President Ronald Reagan.

Once a well-dressed man appeared at one of the Houses for the Dying and asked for Mother Teresa. He was told that she was in the back cleaning toilets. Surprised, he asked where she might be found thus engaged. When he approached her at her task, she mistakenly took him for a volunteer and undertook to instruct him on how to properly clean the toilet. She left, and he spent the next twenty minutes performing this assigned task. Upon completion, he sought Mother Teresa out and explained that, as the head of the airline, he was there with her requested airplane tickets. He had simply wanted to deliver them to her personally. However, he later stated that those twenty minutes of cleaning toilets for the dying were the most important twenty minutes of his life.

The Courageous Little Saint

No discussion of Mother Teresa would be complete without paying tribute to her remarkable courage. She was a very tough woman!

One of her biographers said of her:

> I came to know her humour and her toughness. She was, I discovered, not only humble and small but also strong-willed, resolute, determined and totally fearless, because God was on her side. This assumed union of intention was not one with which everybody easily came to terms. "What Mother wants, she gets" was a truism widely accepted amongst those who knew her.[50]

Her personal courage was evident in the first act of her "call within a call," when she went into Moti Jihl alone, penniless, and began her mission. It was to be demonstrated many times thereafter.

An example of disregard for personal safety occurred in 1982 in Beirut, Lebanon. Beirut was then a war zone because of a civil war between Christians and Muslims that had been raging for seven years. Mother Teresa learned that there were thirty-eight Muslim children stranded at a mental hospital in the middle of the fighting. She led a convoy to bring the mentally and physically handicapped children to safety after they had been largely abandoned by terrified staff members. Two days later, she entered the war zone again to rescue another large group of children.

When Bhopal, India, was struck by a tragic poisonous gas leak and thousands were killed, Mother Teresa was there. When the Soviet Union suffered from the Chernobyl nuclear disaster, she was there. She and her Missionaries of Charity were in Armenia after its great earthquake.

It was her faith—her faith that as long as she was doing God's will she would be protected—that motivated her.

Throughout her life, she displayed not just physical courage but a rare moral courage, the courage to take on the world over an issue that troubled her heart mightily—abortion. Throughout her public ministry, she made the point over and over again, "Abortion is murder in the mother's womb. A child is a gift from God. If you do not want it, then give it to me. I want it."[51]

In 1979, when she received the Nobel Prize for Peace, she might have confined her acceptance speech to championing her causes of fighting poverty and loneliness. But she could not pass up this unique opportunity to address the world and confront the issue of abortion head-on:

> I feel the greatest destroyer of peace is abortion, because it is a direct war, a direct killing, direct murder by the mother herself. . . . Many people are very, very concerned with the children of India, with the children of Africa where quite a number die, maybe of malnutrition, of hunger and

> so, but millions are dying deliberately by the will of the mother. And this is the greatest destroyer of peace today.[52]

In her 1985 speech before the United Nations, again an audience of great diversity and sophistication, she fearlessly asserted:

> This is what is such a contradiction, and today I feel that abortion has become the greatest destroyer of peace. We are afraid of the nuclears [nuclear weapons], because it is touching [i.e. affects] us, but we are not afraid, the mother is not afraid to commit that terrible murder. . . . And let us help each other to strengthen that. That in our countries that terrible law of killing the innocents, of destroying life, destroying the presence of God, be removed from our country, from our nation, from our people, from our families.[53]

In 1994, Mother Teresa was the invited speaker for the National Prayer Breakfast sponsored by the Congress of the United States. To a group that included many of the nation's most liberal elite, she again assailed abortion in extensive remarks mirroring those given to the Nobel audience and the United Nations. Among her most powerful statements: "And if we accept that a mother can kill even her own child, how can we tell other people not to kill one another."[54]

Her courage was always sustained by her undiminished faith in God.

To the end, Mother Teresa displayed courage in the face of her own declining health. She had always had a frail constitution. In 1983 she suffered a major heart attack. Upon recovering, she reengaged in a full schedule. She suffered a second, nearly fatal heart attack in 1989. Again, as soon as possible, she returned to a brutal schedule. In 1997, Mother Teresa was replaced as the head of the Missionaries of Charity, although she remained the organization's spiritual headmistress. On September 5, 1997, Mother Teresa died of a heart attack at the Motherhouse in Calcutta. She was eighty-seven years old.

Sainthood

During her lifetime, Mother Teresa was to receive many honors, including the aforementioned 1979 Nobel Peace Prize. She received the Pope's Peace Prize in 1971 and the Presidential Medal of Freedom from President Ronald Reagan of the United States in 1985. She would receive similar honors or awards from the leaders of India, the Philippines, Great Britain, and Albania. She would be granted numerous honorary doctorates. She was made an honorary citizen of the United States and Albania (after Communism fell).

She would be the respected guest of presidents and prime ministers, friend of first ladies and princesses, including a close friendship with Lady Diana of Great Britain. She would have access to the Pope and leaders of the United Nations and heads of many countries.

Her impact on these distinguished world leaders was profound. The former Indian Prime Minister Indira Gandhi said of Mother Teresa, "To meet her is to feel utterly humble, to sense the power of tenderness and the strength of love."[55] Lord Runcie, Archbishop of Canterbury, stated that when he met Mother Teresa, he felt as if he should "kneel and kiss Mother Teresa's feet . . . [it was] the most humbling and uplifting experience of my life."[56]

She received honors from all over the world. She was featured on magazine covers and in film documentaries. During her life, the awards and medals that she received filled seven army lockers. Following her death, she was designated a saint by Pope John Paul II.

But through it all, she was just what she was when she began, a humble servant of Jesus Christ. She called herself "a little pencil in God's hands."[57]

She was once asked whether all of the honors and awards had made her proud—even just a little bit. Her reply was to point a finger at each ear and say, "It goes in here and out the other side again. And there is nothing in between. It is His work!"[58]

In one of the few examples of her talking about herself, she summed up her life and work: "By birth, I am Albanian. I am an

Indian citizen. I am a Catholic nun. In what I do, I belong to the whole world, but my heart belongs entirely to Jesus."[59]

She was in fact, a very common person. Father Van Exem, who was to become her great mentor, said of her, "Mother was not an exceptional person. She was an ordinary Loreto nun, a very ordinary person but with great love for her Lord."[60] This very ordinariness was evidence to Father Van Exem that her extraordinary call was authentic.

How Did Mother Teresa Change the World?

How was the world changed by this one ordinary woman? In the big picture of things, did a diminutive woman from the little country of Albania, serving primarily among the masses of India, make a difference in the world?

While she was yet alive, Mother Teresa was deemed to be one of the most influential women who ever lived.[61]

The amount of good that she accomplished during her life is immeasurable. The lives that were saved, the children who were given a future, the dignity afforded to the dying, are simply impossible to measure in any tangible way.

The cumulative good done by tens of thousands of people who were inspired by her—whether through donations or volunteer work or individual acts of charity—is impossible of calculation.

The numbers of the earth's inhabitants who were turned to God because of her life and example is beyond reckoning.

To the end, she sincerely believed that none of the awards and honors mattered. She did believe, however: "At the end of our life this is how we will be judged: 'I was hungry and you gave me food, I was naked and you clothed me, I was homeless and you welcomed me.'"[62]

By that measure, at five feet tall, Mother Teresa of Calcutta was indeed a giant![63]

Notes

1. For information about the slums of India, see Gold, *Mother,* 58–63; Langford, *Fire,* 27–29; Spink, *Teresa,* 52; Teresa, *Greater Love,* 23–25, 70.
2. Skopje is today in the republic of Macedonia.
3. Gold, *Mother,* 12.
4. Spink, *Teresa,* 6.
5. Ibid., 7.
6. Maasburg, *Calcutta,* 92.
7. Spink, *Teresa,* 11.
8. Ibid.
9. Ibid., 15.
10. Ibid., 19.
11. Gold, *Mother,* 45.
12. Spink, *Teresa,* 24.
13. Maasburg, *Calcutta,* 26.
14. Spink, *Teresa,* 24.
15. Matthew 25:40.
16. Maasburg, *Calcutta,* 36.
17. Spink, *Teresa,* 24.
18. Maasburg, *Calcutta,* 26.
19. Spink, *Teresa,* 31.
20. Ibid., 32.
21. For information about the years prior to Mother Teresa's leaving the Sisters of Loreto, see Gold, *Mother,* 1–61; Spink, *Teresa,* 1–35.
22. Gold, *Mother,* 64.
23. Ibid.
24. Spink, *Teresa,* 43.
25. Ibid., 44.
26. Ibid., 55.
27. See Maasburg, *Calcutta,* 36; Spink, *Teresa,* 64.
28. Spink, *Teresa,* 80–81.
29. See Gold, *Mother,* 89–91; Spink, *Teresa,* Appendix A; Teresa, *Where There Is Love,* xiv.
30. Maasburg, *Calcutta,* 199.
31. For more information about the life history of Mother Teresa, see Gold, *Mother;* Maasburg, *Calcutta;* Spink, *Teresa.*
32. She is credited with authoring or coauthoring six books.
33. Teresa, *No Greater Love,* 40–41.
34. Ibid., 97–98.
35. Ibid., 127.

36. Ibid., 94–95.
37. Ibid., 26–27.
38. Ibid., 69.
39. Maasburg, *Calcutta,* 75–76.
40. Ibid., 39.
41. Ibid.
42. Ibid., 92.
43. Ibid., 68–69.
44. Ibid., 159.
45. Ibid., 182.
46. Ibid., 192.
47. Ibid., *Calcutta,* 199.
48. Gold, *Mother,* 105.
49. Maasburg, *Calcutta,* 175.
50. Spink, *Teresa,* vii.
51. Maasburg, *Calcutta,* 166.
52. Ibid.
53. Ibid., 167.
54. Ibid., 169.
55. Felder, *100,* 117.
56. Spink, *Teresa,* viii.
57. Gold, *Mother,* 97.
58. Maasburg, *Calcutta,* 175.
59. Ibid., x.
60. Gold, *Mother,* 47.
61. Felder, *100 Women.*
62. Maasburg, *Calcutta*, 181.
63. For information about the life, deeds, and teachings of Mother Teresa, see Felder, *100 Women;* Gold, *Teresa*; Langford, *Fire*; Maasburg, *Calcutta*; Spink, *Teresa*; Teresa, *No Greater*; Teresa, *Where There Is Love.*

Conclusion

Are There Giants among Us?

In this book we have examined the lives of seven men and women who altered the course of history in a variety of ways—all of which enriched and enhanced the condition of humankind.

Because of Abraham's faithfulness, monotheism was established and persevered through the practice of three of the world's great religions: Judaism, Christianity, and Islam. He introduced the spiritual worldview that has been adopted by much of the world's population throughout subsequent history.

Because of Pericles and the two centuries of Athenian democracy, an ideal was given birth, an ideal that was to survive the two and one half millennia that followed. That ideal was the belief that men were truly capable of governing themselves—an ideal kept alive by those who, through centuries of tyranny and darkness, believed that the theory of self-government would someday be proven again. And it was, in the form of the Western political philosophy from which the United States of America came to be.

Paul was the representative of Christianity most responsible for expounding its enlightened doctrine and spreading its message. Among its innumerable virtues, it can be said that Christianity altered the world from a sphere in which only the powerful and dominant could prevail to a world where liberty and self-government can exist. It is a world where adherence to a higher moral law is expected of its citizens.

Through the efforts of these three, a foundation for the remainder of the history of the world was laid. This foundation allowed our world to advance, ever so slowly, toward becoming a world where the right of self-government is ingrained, recognition of fundamental rights and personal liberty endure, the pursuit of equality for all individuals is pursued, a commitment to the rule of law exists, and assuring justice is a goal of society.

The remaining four giants whose lives we examined played vital roles in bettering the lives of their fellow men.

Sir Isaac Newton changed history by making our natural world understandable. This, in turn, led to the advances in science and technology that finally changed the way that men and women lived their daily lives.

Marie Curie wrought great advances in science—advances that dominated the science of the twentieth century. To her credit, although it was never her priority, she also established a precedent whereby the contributions of women could be joined with those of men to improve mankind.

Martin Luther King Jr. committed his life to making a theory—the equality of all under the law and equality of opportunity for all Americans—into a reality. In so doing, he forced changes in our society that made us more true to our founding principles.

Mother Teresa showed that a life devoted to improving the lot of the most unfortunate was a noble life. Her example continues to inspire men and women of many nations to perform unselfish acts of service.

In sum, the giants in our review individually and collectively altered the way that we are governed, the way that we think, the way that we act, the nature of our aspirations, the priorities that we pursue, what we understand, and the comforts that we enjoy. They made our lives better and us better.

In proclaiming their virtues, I do not assert that they were without fault. All seven giants were mere mortals and displayed weaknesses. If one wanted to write a book about all of the mistakes that they made, the personality quirks that they displayed, the sharpness of tongue or quickness to find fault that they suffered from, and the lapses in judgment or morality of which they were guilty, it would be a lengthy book.

But all it would do is prove that imperfect people can still accomplish wonderful things. What can't be honestly disputed is the greatness of their achievements.

Why These Seven?

The introduction to this book posed a series of questions. Those questions included:

What is it about these few that makes them different?

Are there character traits that they share in common?

Were they merely in the right place at the right time?

Do these notable ones craft their own destiny, or are they somehow chosen? Are all of these giants in world history in fact men and women who were called by Providence? Were they all, truly, gifts of God? Or are they the product of their own genius or their own unique gifts?

Were they giants because they were brave, or determined, or full of faith?

It could be noted that three of the seven claimed to be called by God to perform their deeds: Abraham, Paul, and Mother Teresa. Others may have thought they were called but did not publicly declare it. Others may have been called but did not know it. Others just did what they felt they had to do.

Regardless of the reality of a "call," it is easy to argue that they were all gifts from God.

Was it wealth or position that made it possible for these seven to accomplish great things? Did the seven have the advantage of inherited prestige to assist them in their effort?

Only Pericles was born to privilege. Two were farmers (Abraham and Newton). Paul was a tentmaker. Curie, King, and Mother Teresa all emerged from humble backgrounds.

No, their success cannot be attributed to hereditary advantage.

However, there are three qualities that seem to be shared character traits of all seven of these giants of world history. Perhaps these qualities constitute the mark of a giant:

First was personal courage, which included a willingness to challenge the status quo.

Rebuffing the worship of idols, which was the practice of every other person and culture of his time, Abraham put his life at risk to challenge the prevailing value system.

Pericles's mentor, Ephialtes, had been murdered for attempting to break the power of Athenian aristocracy. Undaunted, Pericles took up the cause and forced reforms that made all citizens of Athens equal under the law.

Paul bravely contended with those within and without the fledgling Christian faith who resisted the extension of the full hand of fellowship to the Gentiles.

The young and self-taught Newton was courageous enough to reject the conventional scientific dogma of Aristotle and other natural philosophers more contemporary. He sought only the truth, regardless of the views of his peers, whether they be truths of science or religion.

Marie Curie had the audacity to take on not only the most daunting of scientific challenges but the entire male-dominated world.

Martin Luther King Jr. was bold enough to lead a movement to guarantee those rights that a bloody Civil War, federal legislation, and Supreme Court decisions had failed to assure for black Americans.

Mother Teresa left the comfort of a place among her beloved Sisters of Loreto to live in hell and rely on God for her very sustenance.

None of the seven were cowards!

Second, none of them were easily discouraged. They were all persistent to a fault.

Abraham persevered in worshipping Jehovah and preaching monotheism from the day of his call to the end of his long life. He never doubted or wavered. His resolve serves as an example to the current day.

Pericles worked inexorably for decades to wring concessions from the powerful to assure the rights of citizenship for the lowly. To the end, he defended the Athenian system of democracy despite the fact that he became a victim to its mobocratic tendencies.

Despite persecution and rejection, Paul could not be deterred from preaching Christ. He endured floggings, jailing, and ultimately execution for his insistence upon doing so.

Once Isaac Newton began to focus on a question, he would not abandon seeking the answer until he had satisfied himself. Sleep and food and sociality be hanged!

Taking four years to extract one-tenth of a gram of radium from ten tons of pitchblende might be the epitome of relentless drive. Marie Curie did that.

Fighting injustice from Montgomery to Memphis, Martin Luther King Jr. would not let the racism that permeated America's Southland defeat him. Threats, intimidation, and occasional failure did not slow him in his efforts to make America's soul whole.

And Mother Teresa undertook to assuage the hunger, grief, and pain of individuals one at a time, even though those individuals needing her love and assistance numbered in the millions.

Yes, they were a determined lot.

The final virtue that all seven possessed was faith.

Unlike those who worshipped idols, Abraham preached a God who could not be seen by believers. That requires faith. Abraham displayed his faith through his willingness to sacrifice his son Isaac. He had faith that Jehovah would provide a way for the fulfillment of His promise of a mighty posterity through that son.

Pericles had an abiding faith in human nature. He believed that man could be trusted to vote the broader public interest, not just his own self-interest. He accepted as true the existence of the noble Athenian.

As to Paul, he was commissioned by Jesus Christ to take the word of Christ to the Gentiles. He had faith that the roadblocks would be removed and that the way would be made clear for him to do so.

Despite the scientific truths that he helped to unveil, Isaac Newton's faith in God and his belief in His role in the creation and maintenance of the universe never wavered. To the end he considered his function as simply revealing the magnificence of God's creation.

Marie Curie was motivated by a belief that if she did her best, and if she succeeded in whatever she undertook, she would be recognized for her achievements even though she was a woman. She had great faith in herself.

Even though there were many among his own followers who lost their faith in nonviolence, Martin Luther King Jr. never did. Despite the violence inflicted upon him, his loved ones, and his followers, he had the faith that justice could be achieved without bloodshed.

Mother Teresa undertook a mission to the "poorest of the poor" that would seem to be unachievable to the normal person. But she never wavered in her belief that she had been called to quench the thirst of Jesus Christ through her administration to those who suffered. She had the faith that her earnest efforts would fulfill that commission.

Yes, they were all motivated by faith. In fact, personal courage, persistence, and faith were truly marks of all these seven giants.

Giants among Us

Are there giants among us today? Are there men and women that are accomplishing great things at this very moment because of their courage, persistence, and faith?

Of course, the answer is an emphatic yes! A review of those engaged in the arenas of government, science, business, nonprofit organizations, education, religion, and many other fields would reveal giants in all of them.

However, it would be wrong to suggest that a giant must be someone whom we read about, or whose name we hear mentioned on the news, or who could be identified by a large number of citizens.

It would be wrong to believe that the only giants who matter are those who will someday have their names appear in history books.

No, this world is as good as it is because there are innumerable men and women, old and young, who do great things with only a handful of people being aware of it, or perhaps with no recognition of their acts at all.

For example, only a handful of people alive today recognize the name of Amanda de Lange. Volunteering at a huge government orphanage in China, she made a rather startling discovery—the existence of rooms in which were placed infants who suffered from health problems such as heart defects, spina bifida, cleft palate, severe birthmarks, or any other defect that would make it impossible for the baby to be successfully offered for adoption. Amanda could not bear the thought that such infants were, in effect, being discarded. She decided that she had to do something, small though the effort was, to help those most helpless ones.

Ultimately receiving permission from Chinese authorities to start her own foster home, she made arrangements to go to the official orphanages and retrieve those infants that she had the resources to help. At first, her foster home was a couple of beds in her own small apartment. Amanda nursed the infants to good health by giving them proper food and love. She raised the money needed to have the heart defect, cleft palate, or birthmark repaired and arranged for the surgeries. Once the child was made whole, she would place the child for adoption.

Her one-apartment operation expanded to two small apartments. It continued to grow from there.

At the time of this writing, the operation, known as Starfish Foster Home, has an international board of directors. Amanda supervises a staff of thirty people, and the foster home is currently caring for about fifty infants.

Is Amanda a giant? To the hundreds of babies saved from certain death and given the opportunity for a normal life, she is. To the parents of the adopted children, who have had their lives enriched beyond measure by having those little ones become a part of their families, the answer is yes.

On a smaller scale, I offer the example of Tina. Tina found herself with elderly neighbors who had little in the way of money or support from their children. Tina could not accept their dire circumstances. She determined to take upon herself responsibility for the medical care, financial management, and housing of her neighbors.

As the couple aged, the demands became more challenging. On occasion, Tina would have to personally take the husband a hundred miles in two different directions to attend to his health needs. She had to fight with bureaucrats to assure that the couple received the financial and medical benefits to which they were entitled. She had to arrange for movement to care centers. When the husband died, she had to arrange his funeral.

She did not do it all alone. Her husband and other family members assisted. Other members of the community stepped in on occasion. But Tina wore herself out in providing the care, love, and resources that would otherwise never have been available.

Is she a giant? To that couple whose lives were made immensely more livable in their declining years, the answer is yes.

All those who read these words can summon to mind their own examples of giants in their own lives. It might be a family member, a friend, someone from their faith group, a fellow employee, a neighbor.

They are out there, and this world is a better place because of them.

There truly are giants among us!

What about Us?

We may not be in a position to be a giant who saves the world, but how about our ability to be a giant in our family, our neighborhood, our city or town, our state?

We do not need to wait for a call from God!

Perhaps you want to aim high. There are so many causes, so many important things that must be done, so many wrongs to right, so much change that must be wrought.

If you want a cause, take on the curse of pornography and the degrading of American culture.

If you want to right a wrong, fight those forces and influences that are destroying America's family.

The world is still beset with racism and bigotry. Too many of God's children continue to be judged by the color of their skin or the religion that they choose to follow, instead of by their character.

The world is still in need of noble scientists: honest, unselfish, possessed of the scientific spirit similar to that of Marie Curie. Cures for diseases need to be found. Man has much of nature to discover and understand.

Poverty needs to be alleviated. There is much we can do to ease the burdens of the weakest among us, perhaps not on a global scale, or in a nation, or even in a city, but in our neighborhoods and our own families.

As previously mentioned, the opportunity of self-government is more widespread today than at any time in the world's long history. But, taken for granted and foolishly neglected, all of it can be lost in very short order.

To prevent that, we need more people to leave the mark of a giant on the world!

We need fewer of us sitting back and waiting for others to step forward to take control of the future.

We need more individuals dedicated to preserving freedom where it exists and spreading it farther abroad.

We need more individuals devoted to those proven principles that expand economic freedom and prosperity.

We need more individuals willing to sacrifice to expand equality of opportunity to all of God's children.

We need more individuals willing to dedicate their great minds to the scientific and technological advancement of the human condition.

Yes, we need more dwarfs to become giants!

Should the accounts of greatness recorded in this book somehow motivate a handful of readers to make the conversion from dwarf to giant, in this day and age where greatness in our leaders and our people is so desperately needed, then this book has served its purpose.

Bibliography

Chapter 1
Abraham of Ur

Crim, Keith, ed. *The Interpreter's Dictionary of the Bible.* Nashville: Abingdon Press, 1962.

Dimont, Max I. *Jews, God, and History.* New York: Penguin Books, 1994.

Federer, William J. *America's God and Country.* New York: Fame Publishing, Inc., 1996.

Feiler, Bruce. *Abraham: A Journey to the Hearth of Three Faiths.* New York: Harper Perennial, 2004.

Josephus, Flavius. *The Works of Flavius Josephus.* London: Ward, Lock & Co., Limited.

Levenson, Jon D. *Abraham Between Torah and Gospel.* Milwaukee: Marquette University Press, 2011.

Nicholi, Armand, Jr. *The Question of God.* New York: Free Press, 2002.

Tvedtnes, John A., Brian M. Hauglid, and John Gee, eds. *Traditions about the Early Life of Abraham.* Provo: Foundation for Ancient Research and Mormon Studies, 2001.

Ussher, James. *The Annals of the World.* United States: Master Books, 2005.

Chapter 2
Pericles the Greek

Botsford, George Willis, and Charles Alexander Robinson, Jr. *Hellenic History.* New York: The Macmillan Company, 1969.

Hamilton, Alexander, John Jay, and James Madison. *The Federalist.* Washington, D.C.: Global Affairs Publishing Company, 1987.

Kagan, Donald. *Pericles of Athens and the Birth of Democracy.* New York: The Free Press, 1991.

Plutarch. *Plutarch's Lives.* New York: The Modern Library, 2001.

Robinson, Charles Alexander, Jr. *Athens in the Age of Pericles.* Norman, Oklahoma: University of Oklahoma Press, 1959.

Strain, Jacqueline. *The Contribution of Ancient Greece.* New York: Holt, Rinehart and Winston, Inc., 1971.

Chapter 3
Paul—Apostle to the Gentiles

Boak, Arthur E. R., and William G. Sinnigen. *A History of Rome to A.D. 565.* London: The Macmillan Company, 1965.

Brown, S. Kent, and Richard Neitzel Holzapfel. *The Lost 500 Years.* Salt Lake City: Deseret Book, 2006.

Farrar, Frederic W. *The Life and Work of St. Paul.* London: Cassell and Company, Limited, 1897.

Hart, Michael H. *The 100—A Ranking of the Most Influential Persons in History.* New York: Citadel Press, 1992.

Josephus, Flavius. *The Works of Flavius Josephus.* London: Ward, Lock & Co., Limited.

Stewart, Chris, and Ted Stewart. *The Miracle of Freedom: 7 Tipping Points That Saved the World.* Salt Lake City: Shadow Mountain, 2011.

Wilson, A. N. *Paul—The Mind of an Apostle.* New York: W.W. Norton & Company, 1997.

Chapter 4
The Incomparable Mr. Newton

Bunch, Bryan. *The History of Science and Technology.* New York: Houghton Mifflin Company, 2004.

Gribbin, John. *The Scientists: A History of Science Told Through the Lives of Its Greatest Inventors.* New York: Random House, 2002.

Hart, Michael H. *The 100: A Ranking of the Most Influential Persons in History.* New York: Carol Publishing Group, 1992.

Steele, Philip. *Isaac Newton: The Scientist Who Changed Everything.* Washington, D.C.: National Geographic Society, 2007.

Westfall, Richard S. *The Life of Isaac Newton.* New York: Cambridge University Press, 2007.

White, Michael. *Isaac Newton: The Last Sorcerer.* New York: Helix Books, 1997.

Williams, Henry Smith. *A History of Science.* Lexington, KY, 2011.

Chapter 5
Madame Marie Curie

Brian, Denis. *The Curies.* Hoboken: John Wiley & Sons, 2005.

Cobb, Vicki. *Marie Curie.* New York: DK Publishing, 2008.

Curie, Eve. *Madame Curie.* New York: Da Capo Press, 2001.

Felder, Deborah G. *The 100 Most Influential Women of All Time.* New York: Citadel Press, 1996.

Goldsmith, Barbara. *Obsessive Genius.* New York: W.W. Norton & Company, 2005.

Pflaum, Rosalynd. *Grand Obsession.* New York: Doubleday, 1989.

Chapter 6
Dr. Martin Luther King Jr.

Jackson, Thomas F. *From Civil Rights to Human Rights.* Philadelphia: University of Pennsylvania Press, 2007.

King, Martin Luther, Jr. *The Autobiography of Martin Luther King, Jr.* New York: Grand Central Publishing, 1998.

———. *Stride Toward Freedom.* Boston: Beacon Press, 1986.

———. *I Have a Dream, Writings and Speeches That Changed the World.* New York: HarperOne, 1992.

Landau, Elaine. *The Civil Rights Movement in America.* New York: Children's Press, 2003.

Lawson, Steven F., and Charles Payne. *Debating the Civil Rights Movement 1945–1968.* Lanham: Rowman & Littlefield Publishers, 2006.

McConnell, Michael. "Originalism and the Desegregation Decisions." *Virginia Law Review,* Volume 81, May 1995.

Williams, Juan. *Eyes on the Prize, America's Civil Rights Years, 1954–1965.* New York: Penguin Group, 2002.

Chapter 7
Mother Teresa

Felder, Deborah G. *The 100 Most Influential Women of All Time.* New York: Citadel Press, 1996.

Gold, Maya. *Mother Teresa.* London: DK Publishing, 2008.

Langford, Joseph. *Mother Teresa's Secret Fire.* Huntington: One Sunday Visitor Publishing Division, 2008.

Maasburg, Leo. *Mother Teresa of Calcutta.* San Francisco: Ignatius Press, 2010.

Spink, Kathryn. *Mother Teresa—A Complete Authorized Biography.* New York: HarperOne, 1997.

Teresa, Mother. *No Greater Love.* Novato: New World Library, 1995.

———. *Where There Is Love, There Is God.* New York: Doubleday, 2010.

Index

Abortion, 234–35
Abraham of Ur: legacy of, 3, 16–20, 240; conditions during time of, 8–9; idolatry and, 9–10; journeys of, 10–12; mercy and unselfishness of, 12–13; receives new name, 13–14; Isaac and, 14–16; Christians as children of, 72–73; courage of, 243; faith of, 244; persistence of, 244
Adams, John, 17
Adoption, of Chinese children, 245–47
Alexander the Great, 57
Ananias, 59–60
Anaxagoras, 29–30, 32
Arianism, 95–97
Aristotle, 81–84, 90–91
Assembly, The, 34–35, 36
Athens: impact of, 24; democracy in, 25–29, 34–37; rise of Pericles and, 29–31; Pericles's leadership of, 31–34; height of, 38–39; Pericles on, 39–40; significance of, 41–45; Sparta and, 45n1. *See also* Democracy
Atomic weights, 123
Atoms, 82, 122–23, 140, 152

Babies: saved by Mother Terésa, 221–22; adoption of Chinese, 246–47
Bacon, Sir Francis, 84
Barnabas, 64, 67

Barnett, Ross, 195
Becquerel, Henri, 126–27, 130, 134, 135, 142, 145–46
Becquerel rays, 126–27, 129–32
Beirut, Lebanon, Mother Teresa's work in, 234
Berle, Adolph, 23
Bible, Newton and, 97
Bloodgood, Colt, 152
Bojaxhiu, Agnes Gonxha. *See* Mother Teresa
Bojaxhiu, Drana, 209, 211
Bojaxhiu, Nikola, 208–9
Boycott, of Montgomery bus system, 175–76, 180–92
Bradley, Mamie, 168
Brown v. Board of Education (1954), 172, 173, 187
Bryant, Roy, 168–69
Bus boycott, 175–76, 180–92

Calculus, 99–100
Calcutta, India, 206–8, 222
Cambridge University, 89–92
Cancer, treatment of, 141–42
Capitalism, 178
Carpooling, during Montgomery bus boycott, 183, 184, 185
Cathode ray, 124
Charles I, 80
Children: saved by Mother Teresa, 221–22, 234; adoption of Chinese, 246–47
Christians and Christianity: Abraham and, 18; endurance of, 47–48; spread of, 53–57; persecution of, 57–59; Gentiles converted to, 63–66; Paul and, 71–76, 241; Aristotle's teachings and, 82–83; corruption of, 96
Cimon, 31
Circumcision, 63, 64
Citizenship: Athenian, 36–37; Roman, 50, 70
City-states, 24–25, 45n3
Civil Rights Act (1875), 159, 160
Civil Rights Act (1957), 193
Civil Rights Act (1964), 193
Civil Rights Movement: overview of, 170–72; birth of, 172–76; Martin Luther King Jr. and, 176–80; and Montgomery bus boycott, 180–92; growth of, 192–97
Clark, Kenneth, 162–63, 172
Cleisthenes, 28–29, 31
Colonization, Pericles and, 38
Communism, 177–78, 198
Connor, "Bull," 193
Copernicus, 83
Cornelius, 64
Council of Five Hundred, 28, 35
Council of Four Hundred, 27
Council of the Areopagite, 31
Courage, 233–35, 243
Crookes, William, 124
Curie, Eve, 119, 138, 147, 148–49
Curie, Irene, 128, 148, 149, 151
Curie, Marie: legacy of, 4–5, 110–11, 152–53, 241; early years and education of, 111–15; studies at the Sorbonne, 116–19; Pierre Curie and, 119–21; research of, 127–39; radium and, 139–44;

receives PhD, 144–45; honors given to, 145–47; following death of Pierre Curie, 147–51; courage of, 243; persistence of, 244; faith of, 245
Curie, Pierre: courtship and marriage of, 119–21, 127–28; research of, 133–38; scientific spirit of, 143–44; health problems of, 145–46; honors given to, 145–47; death of, 147–48

Dalton, John, 123
de Lange, Amanda, 246–47
Delian League, 30
Democracy: background to Athenian, 25–26; contributors to Athenian, 27–29; Pericles and, 31–34, 240; functioning of Athenian, 34–37; criticism of Athenian, 36–37; significance of Athenian, 41–45; future of, 45
Democritus, 82, 122–23
Descartes, Rene, 84
Disciples of Jesus Christ: following crucifixion, 54–55; comprehension of, 62–63

Earth, as center of universe, 83
Egypt, 11–12, 23
Einstein, Albert, 110, 141, 152
Eisenhower, Dwight, 195
Elements, 81–82, 122–23, 134
Emerson, Ralph Waldo, 2
Energy, 122–23, 141, 152–53
Ephialtes, 31
Ethiopia, Mother Teresa's work in, 229–30
Europe, Christianity and, 68, 75
Eutychus, 69
Example, Mother Teresa as, 230, 231–33

Faith: of Abraham, 10, 13, 15–16, 19; of Newton, 93–95, 97; of Mother Teresa, 232; of seven giants, 244–45
Farrar, Frederic W.: on need for Paul, 47; on marriage of Paul, 53; on Paul and law of Moses, 66; on Paul's writings, 72; on legacy of Paul, 73; on dispersion of Jews, 76–77n33; on titles of Jesus Christ, 77n40
Faubus, Orval, 195
Founding Fathers, 43–45
Four elements, 81–82
"Freedom Riders," 194
French Academy of Science, 150

Galileo, 80, 83
Gamaliel, 51
Gandhi, Indira, 236
Gandhi, Mahatma, 178–79
Gentiles, converted to Christianity, 63–66
Germany, 157–58
Giving, 229–30
God: Newton's devotion to, 93–94; love of, 179–80, 192, 215; Martin Luther King Jr. on, 197. *See also* Monotheism
Gomes, Alfred, 219

Gravity, 103
Greece: government of, 23–24; development of city-states in, 24–25, 45n3; intellectual strength of, 38–39. *See also* Athens; Sparta
Greek, 57

Hagar, 13–14, 15
Halley, Edmond, 100–101
Heliaea, 27, 36
Herakles/Hercules, 49
Holy Ghost, 54–55
Hooke, Robert, 107
Housing Act (1968), 194
Human sacrifice, 19–20
Humility, of Newton, 107

Idolatry, 9–10, 17
Industrial Revolution, 106–7
Inferiority, propagation of black, 162–63
Integration, 172–73, 189–90
Isaac, 14–16
Ishmael, 14, 15
Islam, 18
Israel, 97

Japan, 157–58
Jesus Christ: as descendant of Abraham, 16, 18; Paul and, 53, 58–59, 60; Christianity following crucifixion of, 53–55; disciples' comprehension of, 62–63; titles of, 77n40
Jews, dispersion of, 55–57, 76–77n33
Jim Crow. *See* Segregation
John of Salisbury, 1
Josephus, 11, 47, 56
Judaism, 17–18
Judging others, 209, 229
Justice, Abraham and, 19

Kelvin, Lord, 150
Kennedy, John, 195
King, Coretta Scott, 179–80, 196
King, Martin Luther Jr.: legacy of, 5, 199–203, 241; on experience of black citizens, 169–70; life of, 176–80; and Montgomery bus boycott, 180–92; and growth of Civil Rights Movement, 193–97; courage of, 243; persistence of, 244; faith of, 245

Labouisse, Eve Curie, 119, 138, 147, 148–49
Lange, Amanda de, 246–47
Law of Conservation of Energy, 122
Law of Conservation of Matter, 123
Law of Moses, 62–65
Laws of motion, 103
Leprosy, 222–24, 228–29
Lincoln, Abraham, 2
Locke, John, 97, 105–6
Loreto Entally, 212–13, 217
Lot, 12
Love: for enemies, 178–79, 186, 191; Martin Luther King Jr. on, 182; of God, 192, 215; Mother Teresa on, 229
Luke, 67–68
Lunch counters, sit-ins at, 194
Lynching, 166–66

Marriage, of Paul, 53
Martyrdom, of Paul, 71
Matter, 81–85, 122–23
Maxwell, James Clerk, 129
Mercy, of Abraham, 12–13, 18–19
Migration, of black citizens, 165
Milam, J. W., 168–69
Military, Athenian, 25–26
Miracles, performed by Paul, 69
Missionaries of Charity, 219–26, 231
Missionary Brothers of Charity, 226
Mithras, 49
Monotheism, 16–17, 19, 240
Montgomery bus boycott, 175–76, 180–92
Montgomery Improvement Association (MIA), 176, 187–88
Morality, 20
Mother Teresa: legacy of, 5, 237, 241; arrives in Calcutta, 206–8; childhood and family of, 208–10; takes vows, 210–11; serves in India, 211–14; receives call, 214–17; begins work among poor, 217–22; expands mission, 222–26; teachings and philosophy of, 226–31; as example, 230, 231–33; courage of, 233–35, 243; honors given to, 236–37; persistence of, 244; faith of, 245
Moti Jihl, India, 206, 217–22, 234
Motion, 81–85; laws of, 103
Muhammad, 18
Natural philosophy, evolution of, 81–85
Navy, Athenian, 25–26
Nazi Germany, 157–58
Newton, Hannah Ayscough, 85–86, 87, 89
Newton, Isaac, senior, 85
Newton, Sir Isaac: legacy of, 4, 106–7, 241; world at time of, 79–80; birth and childhood of, 85–87; early education of, 87–89; attends Cambridge University, 89–92; success of, 93–94; motivation of, 94–97; concentration and tenacity of, 98–99, 244; calculus and, 99–100; *Principia Mathematica* and, 101–5; final years of, 105–6; courage of, 243; faith of, 245
Nimrod, 8
Nixon, E.D., 175
Nobel, Alfred, 148
Nobel Peace Prize: awarded to Martin Luther King Jr., 202–3; awarded to Mother Teresa, 232
Nobel Prize, awarded to Marie Curie, 145–46, 150
"Noble Athenian," 39–41
Nonviolence, 178–79, 180–92, 193, 200–201
Nuclear energy and weapons, 152–53

Obedience, 224–25
"Old Oligarch," 37
Ostracism, 28

Pagan gods, 49–50
Pagan rites, 20
Parks, Rosa, 174–75
Paul: legacy of, 4, 71–76, 241; information concerning, 48–49; background of, 49–53; and persecution of Christians, 57–59; conversion of, 58–61; and Peter's conversion and vision, 62–66; missionary journeys of, 66–69; in Jerusalem and Rome, 69–71; martyrdom of, 71; courage of, 243; persistence of, 244; faith of, 245
Paul VI, Pope, 223
Peace, 228
Peloponnesian War, 39, 41
Pentecost, 54–55
Pericles: legacy of, 3–4, 41–45, 240; rise of, 29–31; leadership of, 31–34; functioning of democracy under, 34–37; accomplishments of, 38–39; "noble Athenian" and, 39–41; courage of, 243; persistence of, 244; faith of, 244–45
Perier, Ferdinand, 216
Persian Empire, 23
Persistence, 244
Persuasion, Pericles and, 33
Peter, 61–66
Pharaoh, 11–12
Pharisees, 50–53
Philip, 63
Piezoelectric scale, 130–31
Pitchblende, 133–38
Plato, 37–38
Plessy v. Ferguson (1896), 160, 162
Plutarch, 37–38, 46n9
Polonium, 134
Pope, Alexander, 79, 107
Poverty: of Missionaries of Charity, 220, 231; spiritual and material, 227–28; fighting, 248
Principia Mathematica (Newton), 101–5
Public offices, selected by lot, 36
Pure democracy, 43–44

"Quaestiones," of Newton, 91–92

Race riots, 165, 198
Racism: following World War II, 158; following Civil War, 159–60; during mid-twentieth century, 160–70; ending, 199–200; fighting, 248. *See also* Civil Rights Movement
Radioactivity, 132–38, 140
Radium, 135–44, 150
Religion, Newton and, 93–97
Republic, 44
Robinson, Jo Ann, 175
Roentgen, Wilhelm, 124–26
Roman Empire: citizenship in, 50, 70; rise of, 57
Royal Society of London, 106
Runcie, Lord, Archbishop of Canterbury, 236
Rutherford, Ernest, 140–41, 152, 155n35

Sacrifice: of Isaac, 15–16; human, 19–20

Sarai, 11–15
Scientific method, 92, 108n6
Scientific Revolution, 83–85
Segregation: in mid-twentieth century America, 160–65; Montgomery bus boycott and, 173–75, 187–89, 190; ending, 178, 200; protests against, 192–94
Sexual morality, 20, 50
Silas, 67–68
Sisters of Loreto, 211–13
"Sit-in" movement, 194
Sklodowska, Bronya, 114–15, 116
Sklodowska, Marie. *See* Curie, Marie
Slavery, 158–59
Smith, Barnabas, 86
Soddy, Frederick, 132, 140–41
Sodom and Gomorrah, 12–13
Solon, 27–28
Sparta, 23–24, 45n1
Spiritual poverty, 227–28
Starfish Foster Home, 246–47
Stephen, 57–58, 62–63
Stokes, Henry, 87, 88, 89
Strategoi, 28–29
Subsizar, 89–90
Suffering, as gift of God, 228–29
Suffrage, 164–65, 173

Tarsus, 49–50
Terah, 9–10
Teresa, Mother. *See* Mother Teresa
Thoreau, Henry David, 178
Thucydides, 33, 34
Till, Emmett, 168–69
Timocracy, 27
Timothy, 67–68
Tina, 247
Toilets, 220, 233
Travel, of Mother Teresa, 231–32
Trial(s): of Abraham, 15–16; Mother Teresa on, 230
Trinitarianism, 95–97

United Nations General Assembly, Mother Teresa addresses, 232–33
United States of America: Athenian democracy and, 42–45; slavery and racism in, 158–60; experience of black citizens in, 160–70
Unmoved Mover, 82, 83
Unselfishness, of Abraham, 12–13, 18–19
Ur, location of, 8
Uranium, 126, 129–33, 136
Ussher, James, 8

Van Exem, Father, 237
Venezuela, Mother Teresa's work in, 225–26
Veterans, racism against, 158, 166–67
Violence: against black citizens, 161, 165–70; during Civil Rights Movement, 171–72, 186–87, 189–90, 195; Martin Luther King Jr.'s aversion to, 201. *See also* Nonviolence
Voting, 164–65, 173
Voting Rights Act (1965), 194

Wallace, George, 195
Ward, Mary, 211
Warfare, Greek, 25
Wickins, John, 90, 92
Wilson, A. N., 74–75
Women's rights, 118
Woodard, Isaac, 167–68
World War I, 150–51
World War II, 157–58, 166–67, 213–14
Wright, Mose, 168

X-rays, 124–26, 150–51